SSSP

Springer
Series in
Social
Psychology

Springer Series in Social Psychology

Springer Series in Social Psychology

SSSP

Miles L. Patterson

Nonverbal Behavior
A Functional Perspective

Springer-Verlag
New York   Berlin   Heidelberg   Tokyo

Miles L. Patterson
Department of Psychology
University of Missouri—St. Louis
St. Louis, Missouri 63121 U.S.A.

Library of Congress Cataloging in Publication Data
Patterson, Miles L.
    Nonverbal behavior.
    (Springer series in social psychology)
    Bibliography: p.
    Includes indexes.
    1. Nonverbal communication (Psychology) 2. Social
interaction. I. Title. II. Series. [DNLM: 1. Nonverbal
communication. 2. Social behavior. HM 251 P318n]
BF637.C45P33 1983   153.6   83-10602

With 13 Figures

Typeset by Publishers Service, Bozeman, Montana.
Printed and bound by R.R. Donnelley & Sons, Harrisonburg, Virginia.
Printed in the United States of America.

9 8 7 6 5 4 3 2 1

ISBN 0-387-90846-3 Springer-Verlag New York Berlin Heidelberg Tokyo
ISBN 3-540-90846-3 Springer-Verlag Berlin Heidelberg New York Tokyo

*To my wife Dianne
and my son Kevin*

Preface

My interest in nonverbal behavior has remained constant for over 15 years. I think this has been the case because nonverbal behavior has proved a very fascinating and challenging topic. Others might suggest that I am just a slow learner. With enough time in any area, however, one begins to feel that he or she has some special insights to offer to others. About the time that I was struck with that thought, approximately two and a half years ago, I was developing the first version of my sequential functional model of nonverbal exchange. It seemed to me that the functional model might provide a very useful framework for a book discussing and analyzing nonverbal behavior. I did not want (nor do I think I had the patience) to write a comprehensive review of research on nonverbal behavior. Other works, such as Siegman and Feldstein's (1978) edited *Nonverbal Behavior and Communication,* and Harper, Wiens, and Matarazzo's (1978) *Nonverbal Communication: The State of the Art,* have provided excellent reviews of the research on nonverbal behavior. Instead, what I have tried to do in this book is to use nonverbal behavior as a vehicle for discussing social behavior. In a very real sense, this analysis of nonverbal behavior is a means to an end, not an end in itself. A consequence of this approach is that this review is a selective one, unlike the comprehensive works mentioned earlier. Nevertheless, that selective review includes several hundred citations on nonverbal behavior; citations that contribute to our understanding of social interaction.

This means-oriented analysis of nonverbal behavior is developed specifically in the context of a functional theory. This theoretical structure provides a system for discussing and analyzing nonverbal behavior in terms of the goals or purposes served by patterns of nonverbal behavior. Through this approach, I hope the reader might share an appreciation of the role that nonverbal behavior plays in social exchanges.

There are a number of acknowledgments I would like to make to those who have contributed to this effort. First, I want to thank my wife, Dianne, and my son, Kevin, for their patience in putting up with me and this project over the last two years. Patience has also been characteristic of the editorial support from Robert

Kidd and the staff of Springer-Verlag. That support and encouragement made this project possible.

There are several important professional relationships that have facilitated the completion of this book. First, Joyce Edinger reviewed most of the research cited in Chapter 6. That work resulted in our coauthored article in the *Psychological Bulletin* (Edinger & Patterson, 1983). Bill Ickes provided many excellent comments and insights in reviewing several of the chapters. He was a demanding yet gentle critic. Over the years I have benefited from constructive exchanges with talented colleagues, especially Bill Ickes, Phoebe Ellsworth, and Eric Knowles. Finally, I would like to note, belatedly, the debt I owe to Erving Goffman, who died just a few months ago. We had never met or communicated directly, but his work certainly shaped much of my thinking. I hope that exposure to his insightful analyses has helped me to become a better observer of human behavior.

The typing of the final manuscript was primarily the skillful work of Deloris Licklider. She never complained when I added a few "minor changes" to a supposedly final copy. That attitude made it easy to continue polishing this manuscript. Katie Danforth, Valerie Wooten, Liz Barker, Rick Prevallet, and Jeanette Collins also helped on the typing chores. Liz Barker also assisted in compiling the bibliography. I am very grateful to all these people for their help on this book.

June 1983   Miles L. Patterson

Contents

Chapter 1
Defining a Perspective on Nonverbal Behavior

Curiosity about the role of nonverbal behavior in everyday life is a widespread phenomenon. For the layman, the study of nonverbal behavior seems to provide an indirect means of knowing more about other people. Presumably the information gleaned from another person's nonverbal behavior is more representative of "true" characteristics, attitudes, and feelings than that offered verbally. That is, most of us assume that nonverbal behavior is spontaneous and sincere, whereas verbal behavior is easily managed and often used to deceive. For example, even though we may have no independent knowledge of the truth of another person's statement, we may judge confidently from another person's nonverbal behavior that a given statement is true.

Of course, nonverbal behavior is relevant not only for deception, but for impression formation, attraction, social influence, aggression, emotional expression, and other interpersonal processes. Throughout history, authors, poets, painters, and sculptors have commonly provided their audiences with insights about character, motivation, or the nature of a relationship through the skillful portrayal of nonverbal behavior. Although such descriptions and analyses of nonverbal behavior have long been of interest to the artist, the intense scientific study of nonverbal behavior seems to be a relatively recent development.

As a gauge of this trend in research, I examined the distribution of citations as a function of year of publication in two comprehensive texts on nonverbal behavior. The first book, LaFrance and Mayo's (1978) *Moving Bodies*, might be described as a general survey of the field of nonverbal social behavior. The second book, Harper, Wiens, and Matarazzo's (1978) *Nonverbal Communication: The State of the Art,* provides a scholarly review of the research. Although the selection of references may be biased by a tendency to cite more recent work, the two citation distributions are remarkably similar and informative. From the 439 citations in *Moving Bodies* and the 998 citations in *Nonverbal Communication*, fewer than 10% were published before 1960. More than half of the citations came from the most recent period (1970-1976) cited in those books. Although I have not tried to assess the pattern after 1976, my impression is that interest in research on nonverbal behavior has continued to increase.

A further indication of the accelerated interest in nonverbal behavior was the initiation of a journal focusing only on that topic—*The Journal of Nonverbal Behavior*. (The journal began as *Environmental Psychology and Nonverbal Behavior* in 1976 and 3 years later restricted its focus to nonverbal behavior.) Contributors to and readers of that journal span such disciplines as psychology, sociology, anthropology, speech and communication, health fields, and management. Furthermore, within each of these disciplines, articles on diverse issues related to nonverbal behavior can be found in a variety of other journals.

The vast majority of this research on nonverbal social behavior is clearly of an empirical nature, which is probably not surprising. In general, developed theoretical integrations have lagged behind the growing body of empirical research. There are, of course, some notable exceptions (e.g., Argyle & Dean, 1965; Ellsworth & Langer, 1976; Firestone, 1977; Patterson, 1976; Sundstrom & Altman, 1976), but each of these approaches is limited in some important way. Typically, these theoretical discussions are inadequate in one or more areas. First, the range of behaviors analyzed is often quite limited. For example, Ellsworth and Langer (1976) attend only to gaze, and Sundstrom and Altman (1976) limit themselves to interaction distance. Even Argyle and Dean's (1965) equilibrium theory and my own arousal model (Patterson, 1976) are limited to a small set of "intimacy" behaviors. Second, all of the theoretical approaches mentioned fail to consider the potential diversity of functions served by nonverbal behavior. Third, predisposing variables are either neglected or, at least, inadequately analyzed. That is, factors such as culture, personality, sex of interactants, or degree of relationship need to be considered as potential determinants of nonverbal behavior. One clear exception here is Sundstrom and Altman's model that does consider predisposing factors in regulating interaction distance. Special emphasis in that model is given to the important role of degree of relationship in determining comfortable interaction distances. It is probably not surprising that theoretical developments lag behind the empirical work in such a rapidly growing area of research. Nevertheless, such a condition does point to a distinct need for a comprehensive, integrated theoretical perspective in the field. This book represents an attempt to address that need.

In developing that integrated theoretical treatment, this chapter will begin by discussing several issues basic to an understanding of nonverbal social behavior. These include the following concerns: (a) emphasizing the importance of *patterns* of nonverbal behavior; (b) identifying nonverbal involvement as a focal construct; and (c) discussing and evaluating a functional approach in analyzing nonverbal behavior.

Patterns of Nonverbal Behaviors

Nonverbal behavior, if defined broadly, might include most of what we do with our bodies. Even certain characteristics of verbal behavior might be included because an important distinction is typically made between the content, or meaning, of speech and vocal characteristics of speech such as loudness, tempo, pitch, and intonation.

Although the content, or meaning, of speech has been traditionally defined as verbal, the vocal characteristics of speech (also termed paralinguistic cues) are defined as nonverbal. In addition to the paralinguistic cues, the term "nonverbal behavior" might incorporate the following:

 1. Interpersonal distance.
 2. Gaze direction.
 3. Touch.
 4. Body lean.
 5. Body orientation.
 6. Facial expressions.
 7. Posture and postural adjustments.
 8. Gestures.
 9. Hand movements.
10. Foot or leg movements.
11. Grooming behaviors.
12. Self- and object manipulations (scratching, adjusting clothes, fiddling with rings, keys or other objects).
13. Pupilllary dilation-constriction.
14. Pauses.
15. Interruptions.
16. Speech duration.

Some writers and researchers would also include behaviorally relevant attributes such as physical appearance and body odor, and artifactual cues such as clothing, glasses, or jewelry. Other behaviors, attributes, and cues could be added, but the present list is probably sufficient for representing the diversity of nonverbal expression.

Although a catalog of specific behaviors can be easily identified, it is important to recognize that these behaviors do not occur in isolation. In general, the integrated pattern of behaviors enacted at any point in time is the critical determinant of the meaning or significance of some action. It may be convenient to isolate a specific behavior for analysis, but without knowing the rest of the behavioral context, inferences about that behavior may be questionable or completely wrong. For example, gazing at another person is an important sign of interest in that person or in what that person is doing. However, an evaluation of the gaze is dependent upon knowing at least the surrounding facial cues. If one is looking at another with open eyes, unfurrowed brow, and a smile, it would appear to indicate a positive feeling, or perhaps even an invitation for interaction. In contrast, a squinting gaze with a stern expression is likely to indicate a rather negative assessment. The amount or duration of gaze in both instances may be equivalent, but their meanings are different and their effects on the target person will also be different. Thus, gaze direction and duration, commonly assessed in research, do not by themselves determine the full impact of gazing behavior. The same is true in trying to interpret other nonverbal behaviors in isolation.

Nonverbal Involvement

My primary goal in this book is the description and analysis of nonverbal behavior from a social process perspective. Such a focus is a common one in the research on nonverbal behavior, but it is not the only one. For example, a diagnostic approach would focus on nonverbal behaviors as indicative of specific traits or states. Thus, inferences about personality, cognitive style, or psychiatric classification might be made from distinct patterns of gaze, the presence of nervous mannerisms, the way in which affect is expressed, or through some other combination of cues. In fact, there is extensive research on differences in nonverbal behavior between normal and psychiatric populations. In addition, a great deal of nonverbal research focuses on personality differences within normal populations (see Patterson, 1982a, for one analysis of personality research). Although nonverbal data may come from inter-active settings, the diagnostic approach emphasizes the utility of the behavior in classifying individuals. Alternately, a communication systems approach might stress an analysis of the meaning of coordinated verbal and nonverbal messages. Here, too, the distinction is not whether the behavior occurs in social interaction or in isola-tion, but how the behaviors are used and analyzed. There is necessarily some overlap among these approaches, but their dissimilarities often lead to different questions, different research strategies, and different ways of analyzing nonverbal behavior. The elements I wish to stress in developing the social process perspective are (a) the need for a multivariate approach and (b) the utility of operationalizing nonverbal involvement.

A Multivariate Approach

The multivariate approach applied in this book will entail a comprehensive, inte-grated description of nonverbal behavior in the service of different social functions. Such an approach is clearly consistent with the earlier emphasis on patterns of non-verbal behavior. For example, in discussing the function of interaction regulation, the coordinated changes among several behaviors such as distance, gaze, gestures, and paralinguistic cues will be analyzed. Such a focus contrasts with the common "channel" approach in which each nonverbal channel or behavior is sequentially examined in isolation (e.g., one chapter on interpersonal distance, one on facial expression, another on gaze). In the channel approach, the topical concerns relating to each behavior are repeated across chapters. This kind of approach is a common one used in many texts on nonverbal behavior. The channel approach may be con-venient for organizational purposes, but it makes difficult an appreciation of the coordinated, interdependent relationships among behaviors as they actually occur.

If one accepts the desirability of a multivariate approach over a channel ap-proach, there is still the issue of deciding which behaviors are most important in understanding the process of social interaction. Fortunately, previous research pro-vides some direction. One example can be found in Hall's (1963) description of a "proxemic" notation system for analyzing social behavior. Included in Hall's system are the following:

1. Posture.
2. Orientation.
3. Functional distance (ease of reaching another person).
4. Touch.
5. Visual behavior.
6. Thermal cues.
7. Olfactory cues.
8. Voice loudness.

Argyle and Dean (1965) have emphasized a set of behaviors that they believe are critical in expressing and managing interpersonal intimacy. Included among the "intimacy behaviors" are interpersonal distance, gaze, smiling, and verbal intimacy. In effect, Argyle and Dean identified one function of nonverbal behavior—the expression of intimacy—and proposed a set of behaviors relevant to that function. In a similar vein, Mehrabian has used the term "immediacy" to refer to the "extent to which communication behaviors enhance closeness to or nonverbal intervention with another" (1969b, p. 203). The behaviors that Mehrabian listed as components of immediacy were:

1. Interpersonal distance.
2. Gaze.
3. Touch.
4. Body orientation.
5. Lean.

In each of these three cases, constructs reflecting some dimension of interpersonal closeness or intensity have been defined in terms of the combined effects of the component behaviors. Common to all three constructs is an appreciation of the coordinated impact of several related behaviors on the process of social interaction. Consistent with this perspective, this book will focus primarily on one set of related behaviors that seems most important for interaction and the social process orientation stressed here. I will use the term *nonverbal involvement behaviors* to identify this set of focal cues.

Nonverbal Involvement and Exchange

The construct of nonverbal involvement overlaps with proxemics, intimacy, and immediacy, but it is more comprehensive than each of those constructs. A tentative list of behaviors that signal nonverbal involvement would include the following:

1. Interpersonal distance.
2. Gaze.
3. Touch.
4. Body orientation.
5. Lean.
6. Facial expressiveness.
7. Talking duration.

   8. Interruptions.
   9. Postural openness.
  10. Relational gestures. (Relational gestures would include hand and arm movements that portray the actual or intended involvement desired with another. An example of such a gesture would be a hand movement by the speaker that goes out toward the listener and back as the speaker is saying "the two of us.")
  11. Head nods.
  12. Paralinguistic cues such as intonation, speech rate, volume, and so forth.

In general, increased involvement would be indicated by decreased distance, increased gaze and touch, more direct body orientation, more forward lean, greater facial expressiveness, longer speech duration, more frequent and/or more intense interruptions, increased postural openness, more relational gestures, more frequent head nods, and more intense paralinguistic cues. Again, modifications may have to be made to this list, and the relative importance of the different cues has yet to be determined. In fact, with respect to the latter point, it may well be that a single overall weighting is not possible, that is, that the importance of different cues changes across situations.

Given this rather extensive list, is there anything left for the noninvolvement category? There is, and ideally it includes those behaviors that are less important in the dynamics of social interaction. For example, most leg and foot movements, grooming behaviors, self-manipulations (scratching, fiddling with one's keys or rings), postural adjustments, artifactual cues (clothing, glasses), and undoubtedly other behaviors, would fall in the noninvolvement category. It should be emphasized that such noninvolvement behaviors can still provide important information about others, but their direct influence on the interaction process is probably less than that of the involvement behaviors.

A thorough analysis of the involvement behaviors of one person in an interaction necessarily requires attention to the complementary behavior of the other person. This joint behavioral pattern might be termed an *exchange*. Exchanges can be seen as coordinated, mutually dependent behavioral patterns. Of course, each person's unique characteristics (e.g., personality or attitudes) and the situation itself also influence the course of an interaction, but the relational nature of each person's behavior is basic. Just as the analysis of a single behavior in isolation is incomplete, so a one-sided analysis of an exchange is incomplete. Obviously, it is difficult to detail everything that two (or more) people do simultaneously in an interaction. However, a focus on the exchange process requires sensitivity to the behavioral context each person constructs for the other.

Functional Analysis

It seems reasonable to assume that our understanding of any phenomenon might begin with a description of its occurrence. As one moves from a description to an attempted understanding of some event or process, it is likely that the question framed will be one of "why?" In pursuing such a question, an analysis of the purposes or functions of nonverbal behavior may be particularly useful. A functional perspective on nonverbal behavior is by no means a new endeavor. Argyle and his colleagues have discussed the functions of nonverbal behavior in several different works (Argyle, 1972; Argyle & Dean, 1965; Argyle, Lalljee & Cook, 1968; Kendon, 1967). Common to these different discussions are those functions relating either to the management of the immediate situation (synchronizing speech, providing feedback, and expressing intimacy) or to the support or replacement of verbal communication.

A communication systems perspective on functions of nonverbal behavior has been advanced by Harrison (1973). In this approach, Harrison proposed that nonverbal behaviors or signs serve the following functions: (a) defining and constraining the communication system; (b) regulating the flow of interaction and providing feedback; and (c) communicating content, usually in a complementary but redundant fashion to the verbal channel. In a similar fashion, Ekman and Friesen (1969b) emphasized the functions of nonverbal behavior relative to verbal communication. Specifically, they proposed that nonverbal behaviors may repeat, contradict, complement, or accent verbal communication. A final function proposed by Ekman and Friesen (1969b), and one common to the other classifications, is that of regulating or managing interacting.

The functional classification proposed here will necessarily overlap with some of the functions already cited. Some new distinctions, however, will also be offered. The purpose of this classification is to provide a relatively comprehensive set of functions that can be related to the management of the involvement behaviors in social interaction. The classification will be at the core of this book's analysis of nonverbal behavior. The specific functional categories proposed here are those of

1. Providing information.
2. Regulating interaction.
3. Expressing intimacy.
4. Exercising social control.
5. Facilitating service or task goals.

The first two functions can be broadly contrasted with the last three functions in terms of a molecular versus molar focus. That is, providing information and regulating interaction are categories descriptive of isolated behavioral patterns. In contrast, the intimacy, social control, and service-task functions are molar descriptions of extended exchanges. Consequently, the last three functions are more important for understanding and predicting the course of nonverbal exchange over the duration of an interaction. The classification of any particular exchange will generally be made on the basis of the apparent purpose underlying an actor's behavior. Such a judgment might be based on some direct self-report or on some analysis of intraindividual or interindividual consistency for the situation evaluated. A brief description of each of the functions will be offered here before they are discussed at length in later chapters.

Information. Perhaps the most basic function of nonverbal behavior might be broadly described as informational. From the point of view of the receiver, or decoder, most of the sender's, or encoder's, behavior can be seen as potentially informative in some way. Specifically, the decoder might evaluate a particular pattern of encoder behavior and infer something about (a) the encoder's characteristic dispositions, (b) his or her more fleeting reactions, or (c) the meaning of a verbal exchange. Of particular importance here are facial expressions. A great deal of specific information is transmitted by the face, even though it can also deceive (Ekman & Friesen, 1974). There is also a second way in which nonverbal behavior may be informative, and in this sense such behavior may relate only indirectly to interaction. Specifically, an actor's own behavior may provide the feedback that helps to define his or her own feeling-states. The hypothesis that our expressive behavior determines the development of our emotional reactions was first proposed by William James (1950/1890, 1968/1884) and is an issue that is still debated today.

Regulating interaction. In many cases, the function of interaction regulation may be the most automatic and least reflective of the proposed functions. Researchers interested in interaction regulation attempt to identify those behavioral patterns that structure the initiation and development of interaction and facilitate smooth conversational sequences. The behaviors that provide the structure or framework for interaction have been called the "standing features" of interaction by Argyle and Kendon (1967). These behaviors, including interpersonal distance, body orientation, and posture, remain relatively stable over the course of an interaction. This group of behaviors sets some rough limits on the opportunity for initiating varying degrees of involvement through other nonverbal behaviors. For example, greater distances in interaction make touch impossible and less directly facing orientations require somewhat greater effort to sustain high levels of gaze. In contrast to the standing features, "dynamic features" such as gaze, facial expression, and verbal intimacy affect the momentary changes in conversational sequences (Argyle & Kendon, 1967). In addition, a variety of paralinguistic cues such as a change in the pitch of the voice, drawl on a final syllable, and decreased loudness are related to the smooth sequencing of conversational turns (Duncan, 1972).

Intimacy. A considerable amount of research on nonverbal behavior in interaction has focused on the function of expressing intimacy, that is, varied nonverbal involvement reflects the differential intimacy desired toward another person. In general, intimacy might be described as a bipolar dimension reflecting the degree of union with or openness toward another person. Practically, increased intimacy is the result of greater liking or love for another, or greater interest in or commitment to another. It should be emphasized that the term "intimacy" in this context refers to the covert evaluative attachment to another person that can be distinguished from the *overt* level of nonverbal involvement manifested toward that person. High intimacy may typically be reflected by high levels of nonverbal involvement, but that is not always the case. Conversely, high levels of nonverbal involvement may indicate something other than high intimacy. Representative of the typical link between intimacy and nonverbal involvement is Rubin's (1970) finding that couples who score higher on a romantic love scale (one aspect of intimacy) spent more time gazing into another's eyes than those scoring lower. Similarly, increased liking or attraction for another person typically results in closer approach distances (Patterson, 1978b).

Social control. The fourth function of nonverbal behavior, social control, is a classification that has received relatively little emphasis in previous discussions of nonverbal behavior. One notable exception to this trend has been Henley's (1973, 1977) work on nonverbal correlates of sex-role differences in power or status. Social control may be described as involving some general goal of exercising influence over other people. More specifically, social control processes would be activated to produce reactions counter to those expected without such influence. For example, social control may be evident in trying to persuade others to our own particular viewpoint. In such a case, one might initiate a moderately close approach, increased gaze, and an appropriate paralinguistic emphasis in attempting to present a convincing argument. Another example would be the use of gaze or touch to institute or reinforce status differences between individuals (Henley, 1973). A less direct means of social control would be the use of any one of a variety of self-presentation patterns designed to cause others to view one more favorably (Goffman, 1967, 1972). For example, a smiling, attentive expression complemented by a forward lean might portray interest in another and create a favorable impression. Such a behavioral strategy might be initiated by an applicant in a job interview.

Service-task. The service-task function identifies bases for nonverbal involvement that are essentially impersonal. That is, the particular level of involvement reflects the consequence of a service or task relationship, and not a personal or social relationship. Heslin (Note 1) described this type of function with respect to touch. The initiation of touch is commonly limited to those having close relationships. In addition to those close relationships, however, touch is appropriate (and necessary) in exchanges between physician and patient, golf professional and student, fireman and fire victim, and barber and customer (Heslin, Note 1). Although high levels of nonverbal involvement are common in these and some other professional relationships, such involvement is merely the means to an end of treating, teaching, or otherwise serving the needs of an individual. Frequently in such professional or service exchanges, the high involvement is unidirectional, that is, no analogous response is expected, or for that matter, even appropriate from the patient or customer. Other occasions of variable involvement appropriate to this function may be less influenced by role relationships but more influenced by the immediate demands of completing a task, for example, standing or sitting in a close arrangement so that materials can be shared. In addition, solitary tasks or activities that have to be performed in the presence of others may be facilitated by low involvement arrangements. These service-task exchanges are also interesting in that they demonstrate the considerable influence that role and situational norms have on the initiation of nonverbal involvement.

Evaluating a Functional Analysis

What are the advantages and disadvantages of a functional analysis of nonverbal behavior? There are at least three distinct advantages. First, a functional analysis attempts to identify the reasons for or causes of a particular behavioral pattern. It is clear that questions of causality may not be easily answered, but they will still be asked. A functional analysis is one means of structuring such questions.

A second advantage is relevant to an issue discussed earlier in this chapter—the advisability of a multivariate approach. An analysis focused on functions cuts across single channel descriptions. Few if any specific functions are manifested in a single channel. Even in an area such as emotional expressiveness that requires special attention toward facial expression, other paralinguistic, postural, and visual cues contribute to a comprehensive and coordinated reaction. For example, we would not judge someone as happy merely because she forced a smile, if her eyes were downcast, her posture slumping, and her comments made in a slow, soft monotone. A functional analysis can facilitate the type of integrated treatment that stresses the patterned nature of nonverbal reactions.

A third advantage of a functional analysis lies in providing a link between patterns of nonverbal behavior and a variety of social psychological processes. For example, in terms of the functions proposed here, expressing intimacy may be particularly relevant for attraction, liking or disliking, and impression formation. In contrast, the social control function may be related to influence processes such as persuasion, social dominance, aggression, or leadership. From the perspective of the nonverbal researcher, such a link can provide a fertile source for generating hypotheses about nonverbal behavior. That is, various psychological processes may provide clues about potential mediators that guide the expression and management of nonverbal behavior. For the social psychology researcher, this link may increase sensitivity to the more subtle behavioral cues or indicators influencing these important social processes.

Of course a functional analysis has some disadvantages too. For example, inferences about functions are often uncertain. Even when we are able to inquire about the intentions or purposes of actors, the actors themselves may not be aware of specific intentions, or they may be biased in their reports of intentions. Fortunately, if the behavior is consistent over time within actors or across different actors, inferences about functions can often be made with confidence.

In addition, it is important to define the perspective from which the inferences about functions are made. As observers of an interaction, we may be in a position to identify the "objective" function of some behavioral pattern. That evaluation may or may not coincide either with the actor's perception of the function of his or her own behavior or with the target's perception of the function of the actor's behavior. In practice, the perceptions of the actor and target are probably more important in determining the course of an exchange than are the objective evaluations. But the actor's and target's perceptions may not always be accessible. That is, either the interactants may not be aware of such functional inferences or there may be no convenient way of assessing those perceptions. In such cases, the best approximation of the functions underlying an exchange may come from the objective assessment of intraindividual or interindividual consistencies across time and circumstances.

Another general limitation of this particular functional classification, and perhaps of all such classifications, is that many behavior patterns serve more than one function. This may be the case either when different people use the same pattern or when one person repeats that pattern. For example, a close approach, supplemented by putting one's arm around another person's shoulders, might serve to express intimacy on one occasion but establish social control on another. In the former instance, such a sequence might be initiated by a husband toward his wife, whereas the latter instance might be initiated by a boss toward a male or female employee. The former instance might simply be a sign of affection, but latter could be part of a coordinated pattern leading to a request to initiate a particular task. No doubt the reactions of the targets in those two instances will probably differ substantially. The wife may reciprocate the husband's behavior (e.g., give him a hug or turn and smile), but the employee would probably be more constrained in his or her reaction. In addition, within a given sequence, a behavioral pattern can often be informative and express intimacy, or alternately, regulate interaction and exercise social control.

At the basis of the potential overlap in functions within a given exchange is the likelihood that the informational and interaction regulation functions may be reflected in specific molecular units or reactions, whereas the expression of intimacy, the exercise of social control, and the service-task function may be reflected in molar units. Thus an isolated gesture, head nod, or smile, alone or in combination, can represent fairly discrete informational or regulatory responses. In addition, it is appropriate to examine extended patterns of involvement over time to make a reliable assessment of the intimacy, social control, and service-task functions.

Obviously, different functional approaches are possible, and alternate schemes may be less susceptible to some of the limitations just described. Moreover, it is anticipated that further research will require modifications in the classification offered here. Nevertheless, the present functional classification should be useful in developing this discussion of patterns of nonverbal involvement.

Summary

The purpose of this chapter was to describe a conceptual orientation from which the book's analysis of nonverbal behavior will proceed. First, the importance of analyzing patterns of nonverbal behavior was emphasized. Although it may be convenient to focus on nominally discrete behaviors (e.g., interaction distance or gaze), such an approach results in a very incomplete and often misleading analysis of nonverbal behavior. Second, because this text emphasizes the interactive nature of nonverbal behavior, a set of involvement behaviors was defined as critical to the interaction process. Third, a specific functional approach to the analysis of nonverbal behavior was described and evaluated. The functional bases for nonverbal behavior proposed here include the following:

1. Providing information.
2. Regulating interaction.
3. Expressing intimacy.
4. Exercising social control.
5. Facilitating service and task goals.

Each of these functions will be discussed at length in later chapters.

Chapter 2

Developing a Sequential Functional Model

The purpose of the first chapter was to provide a general description of the domain of nonverbal social behavior and propose several dimensions important in analyzing behavior patterns. Especially critical for the latter goal was defining a broad set of involvement behaviors and developing a functional classification of nonverbal behavior. This approach has facilitated more than just an organizational structure for discussing nonverbal behavior; it has provided a foundation for developing a general theoretical model for nonverbal exchange (Patterson, 1982a). In this chapter, I will be describing this theory and discussing its special relevance to the content and direction of the remaining chapters. In order to facilitate the presentation of this model, some coverage of the evolution of theories about nonverbal exchange may be helpful.

Theoretical Background

Early in the first chapter, I mentioned that there was a relative paucity of theory in research about nonverbal behavior. In spite of that condition, or perhaps because of it, the few existing models have had a considerable effect on the direction of empirical research. Consequently, these models merit some detailed discussion.

Argyle and Dean's (1965) equilibrium model of interpersonal intimacy is widely acknowledged as the first structured theoretical approach to nonverbal exchange. Equilibrium theory proposed that, in any given interaction, there is a definable appropriate or comfortable level of intimacy between individuals. Intimacy is manifested in terms of involvement behaviors such as distance, eye contact, smiling, verbal intimacy, and possibly other behaviors. (In order to maintain consistency in the intimacy-involvement distinction proposed in Chapter 1, the term "involvement" will be used to refer to the behavioral manifestation of the intimacy function, in place of Argyle and Dean's generic "intimacy" or "intimacy behaviors.") Furthermore, the theory proposes that there is pressure to maintain that involvement at the comfortable or equilibrium level. The critical prediction of the theory is that once a comfortable level of involvement has been established or negotiated, variations in one or more of the component behaviors will require compensatory adjustments. The compensation process may be viewed as analogous to a redistribution of pressure in a closed system, such as a hydraulic pressure system. When the pressure on one component behavior (e.g., distance) increases, then a balanced adjustment has to be made in another component (e.g., gaze). For example, a very close approach by one person may momentarily increase involvement beyond the comfortable level. As a result, the other person may react with decreased eye contact, restoring equilibrium. Comfortable levels of involvement will vary across people and settings, but the predicted compensation process should generalize across those circumstances. Specifically, when there is a condition of disequilibrium (too much or too little involvement by one person), directional compensatory adjustments will be made in one or more of the involvement behaviors.

Equilibrium theory stimulated a great deal of research in the past and continues to influence research today. My review of the early research (Patterson, 1973a) indicated considerable support for the theory. However, a few exceptions (e.g., Breed, 1972; Chapman, 1975; Jourard & Friedman, 1970) provided results directly contradicting those predicted by equilibrium theory. Instead of compensation for increased involvement, these studies showed matching or reciprocity, that is, increased involvement precipitated an *increase,* not a decrease, in the partner's involvement. The existence of the few published studies reporting reciprocal adjustments and the observation that such adjustments are common in everyday life suggested that a more comprehensive theory was needed to explain both compensatory and reciprocal adjustments. In reflecting on this situation, it seemed to me that one had to identify specific mediating events which might be responsible for both compensatory and reciprocal adjustments. Because arousal has frequently been linked to increased nonverbal involvement (e.g., Gale, Lucas, Nissim, & Harpham, 1972; Kleinke & Pohlen, 1971; McBride, King, & James, 1965; Nichols & Champness, 1971), it was a likely candidate. Furthermore, arousal in combination with a cognitive labeling process (Schachter & Singer, 1962) provided a means by which different affective reactions to another's change in involvement could be explained. If sufficient changes in another person's nonverbal involvement produced arousal, contrasting adjustments to that person might be a product of how that arousal was labeled (Patterson, 1976). Decreased arousal, however, also seems to be an important component in some nonverbal exchanges. For example, if a person who is fearful or distressed is comforted by another, the fearful person's arousal level probably decreases. That is, comforting another person, perhaps with a hug or an arm around the shoulder, would be an instance of high involvement that results in decreased arousal. Thus, the arousal component may be generally described as *arousal change.* The sequential steps in the arousal model can be seen in Figure 2-1.

The arousal model's explanation of nonverbal exchange can be briefly described. First, if the change in another's nonverbal involvement is *not* sufficiently great, then neither arousal change nor the labeling process will be activated. The result is no required behavioral adjustment. When the change in the other person's nonverbal involvement is sufficiently great, arousal change and its related labeling process will be initiated. If past experience, the situation, and related cues are positive, the individual will develop a positive affective or emotional reaction such as affection, love,

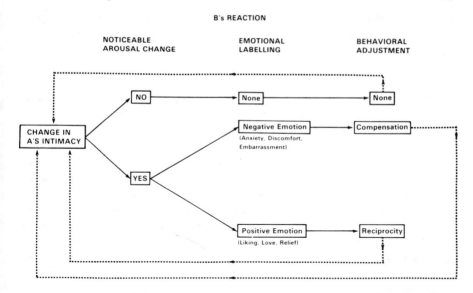

Fig. 2-1. An arousal model of interpersonal intimacy. (Patterson, M.L. An arousal model of interpersonal intimacy. *Psychological Review*, 1976, *83*, 235-245. Copyright 1976 by the American Psychological Association. Reprinted by permission of the publisher.)

or comfort. If those predisposing factors are negative, then an appropriate negative emotional reaction such as fear or anxiety will develop. Positive emotional reactions should facilitate the reciprocation of involvement, whereas negative emotional reactions should facilitate compensation.

The proposed mediating processes provide a coherent explanation for both the compensation effect common in laboratory research and the reciprocity effect common in everyday life. First, in the laboratory, the interactants are almost always strangers (most commonly one is a confederate of the researcher). Next, the subjects are often somewhat apprehensive and probably concerned, if not directly suspicious, about the task before them. Furthermore, the setting for the interaction is usually a rather sterile, minimally furnished laboratory room. Under such circumstances most of the interpersonal and setting cues are sufficiently negative that the labeling process may easily produce some type of negative affect. The result, according to the arousal model, is a predominant pattern of compensation. In contrast, freely chosen interactions with friends, lovers, or family members in settings which are known and under the control of the interactants provide a surplus of positive cues. The result under those circumstances, according to the arousal model, is a predominant pattern of reciprocation. In the former instance, a reaction such as fear or anxiety should result in a compensatory reaction. In the latter instance, a reaction such as liking or love should result in a reciprocal adjustment.

The emphasis on arousal and attribution in responding to changes in nonverbal involvement is not unique to the arousal model. More focused approaches, developed independently at about the same time as the arousal model, similarly stressed the role of arousal and attribution. Specifically, Ellsworth and Langer (1976) suggested that the effect of a confederate's stare on a potential "helper" was mediated by an arousal-attribution process. In addition, Worchel and Teddlie (1976) emphasized the same arousal-attribution process in predicting crowding reactions to personal space invasions.

The roles of arousal and cognition are also highlighted in an ambitious approach toward explaining patterns of nonverbal behavior. This particular theory of nonverbal exchange can be described as a discrepancy-arousal model (Cappella & Greene, 1982). Cappella and Greene proposed that their model of exchange is potentially relevant for all expressive behaviors, both nonverbal and verbal. Their model is an elaboration of Stern's (1974) discrepancy-arousal theory that was generated to explain infant-adult interactions. In contrast to the arousal-attribution models just described, Cappella and Greene's model proposes that the cognitive component precedes rather than follows arousal. That is, arousal in interactions is a product of the discrepancy between the individual's cognitive expectations about the other person's behavior and the actual behavior of the other person. Little or no discrepancy should precipitate no arousal and consequently be perceived as affectively neutral. Moderate discrepancy is assumed to be moderately arousing and therefore pleasurable, whereas high discrepancy is assumed to be highly arousing and unpleasant.

In this way, the amount of increased arousal per se determines the affective reaction of the individual, which in turn specifies the type of behavioral adjustment initiated. Specifically, little or no arousal is affectively neutral and requires no behavioral adjustment. Moderate arousal is experienced positively and precipitates reciprocation of the other's behavior expressiveness, whereas excessive and unpleasant arousal precipitates a compensatory adjustment in behavioral expressiveness. It will be some time before empirical evidence about this model can accumulate, but it does offer considerable promise for a more parsimonious explanation of patterns of nonverbal exchange.

Although it is premature to evaluate the impact of Cappella and Greene's discrepancy-arousal model, it is possible to make some value judgments about the other models—especially Argyle and Dean's equilibrium theory and my own arousal model. Equilibrium theory has been a major stimulus for research on nonverbal exchange and a substantial number of studies offer support for its critical hypothesis of compensation. Although the evidence for compensation is far more common than that for reciprocation (Cappella, 1981; Patterson, 1973a), the inability of equilibrium theory to account for reciprocation, when it does occur, is a major limitation of the theory. In contrast, the arousal change-cognitive labeling process proposed in the arousal model does provide a mediating mechanism capable of explaining both compensatory and reciprocal adjustments. Because of the potentially greater explanatory power of the arousal model, the next section will focus on an evaluation of the empirical research on that model.

Empirical Research on the Arousal Model

Recent research seems moderately supportive of the arousal model. In one study examining interaction patterns among children watching cartoons, friendship pairs matched smiling, looking, and talking responses more than stranger pairs (Foot,

Smith, & Chapman, 1977). The authors interpreted these findings as indicating reciprocation patterns with positively valenced arousal (i.e., with friends), but not with less positively valenced arousal (i.e., with strangers). In a similar study by the same investigators, the reciprocation of intimacy was found between friends, but another prediction of the theory was not supported. Specifically, friend versus stranger pairs did not react differently to different intimacy manipulations (Foot, Chapman, & Smith, 1977). In addition, Storms and Thomas (1977) have reported results from a series of three experiments that are also consistent with the predictions of the arousal model. In particular, the effect of friendly versus unfriendly cues was increased when the confederate sat close to, rather than far away from, the subject. That is, increased involvement produced more favorable reactions with the friendly cues and more unfavorable ones with the unfriendly cues. Presumably, in terms of the arousal model, the close presence of the confederate produced arousal that was experienced positively or negatively as a function of the surrounding friendly or unfriendly cues.

In another study, Whitcher and Fisher (1979) used the postoperative recovery room of a hospital as the setting for manipulating the presence or absence of therapeutic touch. This setting was particularly advantageous because patients in recovery were being physiologically monitored. The results showed that female patients reacted to the touch with decreased physiological arousal and more positive behavioral and judgmental responses, whereas male patients reacted to the touch with increased physiological arousal and more negative behavioral and judgmental responses. An explanation of these results in terms of the arousal model is straightforward. Specifically, the positively valenced decreased arousal of females facilitated a reciprocation of involvement and more positive subjective impressions, whereas the negatively valenced increased arousal of males facilitated a compensatory decrease in involvement and more negative subjective impressions.

In one study designed specifically to test the arousal model, additional support for the model's predictions was found. A confederate's increased involvement (manipulated by increased gaze, more frequent smiles, and a more directly facing body orientation) did increase a heartrate measure of arousal (Coutts, Schneider, & Montgomery, 1980). The prediction regarding an affect manipulation, however, was not supported. Specifically, it was hypothesized that bogus negative feedback would induce negative affect and facilitate a compensatory adjustment to the confederate's involvement. Bogus positive feedback was hypothesized to induce positive affect and facilitate a reciprocal adjustment to the confederate's increased involvement. There were two unexpected results here. First, subjects exposed to negative feedback followed by the confederate's increased involvement *increased* their liking for the confederate, contrary to the change anticipated. Coutts et al., however, suggested that these results were understandable in terms of Aronson and Linder's (1965) gain-loss consideration in attraction. That is, the increased nonverbal involvement of the confederate following negative feedback apparently signaled a gain in the confederate's attraction toward the subject. That in turn induced greater liking (more positive affect) toward the confederate. In other words, the *relative impact* of the increased involvement after the negative feedback was a positive one. A second unexpected result was the pattern of reciprocated involvement in the negative affect condition, and no involvement change in the positive affect condition. Given the increased liking of the confederate in the negative feedback condition, however, the latter result is completely consistent with the arousal model. That is, because the condition designed to induce negative affect apparently did just the opposite, it is reasonable to expect reciprocation under such circumstances. Further, because the positive feedback condition did *not* produce increased liking, the failure to find the predicted reciprocation of the confederate's involvement is not surprising. In summary, after the fact, the results can be viewed as consistent with the predictions of the arousal model. Although such a conclusion indicates support for the model, it also reflects a weakness. Specifically, is it possible to identify beforehand the circumstances that lead to one or another affective reaction, or is the theory simply limited to explaining results after the fact, as in the Coutts et al. study? An alternate interpretation of the results from the Coutts et al. study will play an important part in the discussion of impression management as social control in Chapter 6.

I wish I could claim that the results discussed here are representative of all the research on the arousal model. That is not the case. In fact, it is a little embarrassing to admit that research from my own laboratory has not been very supportive of the arousal model. First, in a study of nonverbal involvement and crowding (Patterson, Roth, & Schenk, 1979), we found that placing groups in a more confronting, circular arrangement versus a less confronting, L-shape arrangement provided only limited support for the model. As hypothesized, subjects in the circular arrangement (high involvement) rated the room more negatively than those in the L-shape arrangement (low involvement). But there was no evidence for increased arousal mediating the more negative reactions. Specifically, both self-rating and task performance (anagram-type problems) measures of arousal were unaffected by the involvement manipulation.

In a study of confederate-subject interaction during a waiting period, the prediction of increased arousal and its related behavioral adjustment was supported in only one of four experimental conditions (Patterson, Jordan, Hogan, & Frerker, 1981). In this study two relatively high involvement patterns (discrete touch plus 50% gaze and 80% gaze alone) were manipulated in a within- and between- (order of conditions) subject design. Only the touch plus 50% gaze condition produced evidence for increased arousal, and then only when it occurred in the middle (but not at the beginning) of the waiting period. These results suggest that the same or comparable levels of involvement can have a different meaning depending on the order and the context in which they appear.

Finally, in an ambitious study that factorially manipulated level of nonverbal involvement, expectancy, and sex composition of subject-confederate pairs, *no* effect of confederate involvement level was found on either the subject's arousal response or his or her behavioral adjustment (Ickes, Patterson, Rajecki, & Tanford, 1982). This study, however, like the Coutts et al. study, has considerable relevance for the social control function. At this point it is sufficient to note that the manipulation of confederate involvement did not produce the effects predicted by the arousal model. But there were some very interesting expectancy effects from that study that will be analyzed in some detail in Chapter 6.

Overall, the pattern of findings from published research shows moderate support for the arousal model. Our own research, however, suggests some important limitations of the model. With this concern in mind, I want to move to a different kind of evaluation of the existing theories, namely, an evaluation of their structural comprehensiveness.

Comprehensiveness of Existing Theories

Although empirical tests of theories are of obvious and critical importance, comparisons of the relative breadth of phenomena covered by theories provide a different basis for evaluating their adequacy. The focus of this latter evaluation will be on the three general models discussed in this chapter: (1) equilibrium theory, (2) the arousal model, and (3) Cappella and Greene's discrepancy-arousal model.

A first concern is the range of behaviors treated by the models. Equilibrium theory and the arousal model are limited to small overlapping sets of intimacy behaviors. Important dimensions such as facial expressiveness, duration of speech, postural openness, and paralinguistic cues are not included in those two models. In contrast, Cappella and Greene's discrepancy-arousal model incorporates a broad range of verbal and nonverbal expressive behaviors. On this point the discrepancy-arousal model fares much better than either of the other two models.

Next is the issue of analyzing different functions of nonverbal behavior. Here all three models are deficient. The recognition that expressing intimacy is but one function of the intimacy behaviors is developed first by Argyle and Dean (1965) and repeated in my later model (Patterson, 1976). Alternate functions, however, are not formally treated in either of those theories. Cappella and Greene have proposed a distinction between expressiveness with an interpersonal focus and expressiveness with a task focus. But specific functions do not play a discriminating role in their discrepancy-arousal process.

A final concern focuses on a consideration of antecedent factors influencing nonverbal exchange. Each of the models recognizes some factors that may potentially qualify the way nonverbal behavior is expressed. That is, there is a general appreciation of the fact that differences in sex, age, or personality may influence the initiation of nonverbal involvement. These antecedents, however, are not classified in any consistent fashion and their relationships to central processes are left indeterminate.

The structural limitations of all these theories and the mixed empirical support for both the equilibrium and arousal models suggest that there is room for improvement in our theories about nonverbal behavior. An empirical evaluation of Cappella and Greene's discrepancy-arousal model is not yet possible, but the discrepancy-arousal model does suffer from some of the same structural limitations that the other models do. It seems clear that a more comprehensive model is needed, one that resolves the deficiencies discussed in this section. In the remainder of this chapter, I will discuss and analyze a sequential functional model of nonverbal exchange (Patterson, 1982a). In developing the new model of nonverbal exchange, it will be important to identify and discuss three critical components: (1) antecedent factors, (2) mediating mechanisms, and (3) the exchange outcome. In the first chapter, the groundwork for this model was developed, both in operationally defining the construct of nonverbal involvement and in proposing a functional classification of nonverbal behavior. The construct of nonverbal involvement identifies a broad range of behaviors most important for the process of nonverbal exchange. The functional classification provides a means for differentiating among the various uses of the involvement behaviors in social settings. Although the involvement behaviors and the functional classification are central to the present theory, an understanding of their dynamic influence on the process of nonverbal exchange requires attention first to the antecedent factors.

Antecedent Factors

Antecedent factors play an important role in understanding the course of nonverbal exchange because they predictably influence both the patterns of involvement and the functions underlying involvement. These antecedent influences can be classified into three general categories: (1) personal, (2) experiential, and (3) relational-situational factors. The antecedent factors will be briefly reviewed here. Later, in Chapter 9, there will be a more thorough review and analysis of these factors.

Personal Factors

Personal factors include those individual or group characteristics that contribute to variability in nonverbal involvement. For example, Hall (1966, 1968) has described differences in closeness and intensity of interactions as a function of *culture*. One contrast identified by Hall was that between Arab, southern Mediterranean, and Latin American people who exhibit higher levels of involvement versus English and northern European people who exhibit lower levels of involvement (Hall, 1966). Next, *sex differences* also seem to contribute to different patterns of nonverbal involvement. Females generally engage in higher levels of nonverbal involvement than males. This is manifested by the following patterns: interacting at closer distances (Aiello & Aiello, 1974; Patterson & Schaeffer, 1977), exhibiting higher levels of gaze (Dabbs, Evans, Hopper, & Purvis, 1980; Exline, 1963; Exline, Gray, & Schuette, 1965), and engaging in touch more often (Jourard, 1966). *Age* may also be a factor influencing nonverbal involvement. Apparently, as children grow older they require more space in interactions (Aiello & Aiello, 1974). Of course, one might argue that such age trends simply reflect the learning of adult norms and do not necessarily imply any change in the underlying "need" for greater space. Another important factor is that of *personality*. The research on personality correlates of nonverbal involvement is extensive. Among the more promising dimensions predicting differential involvement are social approach-avoidance, internal-external locus of control, field dependence-independence, and self-monitoring (Patterson, 1982b). Of course, additional factors such as socioeconomic class, occupation, or religion, among others, might also be related to differential preferences for nonverbal involvement, but there has been relatively little research on these variables.

Experiential Factors

Experiential factors concern the influence of recent and/or similar experiences on interactions. Two different general perspectives might be employed in describing these experiential influences. The first is a general learning-reinforcement perspective. According to this orientation, selective reinforcement of previous involvement patterns and their related functional strategies facilitate their learning and increase their probability of activation in similar future settings. Learning reinforcement could affect the individual vicariously (social learning) or directly (operant or classical conditioning).

An alternate explanation would focus on the regulation of stimulation levels associated with interaction. Milgram (1970) has applied a homeostatic model to the explanation of crowding in high density urban areas. Specifically, Milgram has proposed that crowding is the result of overstimulation or overload of social stimuli. The opposite of the overload circumstance is understimulation. Altman (1975) has integrated both of these notions in developing his model of privacy regulation. Altman's homeostatic model assumes that, in any situation, too little privacy (overstimulation) or too much privacy (understimulation) leads to behavioral adjustments designed to approximate the ideal level of privacy. A similar perspective, but one grounded in physiology, proposes that there is a reliable periodicity in the timing and intensity of social interaction (Chapple, 1970; Hayes & Cobb, Note 2). That is, the preference for social interaction follows a cyclical pattern just as other biorhythms do. Another stimulation-based process, adaptation-level (AL), would predict that repeated deviations from the AL would be incorporated into a new AL, making the same objective levels of stimulation appear less extreme on their next occurrence (Helson, 1964). In terms of involvement behavior, repeated instances of high involvement should be judged as less intense over time, resulting in fewer or less extreme adjustments. It is interesting to note that the stimulation-regulation and AL models seem to make directly opposing predictions.

Relational-Situational Factors

Relational and situational factors are grouped in a common category because they often interact with one another in specifying a particular influence on nonverbal involvement. That is, the influence of the type of relationship between individuals is often moderated by the nature of the setting. Thus, the way one acts toward one's spouse, friend, or boss depends on whether one is at home, at work, out in a restaurant, or in a church. In fact, although there is considerable research on relationships and nonverbal involvement, there is relatively little research on the influence of the situation on nonverbal involvement. Representative of the former type of research is the tendency for those in more intimate relationships to stand at closer distances (Patterson, 1978b), engage in more eye contact (Rubin, 1970), and touch more frequently (Jourard, 1966) than those in less intimate relationships.

One useful perspective for describing and evaluating the influence of the situation is the behavior setting approach of ecological psychology (Barker, 1968; Wicker, 1979). This approach emphasizes the influence of the physical, social, and selection characteristics of a setting on the homogeneity of behavior across individuals. For example, a setting like a small neighborhood bar has a distinct physical design including, perhaps, most of the seating on stools in front of the bar. Such a design is likely to inhibit easy interaction among small groups more than a table or lounge pattern would (Sommer, 1969). The social norms for such bars are usually unwritten but nevertheless closely held. There is often a direct, subtle selection of customers on the bases of race, sex, social class, or other characteristics. In a complementary fashion, customers exercise a selection in choosing to patronize such a setting. The result of all of these converging forces is a group of customers, more similar to one another than to a randomly selected group, responding to common limiting physical and social constraints. Thus, their involvement patterns in this setting should be relatively unique compared to involvement patterns in other settings, even those in which the same actors take part.

Mediating Mechanisms

The effects of the antecedents on the course of an impending interaction are assumed to be mediated by more covert processes. Similarly, when adjustments in nonverbal exchange are precipitated in the interaction itself, specific mediators may also be identified. Thus, mediating mechanisms exercise their influence both in anticipation of the interaction and during the interaction itself. The mediators proposed here include behavioral predispositions, potential arousal change, and cognitive assessment.

Behavioral Predispositions

The habitual nonverbal patterns reflecting stable individual characteristics will be termed "behavioral predispositions." It is assumed that these predispositions are usually more or less "automatic" and often not well represented cognitively. For example, behavioral predispositions may commonly mediate the influence of personal factors on nonverbal involvement. That is, the involvement differences described earlier as a function of culture, sex, age, or personality apparently represent relatively stable preferences requiring little or no cognitive reflection. For example, the tendency for females to exhibit higher levels of nonverbal involvement than males is a fairly general behavioral tendency which probably operates outside of the individual's awareness. Even when there is some reason for the actor to analyze his or her own behavior it is likely that attention will not be focused on the personal antecedents. Instead, the actor's cognitions surrounding some anticipated or actual interaction probably focus on the influence of the situation, and not on one's own characteristics or dispositions (Jones & Nisbett, 1971).

Arousal Change

A second mediator is *arousal change*. Traditionally, interest in arousal and behavior has focused on arousal as an activator. The Yerkes-Dodson law (Yerkes & Dodson, 1908) specifies this view in describing the inverted U relationship between arousal and performance. Although the specific optimal level of arousal varies as a function of task complexity, performance tends to increase, level off, and then decrease as a function of increased arousal. More recently, the emphasis is on the ability of arousal to serve as a signaling or triggering event that stimulates some cognitive or affective activity (Mandler, 1975; Schachter & Singer, 1962). The most obvious examples of arousal producing either of these consequences are those involving *increased* arousal. That is, increasing arousal from some resting state tends both to improve performance (up to a point) and to precipitate cognitive activity. Because the Yerkes-Dodson law describes a continuous relationship between arousal and performance, there is the obvious application of this law to instances of decreased arousal too. But the application of the signaling function to instances of decreased arousal is a little more questionable. Nevertheless, it is certainly reasonable to assume that if an individual has some sensitivity to increased arousal, a similar sensitivity may exist for decreased arousal. Thus, it might be proposed that when a *difference* threshold in arousal is exceeded, some cognitive assessment is required.

There is a practical reason for considering the role of decreased arousal in nonverbal exchange. A number of important and intense interactions are characterized by both high levels of nonverbal involvement and decreased arousal. For example, one who is fearful, anxious, or distressed may be comforted by an embrace or a hug. The initiation of such behavior probably decreases arousal and alleviates some of the negative affect. One study reported contrasting arousal, behavioral, and affective reactions to touch as a function of the sex of the person touched (Whitcher & Fisher, 1979). In this study, the manipulation was the presence or absence of touch by nurses toward patients in postoperative recovery. Because these patients were continuously monitored physiologically, arousal change data were conveniently available. The female patients reacted to touch with decreased arousal and more positive behavioral and judgmental reactions, whereas males reacted with increased arousal and more negative behavioral and judgmental reactions. Thus the direction of the arousal change was predictive of contrasting behavioral and affective reactions.

Although arousal change can be an important factor in nonverbal exchange, it is probably not as pervasive as suggested in the arousal model (Patterson, 1976). The Whitcher and Fisher study provided strong support for the mediating role of arousal change, but our own research has not consistently demonstrated such an effect (Ickes, Patterson, Rajecki, & Tanford, 1982; Patterson, Jordan, Hogan, & Frerker, 1981; Patterson, Roth, & Schenk, 1979). In these studies, there was not always a clear correspondence among the arousal, behavioral, and affective reactions of subjects to manipulated involvement, as the arousal model predicted. At the same time, it seems important to recognize even a tentative role for arousal change because it may affect the pattern of behavioral adjustment in one or both of the ways mentioned earlier. That is, changes in arousal might affect either the specific form of behavioral adjustments or serve as a signal to initiate an analysis of the meaning of changing circumstances (Mandler, 1975, chap. 4). In the former case, arousal level may either affect the performance of behavioral adjustments as predicted by the Yerkes-Dodson law or differentially facilitate dominant adjustment patterns (Zajonc, 1965). In the latter case, arousal change as a signal would serve to initiate a cognitive-affective evaluation of the interactional context. The cognitive-affective assessment identifies the last mediator and the topic of the next section.

Cognitive-Affective Assessment

Cognitive-affective assessment involves any kind of evaluative response, from simple affective judgments to more complex patterns of cognitions. Representative of the former are those affective reactions or preferences that are primary responses to stimuli, distinct from cognitions about the same stimuli (Zajonc, 1980). In reviewing a number of studies on such affective reactions, Zajonc (1980) concluded that these primary preferences can develop before subjects are even able to identify the stimulus. That is, not only are these preferences distinct from cognitive reactions to the stimulus, but they can occur *before* the stimulus is even recognized. Zajonc notes that the first impressions of like or dislike we have when meeting strangers are examples of these affective reactions. Such reactions, often developing in a fraction of a second, seem to be dependent primarily on nonverbal cues. Obviously, such simple affective reactions can set the tone for subsequent interaction and provide a further stimulus for additional cognitive work.

More complex cognitive processes may focus on either self-other or setting-activity characteristics. These processes may be especially important in the form of expectancies. Self-other cognitions are the general focus of expectancies like the self-fulfilling prophecy (Merton, 1948, 1957; Rosenthal, 1966, 1974) or the behavioral confirmation process (Snyder & Swann, 1978; Snyder, Tanke, & Berscheid, 1977; Swann & Snyder, 1980). In general, it is assumed that the presence of the expectancy causes the perceiver to behave in a fashion that elicits confirming reactions from the target person. For example, if I hear that George is a rather cold and insensitive person, my first encounter with him may be less enthusiastic and more controlled than if I had heard the opposite. Consequently, my behavioral reserve facilitates George's responding in kind, which in turn supports my original expectancy.

Detailed expectancies about a setting or an activity can also be critical in directing one's behavior. The concept of a script has been used to describe such a related series of expectancies (Abelson, 1981; Schank & Abelson, 1977). In its stronger sense, a script includes expectancies about the occurrence of particular events and their sequential ordering (Abelson, 1981). For the purpose of the present discussion, scripts are important because of their effect in determining behavior sequences in a setting. In contrast to specific expectancies about others, scripts are generalizations about a situation that are relatively stable and independent of the specific identity of the other actors. Thus, the information in a script permits us to anticipate and initiate a series of related interpersonal behaviors. For example, at a party, an acquaintance might say, "There's someone I want you to meet." This invitation, which might pair you with an obnoxious boor, a social stiff, or a pleasant companion, activates the old "meet another character" script. Independent of the initial affective reactions (Zajonc, 1980), the early sequence of events is fairly predictable. When you follow your acquaintance to the other person, you stand back a bit and let the introduction develop. You shake hands (most likely when males are involved), nod slightly, smile, and wait to see if there are any further elaborations made by your acquaintance. If not, you can expect at least a brief conversation, perhaps focusing on your mutual acquaintance, work, or others at the party. Disengaging an uncomfortable interaction can be unpleasant, but excusing yourself to get a drink or snack or having to talk to someone else are possible "covers." Other situations that may provide script-like expectancies include a variety of business, professional, or service encounters.

Whether the focus of these cognitive-affective reactions is the self, the other, or the situation, expectancies can have a substantial effect on subsequent behavior. Furthermore, cognitions relevant to interaction are not merely anticipatory in nature. Although expectancies have been emphasized in social psychological research, cognitive evaluations also often accompany ongoing behavior. This is likely to be the case especially under one or more of the following conditions: (a) a personal or interpersonal expectancy is not fulfilled; (b) the cognitive content of the script disagrees with its behavioral manifestation; and (c) evaluation apprehension is high. Under these circumstances, some continuing cognitive assessment is often necessary to facilitate a desirable outcome.

Finally, it can be suggested that this cognitive activity may occur within or outside of awareness. Nisbett and Wilson's (1977) critique of the verbal reporting of mental processes concludes that, in many situations, people cannot accurately verbalize the cognitive processes that apparently guided their behavior. The issue of accessibility to one's cognitive processes or the accuracy of verbal reports about them is clearly separate from positing that such cognitive processes occur. But practical testing of hypotheses about the influence of various cognitive processes would indeed be difficult if such verbal reports were not valid. In fact, the opposing view, that is, that verbal reports of cognitive processes can be valid (at least under the right conditions), has been gathering support (Cotton, 1980; Ericsson & Simon, 1980; Smith & Miller, 1978; White, 1980). The assessment of such cognitions will be addressed in a later section.

Exchange Outcome

Other models of nonverbal exchange (Argyle & Dean, 1965; Cappella & Greene, 1982; Patterson, 1976) have attempted to explain and predict the type of reactive behavioral adjustments following an initial change in another person's nonverbal behavior. The classification of behavioral adjustments common to these models includes reciprocal or matching reactions, compensatory reactions, or no behavioral change. It is convenient, and usually necessary, to analyze interactive sequences in terms of these individual reactive changes. An exclusive focus, however, on individual behavioral adjustments may be inappropriate for describing complex coordinated sequences.

The emphasis in the last section on expectancies, and especially on scripts, points to the importance of these directing cognitions in determining the behavioral course of an interaction. Thus, each person can have a behavioral program that follows a number of sequentially related adjustments. In this way, each person's behavior is as much a result of activating that script or program as it is a result of reacting to the other person. Thus, the coordinated and mutual involvement of an interaction is not simply the sum of each person's sequential adjustments to the other person's behavior. Even if one can determine with precision the sequencing of each person's behavior, it does not necessarily mean that one person's behavior was a response to the other's earlier behavior. For example, if Joe raises his hand for a handshake two-tenths of a second before Harry does, there is no certainty that Harry is reacting in response to Joe. Harry may not even be attending to Joe's move. Instead, both of them may be *independently* activating a greeting script, and the slight time difference does not necessitate an inference that Harry was reacting to Joe. To the extent that such shared scripts or expectancies determine mutual involvement, a reactive explanation of behavioral adjustment may be inappropriate and inaccurate.

At the same time, it is important to appreciate that reactive adjustments also occur. There is no need to reject such descriptions to provide a place for a mutual index of nonverbal exchange. In fact, I would suggest that a two-level analysis of exchange outcome be initiated. First, at the dyadic level, one could examine the degree to which mutual involvement represents a coordinated enactment of shared scripts. As situations become more structured by social norms and/or past experience, the interactants should share increasingly similar expectancies or scripts about the interaction. This in turn should produce a more stable, coordinated series of mutual adjustments. Some encounters, such as those involving shared scripts about greetings or departures, may often have the appearance of reciprocation when analyzed from an individual reactive level. In contrast, as the situation is less structured by social norms and/or past experience, there should be less communality in expectancies or scripts, leading to a greater opportunity for one or the other interactant to initiate an inappropriate level of involvement. Under these circumstances, a stable, coordinated series of mutual adjustments is less likely and reactive adjustments at the individual level are more likely.

By being sensitive to the programmed nature of at least some interaction, it is possible to differentiate between instances of scripted exchange and those that are primarily reactive. In the former circumstance, correctly anticipating the appropriate behavior provides a kind of cognitive and behavioral economy for the interactants. In the latter circumstance there is probably a greater need for increased cognitive work in evaluating one's own behavior and that of the other in making an adjustment. In general, interactions characterized either by shared scripts or reactive reciprocity will tend to be more stable than those characterized by reactive compensation. That is, when the matching of behavioral patterns is facilitated by shared scripts or by reciprocal individual adjustments, the input of the interactants necessarily tends to be balanced and reflective of some underlying communality. In the case of scripts, communality is a shared perception of sequential steps in the interactive process. In the case of reciprocal reactive adjustments, communality may be comparable interpersonal judgments or shared affective reactions. In contrast, when there are compensatory reactive adjustments, the absence of behavioral matching suggests some underlying differences that can contribute to instability.

The stability-instability continuum is a critical dimension along which a joint or dyadic description of the exchange can be made. For the purposes of the present model, an unstable exchange will be defined as one in which at least one party perceives some inappropriateness and/or lack of synchrony in the behavioral exchange. Such a sensitivity can focus either on one's own behavior or on that of the other person. If the focus is on the other person's behavior, such an evaluation may take the form of Cappella and Greene's (1982) discrepancy analysis of expected versus actual behavior. According to Cappella and Greene, when the discrepancy is too great, the resulting large change in arousal will be experienced negatively and lead to compensation. Regardless of its focus or form, instability is meant to describe an immediate, evaluative reaction to the momentary status of the exchange. Furthermore, it is assumed that individuals do not generally have a conscious awareness of instances in which the exchange is stable. As such, that evaluation takes the form of a negative feedback mechanism. That is, when the discrepancy is too great, the individual is sensitized to it and reactive adjustments are required. The exception, of course, is the situation in which one anticipates instability and the opposite occurs. In that circumstance awareness of the stability of the exchange may be high. The perception of instability is important because it triggers arousal and cognitive-affective processes that mediate nonverbal adjustment. This point will be covered in greater detail in the section on the interaction phase of the model.

A Sequential Functional Model

Now that the critical components have been reviewed and described, they can be assembled into a general model of nonverbal exchange. This may be best accomplished by starting with the antecedent influences and then proceeding sequentially through the stages of the model. The three antecedent factors are ordered in terms of their direct salience to the focal interaction. Most remote are the personal factors such as culture, gender, personality, social class, or age. That is, these individual difference variables have a history and stability that are independent of the focal interaction, even though they influence the course of an exchange. The experiential factor refers to the residual effects of previous interactions, particularly those that are most recent and more similar to the impending interaction. The relational-situational factor refers to the anticipated social and physical constraints structuring the interaction. For example, we often know whom we will see in the near future and we can usually anticipate the circumstances of the interaction. Such information determines our expectancies about the interaction. These expectancies, in turn, may lead to different strategies of involvement.

Preinteraction Influences

What are the practical influences of antecedents on interactions? In general, it is assumed that the effects of the antecedent factors are manifested primarily in the preinteraction mediators. The personal, experiential, and relational-situational antecedents, however, have an earlier and broader effect in developing complex and interrelated self-, other-, and setting-selection processes that necessarily limit the range and circumstances of future interactions. That is, the fact that one is male or female, young or old, black or white, introverted and extraverted, results in some

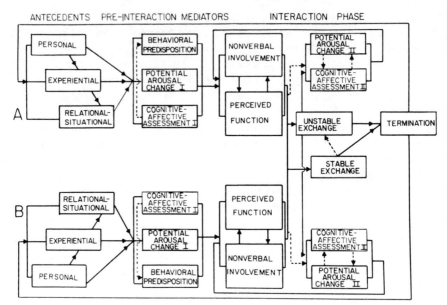

Fig. 2-2. The sequential functional model of nonverbal exchange. (Patterson, M.L. A sequential functional model of nonverbal behavior. *Psychological Review*, 1982, *89*, 231-249. Copyright 1982 by the American Psychological Association. Reprinted by permission of the publisher.)

broadly predictable self-selection tendencies. These self-selection tendencies are complemented by the influence of the experiential and relational-situational factors. Specifically, the experiential factor summarizes the impact of one's past experience on selecting future interactions. For example, past experiences that have been unpleasant and/or overstimulating or understimulating will be avoided. The relational-situational factors represent further selection pressures initiated by others and by the settings of the potential interactions. In this way, the practical availability of specific others and specific settings for future interactions is quite limited, even within the geographical area accessible to the individual. Thus, the initial influence of the antecedent factors involves a kind of screening or filtering device controlling the opportunity for future interaction, and the number of interactions that actually occur represents only a very select portion of those practically possible for any individual.

The complex selection processes that develop as a function of the antecedents are obviously important. The concern of this model, however, is the manner in which antecedents influence the development of interaction, not just the selection of occasions for interaction. Although the relationships between antecedents and preinteraction mediators are quite complex, some of the simpler patterns can be described here.

The direct influence of the personal factors (as opposed to their interactive effects in combination with the other antecedent factors) probably relates more to behavioral predispositions than to arousal change and cognitive-affective assessment. That is, various individual difference dimensions are related to consistent patterns of nonverbal involvement. For example, females typically interact at closer distances (Patterson, 1978b), maintain higher levels of gaze toward others (Ellsworth & Ludwig, 1972), and touch more frequently (Jourard, 1966) than males do. In addition, personality differences may be predictive of differential spacing preferences (Patterson, 1978b, 1982a) or contrasting patterns of paralinguistic behavior (Siegman, 1978). Such behavioral predispositions probably operate outside of awareness, unless something unusual or unexpected occurs, for example, someone reacting very strangely in response to us. Even then, the actor probably attributes another person's unusual reaction to that person's dispositional characteristics rather than to his or her own habitual behavioral patterns (Jones & Nisbett, 1971). The influence of personal antecedents on nonverbal involvement will be examined in detail in Chapter 8.

Experiential and relational-situational factors are more likely to exercise their influence on nonverbal involvement and exchange through the mediation of arousal change and cognitive-affective assessment. That is, the residue of past experience and the knowledge of various interpersonal and situational constraints may activate some cognitive-affective assessment and arousal change processes. In general, it is probably safe to say that the more important and more salient the experiential and relational-situational factors are to the individual, the more likely cognitive and arousal mechanisms are to be triggered. In addition, cognitive and physiological activity should increase in anticipation of an interaction when the experiential and relational-situational cues suggest one of the following: (a) the interaction may be uncomfortable or even threatening; (b) the perceived differences between the actor and the other increase; (c) the setting for the interaction is a novel one; and (d) evaluation apprehension in the interaction increases.

Some recent data we have collected in our laboratory shows support for the predicted increase in cognitive and arousal activity under the first two conditions. In one experiment, an expectancy manipulation involved informing the subjects that the other subject (confederate) was either similar or dissimilar on personality tests taken previously. Those in the similar condition were also told that the other person was probably the type of individual they would choose for a friend, and consequently the interaction should be enjoyable. Contrasting information was given to the subjects in the dissimilar condition. Subjects in the dissimilar condition, compared to those in the similar condition, showed increased arousal (as measured by electrodermal responses) immediately after hearing the expectancy instructions (Ickes et al., 1982). Current research in our laboratory is attempting to determine if cognitive activity also increases as a function of expectancy manipulations. Some of these procedures will be discussed in Chapter 9.

In the arousal model (Patterson, 1976) it was assumed that the arousal and cognitive components mediated nonverbal exchange by operating in the fashion described by Schachter and Singer (1962), that is, arousal triggers the cognitive labeling process that in turn specifies the feeling-state experienced. A similar position was proposed by Mandler (1975) who suggested that the recognition of increased arousal initiates a meaning analysis culminating in the experience of different feelings or emotions. In line with these views, Wegner and Giuliano (1980) recently found that the arousal produced by physical activity stimulates a particular type of cognitive response—increased self-focus. The present functional model, however, recognizes that a bidirectional relationship between arousal and cognitions is most defensible. For example, cognitive input produced by instructional manipulations can substantially affect the level of arousal resulting from some standard stimulus (Lazarus, 1964, 1968). It might also be recalled that Cappella and Greene's (1982) model is based on the assumption that arousal is a direct product of the degree of cognitive discrepancy. To the extent that the interactional context and the available cues are ambiguous or novel, arousal change may stimulate the cognitive activity needed to determine the meaning of events. However, most situations in which we find ourselves are probably meaningful as soon as we know the setting, for example, meeting an old friend, saying goodbye to a loved one, or waiting to get chewed out by the boss. In such instances arousal change may be the *product* of the initial cognitive activity. Presumably, arousal change does not usually happen in a vacuum, with the meaning of the event only developing later.

Finally, the more clearly cognitive-affective assessment defines the anticipated interaction (accurately or inaccurately), the easier it is for the actor to think of the interaction in functional terms. For example, as one anticipates meeting a loved one, a skeptical superior, or a physician administering a physical exam, one will be thinking in terms descriptive of the intimacy, social control, and service-task functions, respectively. The more explicit interpersonal or situational expectancies (scripts) are, the more likely that behavioral strategies will be selected and even rehearsed. For example, a woman going on a job interview may try to anticipate the employer's questions, how to answer them, and how to present herself. When such expectancies are not well defined or in cases of unanticipated exchanges, the apparent functions underlying an interaction may be inferred only from the developing interpretation of the exchange. In such instances, one might be especially sensitive to any cues that would help to define the interaction. As an apparent function is tentatively identified, the behavioral options become more limited and uncertainty about appropriate behavior can be reduced.

The link between the preinteraction mediators and the initiation of the interaction can be briefly summarized. Behavioral predispositions represent some general behavioral tendency, usually outside of awareness, to initiate relatively stable levels of nonverbal involvement across differing interactions. The cognitive-affective assessment and arousal change processes combine to elicit more specific patterns of nonverbal involvement, often within awareness. Further, the cognitive input itself can often trigger a functional analysis that in turn defines the level of involvement enacted.

Interaction Phase

At the time of initiating an interaction the converging effects of the preinteraction mediators have constrained the level of involvement and structured the potential functions of the interaction. The course of nonverbal exchange is primarily determined by the relative intensity of each person's nonverbal involvement and by the degree of correspondence between their perceived functions. Extreme levels of involvement can precipitate increased arousal that is often experienced negatively, resulting in instability and compensatory adjustments (Patterson, 1976). Cappella and Greene (1982) suggest that an extreme level of involvement initiated by one person produces negative affect and compensatory adjustment in the other person because it is too discrepant from the latter individual's expected level of involvement. Presumably, a large discrepancy between the preferred and actual level of involvement results in a high level of arousal that is necessarily experienced negatively. The negative affect in turn precipitates compensatory adjustments. It might be noted that the likelihood of a mismatch in preferred levels of involvement should be greater as differences between the interactants (in terms of personal factors) become greater. That is, as individuals are less similar in culture, sex, age, social class, or personality, the greater the probability that their preferred levels of involvement will be discrepant. Even this general prediction, however, is necessarily qualified by the characteristics of the situation.

A greater disparity between the functional expectancies of the interactants should also create instability and increase the likelihood of compensatory behavior. Of course, similar functional interpretations of an interaction will not guarantee stability if the interactants are at cross purposes. For example, two co-workers may view a particular exchange in a social control manner (i.e., a power struggle) with each trying to dominate the other. Alternatively, a male might make a sexual advance on an unwilling female. In both cases, each party knows the meaning of such behavior, and obviously simply knowing the purpose or function of that behavior does not lead to stability in the exchange. Even in these cases, however, stability might be reached before the exchange is terminated because the interactants are able to interpret and react appropriately to the other's behavior. For example, the struggle for dominance is settled or the sexual advance is rejected, and consequently further behavioral manifestations of those functions are inappropriate.

Although the involvement levels and perceived functions are separate elements in this model, their impact on one another is substantial. When functional expectancies are particularly explicit they can determine the level and pattern of nonverbal involvement. Thus, script-like expectancies of meeting a long-absent loved one versus meeting a personnel manager about a new job lead to contrasting patterns of nonverbal involvement. Furthermore, if the actual involvement level of the other person disagrees with some appropriate normative level, one is likely to reevaluate the underlying function of the interaction.

An illustration of the adjustment process in the interaction phase may be useful at this point. The left side of Figure 2-3 depicts A's reactions to B's initiation of an extremely high level of involvement. B's initial involvement level, presumably discrepant with A's preferred level, results in A's perception of instability in the interaction (unstable exchange cell). This recognition in turn initiates A's cognition-arousal processes. Again, the sequential development of the arousal-cognitive process is variable, but A is likely to experience some increased arousal and assess his or her own feelings and/or the meaning of B's behavior. The result of these mediational processes should be some adjustment in nonverbal involvement and possibly a reevaluation of the function of the interaction. If A's involvement adjustment and assessment of the function are satisfactory and A feels more comfortable, the exchange will tend to stabilize. Of course, because A's reactions represent only one side of the exchange, they cannot ensure a stable exchange. If A's adjustment is not

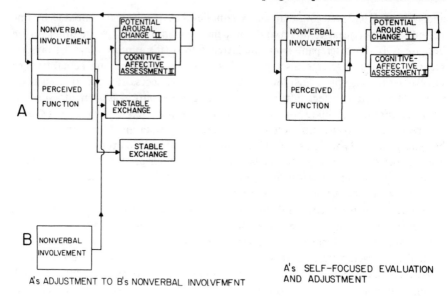

Fig. 2-3. Alternate adjustment sequences of nonverbal exchange.

satisfactory, A will cycle through another loop until the adjustment is satisfactory or the interaction is terminated.

The arousal-cognition processes need not be solely the product of the other person's involvement level. Occasionally, cognitive-affective assessment and the related arousal change may focus primarily on one's own behavior (e.g., did I act the way I wanted to act?). Such a self-focus has been described by Carver (1979) in his cybernetic model of self-attention processes. Specifically, an individual may evaluate the appropriateness of his or her own involvement behavior with or without some instigating arousal concerning its intended effect. Generally, the greater the evaluative concerns, the more likely this self-focus will be accompanied by arousal. Although some instability in the exchange may be the stimulus initiating such a self-focus (e.g., the other person appeared uncomfortable when I moved closer), self-reflection might occur without a potentially negative reaction from the other person. In this latter case, one might have a standard against which one's own behavioral patterns are judged. Usually such standards must be evaluated in terms of the other person's reaction, but some evaluations may be guided more by the actor's own performance or self-presentation expectancies than by a concern about the other person's assessment. In effect, such an individual would have a self-focused script for the interaction.

This situation is represented in the right side of Figure 2-3. Here A's involvement behavior relative to the perceived function of the interaction becomes evaluated after the fact and is potentially modifiable by a second cycle through the system. Although such self-reflection and adjustment obviously affect the degree of stability in an exchange, this is more a side effect in this instance. That is, A's own performance concerns would be focal in the arousal and cognitive processes. This kind of reaction might be expected more frequently when a social control function is activated, especially by individuals who are experiencing evaluation apprehension; in other words, when the actor is more concerned about self-evaluation than about relating to the other person. Of course, such extreme self-focus is probably infrequent and also a luxury for people who have to live with the interpersonal consequences of their behavior. It is unlikely that a low-status person could risk managing his or her interactive behavior independent of the reactions of surrounding high-status people.

Successful adjustments in nonverbal involvement and/or in the perceived functions of the interaction, by definition, increase the stability of the exchange. When there is instability, however, the recognition of this instability in the exchange should again activate the arousal-cognition processes in one or both interactants. Should an interaction prove to be consistently unstable and unaffected by the adjustments of one or both parties, an earlier termination would be expected.

Finally, the termination of an interaction leaves a residue of cognitive and affective reactions that feed back to influence the antecedent factors. Of course, with respect to personal antecedents, such feedback is unlikely to change one's age, race, or sex, but this feedback may alter interpersonal attitudes or values associated with such individual characteristics. Further, changes in one's personality, though probably not great after any single exchange, are certainly possible over time. The experiential factor, by definition, includes residual influences from recent and/or important previous exchanges. The outcome of a given exchange influences complementary self-, other-, and setting-selection processes described in the relational-situational factor. For repeated or similar exchanges, the consequences of the previous exchange can often determine the quality and development of future interaction.

Summarizing the Model

The present model attempts to address some of the weaknesses inherent in previous theoretical formulations. Of greatest importance is the emphasis on a functional analysis of nonverbal involvement. Although other models of nonverbal exchange recognize some variability in the functions served by nonverbal behavior, they do not integrate these functions into a framework for predicting patterns of nonverbal involvement. The sequential process proposed in this model starts with the antecedent factors, including personal characteristics, past experiences, and relational-situational constraints. This set of antecedent factors exercises its influence covertly at the preinteraction stage by (a) determining behavioral predispositions for differential involvement, (b) precipitating arousal change, and (c) developing cognitive and affective expectancies. The joint effect of these three mediators shapes each person's perception of the interaction's function and limits the range of involvement initiated. Each person's preferred level of involvement and functional cognitions determine expectancies about the other person's level of involvement. A stable exchange may be defined as one in which the discrepancy between the expected and actual involvement with the other person is minimal. Thus, further cognitive work is unnecessary and major behavioral adjustments are not required. When the discrepancy between expected and actual involvement is large, a condition of instability is created. That instability stimulates additional cognitive-arousal processes.

These processes, in turn, lead to adjustment in nonverbal involvement that may or may not be accompanied by a reassessment of the interaction's function. When there is instability, additional arousal and cognitive activity will occur until either the interaction is stable or it is terminated.

Summary

This model of nonverbal exchange views interaction behavior as the product of a sequence of related events. At the foundation of the model is the distinction proposed between the interaction behaviors per se and the functions served by them. This distinction is supported by the recognition that the same behavioral patterns can serve very different functions in an interaction. Thus, an understanding of nonverbal exchange requires not only that we can describe the interactive behavior, but also analyze the purpose of that behavior. The pursuit of the function or purpose of some behavioral pattern necessarily gives rise to questions about attributions, cognitive focus, scripts, and other issues that are central in cognitive psychology today. Consequently, this theory complements current cognitive approaches to understanding behavior.

The sequential functional model represents an attempt at a comprehensive theory of nonverbal exchange. In the abstract, this would certainly seem to be a desirable goal, but such an effort cannot be attempted without some corresponding cost. In this case, it is likely that there is some loss in the specificity of predictions relative to those of previous theories. In the arousal model, and especially in the equilibrium model, the derivation of testable hypotheses is reasonably straightforward. The hypotheses may often not be supported, but they are easily testable. One reviewer of the first version of the present theory noted that the testability of equilibrium theory made it more desirable than the functional model. Testability is certainly an important element in evaluating a theory. But if the most favorable comment one can make about a theory is that it is refutable, it is time for an alternate perspective on the issues.

I think that the functional model represents such a useful perspective on nonverbal exchange, though it may not be as "refutable" as earlier models. The discussions in the next five chapters will be developed around the different functions proposed by this model. In this way I hope to provide some insights into the complexities of nonverbal behavior *and* propose a few testable (and refutable) hypotheses.

Chapter 3

The Informational Function

In this chapter the first of the five proposed functions of nonverbal behavior will be discussed and analyzed. It may be recalled that in Chapter 1 the first two functions—the informational function and the regulating interaction—were described as having a molecular focus. That is, they identify isolated patterns of behavior. In contrast, the last three functions—expression of intimacy, social control, and the service-task function—have a molar focus. That is, these three functions describe the theme or motive underlying the whole encounter. Thus, the last three functions are critical over the course of an interaction.

The molecular and molar levels of analysis represent orthogonal dimensions of classification. Consequently, a given behavioral sequence might be described as either informational or regulatory, and at the same time occur within the larger context of an intimacy, social control, or service-task function (Eric Knowles suggested this distinction to me in reacting to an earlier description of this classification of functions). It may be useful to start the discussion of functions with the molecular focus and work up to the molar focus in later chapters.

Any nonverbal behavior in a social setting is potentially informative for observers. Such behavior may tell us something about the actor's characteristic disposition, relationships to others, or reactions to various objects or topics of conversation. Although all behaviors can be classified as informational, some behavioral patterns probably merit a special classification. Specifically, patterns that serve to control the development of an interaction deserve separate classification under the function of regulating interaction, even though those patterns may also be informative. It might also be suggested that a distinction between the informational and interaction regulation functions can be made in terms of a contrast between content and form. That is, the informational function stresses the meaning of a behavioral pattern, whereas the interaction regulation function stresses the form or structure of an exchange. This distinction provides some sense of the contrast between the informational and interaction regulation functions, but it is not without exception. Obviously, the form or structure of an interaction can also provide meaning-related information. Specifically, one's willingness to interact with others and to participate in the regulation process may be seen as basic information about an individual's disposition (I am grateful to Bill Ickes for suggesting the basic informational quality of one's habitual pattern of regulating interaction).

Although it is necessary to note these similarities in the two functions, their differences are important. The utility of the informational versus regulational contrast should be evident in the next two chapters. Let us turn our attention first to the informational function.

A general description of the informational function is necessarily broad and hardly controversial, but a finer distinction within this function is a matter of considerable debate. In particular, the differences revolve around the contrast between *communication* and *indication*. Much research on nonverbal behavior has appeared under the label of "nonverbal communication." Assumptions about the nature of communication, however, are usually not made explicit, and in fact are rarely discussed at all in research on nonverbal behavior. Yet such assumptions can considerably influence not only one's approach to analyzing nonverbal behavior, but also the interpretation of the product of that analysis.

Most of us can probably think of a variety of behaviors that we would intuitively classify as meaningful. The pleasant smile and nod of approval from a friend in response to something we say or do is clearly and immediately interpreted. Similarly, a grimacing reaction leaves little doubt that the behavior in question has met with disapproval or rejection. In addition to these and other changes in facial expression, various other body movements, postures, and gestures supply the observer with considerable information about an individual and his or her reactions to varying circumstances. Like facial expressions, some other behaviors may be fairly explicit and immediately understood, as in the case of raising and extending an open hand outward in signalling someone to stop, or in using an obscene gesture. Still other behaviors may not provide such unambiguous information, but only hint at a general feeling. In this last instance, an acquaintance might be physically withdrawn, avoid eye contact, and frequently change postures. The total picture of such a person's behavior leads to a negatively toned evaluation, but details about the origin, extent, and specific meaning of the acquaintance's behavior may not be immediately obvious. Examples such as the last one are probably common experiences for most of us.

There can be little doubt that we are affected by or react to such nonverbal behaviors in our interactions with others who display them. But the question of whether or not these behaviors should be described as communication is not so easily answered. There is, of course, no single ultimately correct answer to this question; instead there are alternative answers that vary in the degree to which they make sense, are internally consistent, or are useful in furthering our understanding and pursuit of related issues. Furthermore, different perspectives on nonverbal communication often suggest different strategies for asking research questions and for describing the general process of social interaction. At this point it is appropriate to discuss these different perspectives on communication and examine their implications for the functional approach proposed in this book.

Perspectives on Communication

All Behavior Is Communication

One approach to communication involves the simple encompassing assumption that all social behavior is communication. That is, any verbal or nonverbal behavior in the presence of another person is defined as communicative (Watzlawick & Beavin, 1967). This particular orientation is based on the judgment that communication itself is a system that cannot conveniently be segmented into encoder and decoder elements. According to this perspective, designating one person as an encoder or a decoder in an interaction or focusing only on certain behaviors does violence to the whole communication process by destroying the basic interpersonal and multichannel relationships in that process. Furthermore, communication always occurs in a context that structures the nature of the communication. Important contextual elements would include culture, the nature of interpersonal relationships between the interactants, the purpose of the interaction, and the many personal characteristics of the interactants. Birdwhistell (1959) characterizes this perspective on communication in proposing that we do not really communicate; rather, we become a part of communication. That is, individuals do not originate communication but instead participate in it. Birdwhistell makes this judgment because he views communication as a system rather than an activity initiated by the individual. Consequently, according to this perspective, communication as a system must be understood at the transactional level.

Scheflen (1974, pp. 185-196) has elaborated on this position by noting that a typical communications analysis is constrained by the assumption that communication is the force that relates one individual to another. Once these communication forces were postulated, the source for them had to be identified. The forces were held to be internal and not observable, taking the form of instincts, drives, or motivation. According to this view, a person's behavior (the product of his or her internal state) supposedly communicates something to another individual that modifies this person's internal state and produces a behavioral reaction. Scheflen argued, however, that as a consequence of postulating an imaginary force of communication, theorists and researchers have been inclined to develop other nonobservable constructs in the form of internal causes. According to Scheflen, the unfortunate consequence of such an approach is that the communications researcher ignores the structure and patterning of behavior as a system. The structure and patterning of behavior are the most important characteristics of communication to those, like Birdwhistell and Scheflen, who support a systems approach.

What are the consequences of taking a systems approach to communication? Obviously, the encoder-decoder distinction is deemphasized. Instead, behavior has to be analyzed as part of a larger whole involving other individuals and a variety of contextual factors. In addition, concerns about the motivation for behavior, which are an individual matter, are also deemphasized, whereas questions about the regularity of communication patterns across interactions are stressed. This emphasis on the similarities rather than the differences among individuals is more compatible with the task of examining converging processes in social interaction and culturally determined patterns of behavior than with the task of analyzing the meaning of an isolated behavior sequence.

Only Some Behavior Is Communication

In contrast to the systems approach, in which all nonverbal behavior is defined as communicative, another perspective suggests that only a few nonverbal behaviors are communicative. This position has been presented by one group of researchers (Wiener, Devoe, Rubinow, & Geller, 1972) whose discrete analysis of interactive behavior is grounded in a very specific and tightly defined conception of communication. In fact, the approach advocated by Wiener and his colleagues may be seen as a reaction to theorists such as Birdwhistell and Scheflen who refuse to distinguish between behavior and communication. Wiener et al. propose that three distinct characteristics in any interactive behavior pattern must be present before it can be considered communication. They argue that communication requires that there be (a) a socially shared signal system or code, (b) an encoder who uses this system to make some message public, and (c) a decoder who uses the code to interpret the sign. But Wiener et al. see a distinct need to clarify and limit this description by a detailed analysis of the operations involved in defining these characteristics.

There are several critical elements that can be specified in this approach to communication. First, Wiener et al. propose that an encoding approach is the perspective necessary for analyzing communication. Because most analyses of nonverbal behavior have dealt with its effects on the target or observer of the behavior, the typical emphasis has necessarily been on decoding. That is, the common focus of attention is the decoder's reactions following a particular behavioral sequence by the encoder.

For example, suppose that Byron and Zelda are having a friendly conversation over a cup of coffee when Byron begins looking around, fidgeting, scratching his nose, and occasionally glancing at his watch. Zelda, nobody's fool, quickly comments that she had better be going, and both of them leave in different directions. From observing the incident and questioning Zelda about it, we can conclude that she interpreted Byron's behavioral signs as indicating that he was anxious to leave. Wiener et al. would agree that such a description is appropriate. However, they claim that a transformation from *indicating* something to *communicating* it is all too easily, and incorrectly, made. Wiener et al. would claim that a judgment that Byron communicated necessarily requires focusing on Byron as the encoder and source of the behavior. Again, there is no doubt that Zelda evaluated Byron's behavior, but in itself that is no assurance that Byron communicated his interest in leaving. Thus, there is a distinction made between the decoder *inferring* a particular motivation or experience from the encoder's behavior and the encoder behaviorally *communicating* that motivation or experience.

According to Wiener et al. inferences can be made from idiosyncratic behaviors that have no socially shared referent, that is, where there is no code linking behaviors to some referent meaning. In our example, Byron's nose scratching permits Zelda to make an inference of anxiety because in the past Byron has scratched his nose when he was anxious. Other decoders, however, might not make that inference from Byron's behavior, and Zelda would not necessarily infer anxiety of other encoders who scratched their noses. In addition, there is no independent evidence of Byron using a particular behavior to stand for the referent of being anxious to leave. Consequently, Wiener and his colleagues would judge that Byron is *indicating*, not communicating, his anxiety. The fact that Zelda is a keen observer and makes a correct inference about Byron's anxiety is irrelevant to the communication-indication distinction because this distinction requires an analysis of the encoder's behavior, not the decoder's reactions.

Once the focus has shifted to the encoder, the next step in defining communication is to provide independent evidence for the existence of encoding. Working from an analysis of verbal language, Wiener et al. propose that some indication of code usage by either the encoder or decoder must be established. For example, from the standpoint of the encoder, this may involve the encoder's looking at the decoder at the end of a statement to determine if the decoder understood the message. Such behavior suggests that the encoder is trying to evaluate the reaction to his message. Alternately, a pause at the end of a statement, combined with rolling one's eyes upward or to the side, might signal that the encoder is thinking and will continue speaking. This kind of search for the appropriate continuation is a signal that encoding is taking place at that very moment. Thus, encoder behavior, independent of the nonverbal message per se, offers evidence for the presence of encoding. A pause after the encoder's comment in conjunction with a sideways or upward movement of the eyes on the decoder's part signals that the decoder is weighing the encoder's statement and will respond, that is, the previous decoder is now encoding a reply. In this case, the distinct behavioral pattern of the decoder immediately before taking a conversational turn suggests that encoding is taking place. Another type of decoder response is a quizzical or blank look that suggests that the decoder has not understood the message. Such a reaction will usually result in the encoder attempting some clarification. The occurrence of the decoder's "facial doubt" and the encoder's subsequent initiation of a clarification also suggests that encoding was necessarily involved in the encoder's restatement. In each of these examples, the presence of such regulatory and/or search behaviors suggests that encoding has occurred or is occurring. Furthermore, evidence for encoding is independent of the content of the message. These behaviors are important to this analysis not for what they mean, but rather because they provide evidence for the encoding process.

According to Wiener et al., the next requirement in defining communication is that the behaviors must share a common code for the particular group or population studied. This requirement would exclude any behaviors that do not have commonly held meanings within a particular population. For example, a specific gesture meaningful to good friends but to no one else would not be considered communication. The last requirement is that communicative behaviors should be essentially interchangeable with, or substitutable for, a corresponding verbal form. This means that the decoder's reaction to critical nonverbal behaviors should be the same as that made to the corresponding verbal form of the message.

Clearly, such demanding requirements (particularly the last one) would result in relatively few nonverbal behaviors being classified as communication. Some examples given by Wiener et al. are the palms up gesture indicating some degree of uncertainty or the palms out gesture indicating that the encoder does not want to be interrupted or stopped. Although Wiener et al. recognize that many, or even most, nonverbal behaviors affect the reactions of others in an interaction, they feel that such a judgment is not sufficient to warrant calling such behaviors communication. An important characteristic of their approach is its distinction between encoding and decoding analyses and the resulting contrast between communication and inference. Such distinctions are also critical in a final perspective on communication that will now be discussed. This last orientation falls somewhere between the first two in terms of the inclusiveness of those behaviors classified as communicative.

Intentional or Goal-Directed Behavior Is Communication

The third theoretical perspective relies on the concept of intention (Ekman & Friesen, 1969b) or goal directedness (MacKay, 1972) to define communicative behaviors. It should be noted that the first two perspectives reject the necessity for considering underlying intentions, although they do so for different reasons. In the first approach, because all interactive behavior is defined as communicative, distinctions regarding intentions are superfluous. In the second approach, Wiener and his colleagues reject the utility of analyzing intention because they believe it cannot be operationally defined in terms of observable behaviors. Consequently, they focus their attention on behaviorally identifiable correlates of the encoding process.

The third orientation to communication, as represented in the position of Ekman and Friesen (1969b), assumes that communication takes place when the encoder *consciously* uses his or her behavior to send a message to the decoder. This approach, like that of Wiener et al., is one based on an encoding perspective, but the communality between the two orientations ends there. The focus on the encoder's conscious intention alleviates some of the difficulty with making inferences about unconscious motivation, but such a criterion is not as easily operationalized as the criteria offered by Wiener et al. Furthermore, how explicit does an intention have to be before the resulting behavior is considered communicative? Does the encoder *always* have to be aware of his intentions, especially when a given behavior is so frequent as to be almost automatic? These are questions that are not easily answered. Ekman and Friesen's position also diverges from that of Wiener and his colleagues in positing that communication may be idiosyncratic, that is, no commonly shared code is required. Thus, any particular intentional movement or gesture between husband and wife or between good friends which has meaning for the individuals involved, but for no one else, would qualify as communication.

MacKay (1972) discusses the concept of communication in a manner consistent with Ekman and Friesen's distinctions. MacKay, however, assumes that communication requires some attempt by the encoder to represent behaviorally an internal state or organization. More specifically, this means that an encoder's behavior must be goal-directed, that is, that behavior is designed to affect one or more decoders in a particular way. In addition to goal direction (or intention in Ekman and Friesen's terms), the effect of the communication attempt must be evaluated in some fashion by the encoder. That is, the encoder must determine if the behavior had its intended effect. This view assumes, therefore, that a negative feedback system operates in evaluating the consequences of the initial communicative behavior. Thus, goal-directed behavior that does not have its intended effect is changed in some manner (if only intensified or exaggerated) in order to achieve the desired goal. MacKay's inclusion of the evaluative feedback component suggests a means by which intention or goal direction can be operationally defined in at least some cases. For example, when an encoder repeats, exaggerates, or uses different variations of a particular behavior until a discrete reaction occurs in the decoder, we can often assume that those behaviors were intentional or goal-directed.

A specific example depicting the application of this behavioral criterion of evaluation may be informative. Academics or others who often work in accessible office locations are vulnerable to frequent interruptions that can disrupt work schedules. Some of these interruptions seem much more obnoxious than others. One I find occasionally intrusive is a visit from a sales representative of a textbook publisher. The sales rep's technique usually involves an entree of "Hello, I'm from Acme Publishers, do you have just a minute?" It has been my uncontested opinion that sales reps are not lacking in assertiveness or they would not be long in their jobs. Once the portal of the office door is crossed, it can be very difficult to terminate interactions with them, even if one shows no interest in their texts. To supplement my verbal disinterest in their product, I occasionally resort to my "I'm awfully busy" performance. This involves glancing at my watch once or twice, fidgeting in my chair, and checking both my desk calendar and the work in front of me. This routine usually evokes a statement by the intruder that he or she has to get going and will stop by next semester. With considerable relief, my performance stops, I smile, relax, and say goodbye to the visitor.

Sometimes a behavioral routine that is usually communicative serves other needs unrelated to the apparent meaning of the behavior. This has happened with one of the behavioral components that I just described, specifically, glancing at my watch. I happen to be a tea drinker, and I try to keep the brewing time to about 4 minutes. Usually this presents no problems. But when I have a visitor in my office and it is obvious that I am checking my watch, I often get a concerned look. In order to set the visitor at ease and clarify my behavior, it is sometimes necessary to offer an explanation for my behavior, that is, "I'm simply checking the time on my tea; I don't want it to get too strong." In fact, it is awkward to have to explain such a simple behavior and deny the "I'm too busy" message. Without such an explanation, however, a colleague may easily assume that I am too busy, or worse yet, too busy for him or her.

If one applied the evaluational criterion proposed by MacKay, one might confidently judge that my behavior with the sales rep was communication. That is, my routine developed or intensified until the desired departure of the sales rep was achieved and then it stopped completely. In contrast, my time checks for tea occur consistently whenever I have tea, whether or not there is a visitor. Thus, that behavior is not directed toward the goal of getting the visitor to leave. In the latter case the time check might be described as simply indicative of a fussy tea drinker, and clearly not communicative.

As in the case of many simple criteria, however, there are exceptions. Sometimes an encoder's specific behavioral performance will increase or intensify until the decoder makes a critical response, then suddenly change or stop without an identifiable purpose or goal direction. An example of such an occurrence would be the anxious employee who presents an innovative proposal to his superior. In doing so, he indicates his anxiety by frequently rubbing his hands together and adjusting his position in his chair. These behaviors increase up to the conclusion of his presentation when the superior remarks that the proposal is a great idea. At this point the employee relaxes and his anxious mannerisms stop. It is not likely that the employee *managed* these anxious behaviors to influence his superior's decision. In fact, if he were aware of the behaviors he would probably try to control them. Thus, the anxious behaviors happened to increase up to the point of the positive response by the employer, but they were not intended to generate that response. Consequently, such behavior should not be considered communicative. Although this example shows that all situations of criterion-related change cannot routinely be judged communicative, some assessment of the change in the encoder's behavior as a function of the decoder's reaction can often help to identify goal-directed or communicative behaviors.

Evaluating the Three Perspectives

The three perspectives just described differ considerably on important issues. Given that constructs like communication are simply our own inventions designed to help our understanding, contrasting perspectives cannot easily be compared in terms of how correct they are. It is possible, however, to examine their relative utility. I would like to pursue such an evaluation by selecting from the three perspectives those characteristics having the greatest utility in developing the functional approach of this book.

First, some emphasis should be placed on the motivation underlying an individual's behavior; that is, a functional approach necessarily focuses on motivational issues. The obvious solution would seem to be Ekman and Friesen's (1969b) criterion of a conscious intention. But because there are problems with operationally defining an intention in conscious awareness, reliance on purpose or goal direction, as suggested by MacKay (1972), may be preferable. Clearly, the specificity of an intention can vary considerably, from a vague awareness on the one hand to a detailed explicit purpose on the other. If one accepts the latter description as an appropriate standard for an intention, it is likely that relatively few behaviors should be considered communicative. In fact, there may be many instances of verbal language behavior that would not be considered communicative if such an explicit intention had to precede a comment. In reality, however, awareness of an intention for a specific behavior sequence may fade over time as it becomes overlearned. That is, the responses can become conditioned and the intention to perform them can become less likely to be represented in awareness. Thus, a conscious intention may be present at the time a specific reaction is learned, but gradually fade and no longer be available. Nevertheless, an encoder's behavior may be described as goal directed if there is evidence that an evaluation of the consequences of the behavior leads to a change in its occurrence. As the example at the end of the last section indicated, however, this criterion is not an infallible one.

A second critical characteristic is that an idiosyncratic code should be a sufficient vehicle for communication. Thus, if goal direction of some sort is present and the encoder uses a sign known to the decoder in attempting to influence the decoder, it seems unimportant whether such a sign has a relatively universal or a very limited usage. The purpose, function, and reaction may be comparable regardless of whether the code is universal or idiosyncratic.

A third characteristic is an emphasis on a multichannel approach to analyzing communication—an emphasis that has been stressed in the systems perspective. It may be convenient to examine one behavior in isolation to determine its meaning, but it is also frequently misleading. One cannot understand the significance of a particular cue unless the rest of the behavioral context is known. A simple example involves the significance of a physically close approach to another person. Such a manipulation was typical of much of the early research on personal space. Even if we control for relationship effects on such a close approach, many other related behaviors interact with interpersonal distance to determine its meaning. For example, is the approacher gazing directly at the other person? Is he or she smiling? Is the approach frontal or from an angle? What is the rate of approach? Is any conversation initiated? It is unreasonable to assume that one must specify each possible characteristic of an encounter before a defensible interpretation is offered. That, however, does not excuse an arbitrary focus on a single behavior in representing a complex interaction. To understand the significance of any single behavior, we have to be sensitive to the broader behavioral context in which the behavior occurs.

A fourth and final characteristic is a recognition of the importance of distinguishing between informative behaviors that are communicative and those that are not, as Ekman and Friesen (1969b), MacKay (1972), and Wiener et al. (1972) have done. The distinction that I would like to propose rests on the first two characteristics discussed in this section. Specifically, communicative behavior that employs at least an idiosyncratic code would be defined as goal-directed behavior. Goal direction may be determined either by expressed intention (Ekman & Friesen, 1969b) or by some evaluation of the behavioral consequences of the focal behavior (MacKay, 1972). Those informative behaviors that are not goal-directed would be classified as indicative behaviors, for example, Byron's anxious mannerisms. Thus, various behaviors such as those that are characteristic of anxiety may inform the decoder of the encoder's reactions, but the encoder would typically be described as indicating, not communicating, that reaction.

Communication, Indication, and Attribution

Besides emphasizing the purpose of goal direction, the distinction between communication and indication is important because of its relevance to attributional analyses of social behavior. The basic concerns of an attribution perspective include a focus on intentionality in and responsibility for behavioral outcomes. In fact, Heider (1958) indentified intention as a component contributing to the personal force that an individual exerts to produce a particular effect. Because communication has been defined in terms of goal direction, a communicative pattern should involve a person's attempt to produce a certain effect. Consequently, the individual should be judged as having a high degree of responsibility for this effect. In contrast, if the same behavior were indicative, the pattern should be seen as less purposeful. In this way the individual should be judged as less responsible for the behavior's effects. In other words, communication would be judged as managed or deliberate, whereas indicative behavior would be judged as spontaneous.

This distinction between attributions of communicative versus indicative behavior is discussed from a complementary perspective by Schneider, Hastorf, and Ellsworth (1979, pp. 123-128). These authors suggest that because most nonverbal behavior is assumed to be unintentional and uncontrollable (indicative in the terminology of this chapter), attributions regarding the purpose of a behavior are uncommon. That is, if the behavior is not intentional or controllable, it is usually inappropriate to infer that it occurred for the purpose of producing a specific effect. On the other hand, although *purposive* attributions may be uncommon, *reactive* ones are not. Reactive attributions are inferences designed to identify the stimulus producing the reaction rather than inferences about the purpose served by the behavior. The precipitating cause for a reactive behavior may be an environmental event, a feeling-state, or even a personality characteristic.

The contrast between communicative and indicative behavior is important because of its consequences for the decoder's attributional and behavioral reactions. In order to understand this contrast better and to appreciate its implications for interaction, the next section will focus on the predisposing factors contributing to the initiation of communicative behavior.

Determinants of Communication

What circumstances are likely to contribute to a communicative reaction? In analyzing the factors facilitating communication, I will ignore those instances in which explicit signals or gestures are used as direct substitutes for a specific verbal message, for example, motioning someone to stop or go, using the OK sign, or initiating an obscene gesture. Ekman and Friesen (1969b) use the term emblem to identify gestures that have a direct literal translation. Such behaviors are obvious instances of communication, but they have little direct relevance for interpersonal involvement. Consistent with the theme of this chapter, the emphasis here will be on the communication-indication contrast in nonverbal involvement.

There are at least three different conditions that may increase the likelihood of initiating a goal-directed or communicative behavioral pattern. They include the following: (1) the presence of evaluational pressures in an interaction; (2) the relaying of sensitive judgments; and (3) the amplifying of verbal reactions.

Evaluational Pressures

In highly evaluative situations, individuals often monitor and manage their own behavior closely to create a favorable impression (Snyder, 1981). For example, in an interview setting, the job applicant is likely to modify his or her behavior in some predictable fashion in order to impress the interviewer. Attention toward or interest in the interviewer might be signaled by increased gaze and forward lean. A moderate level of smiling and an occasional nod of agreement would reflect a pleasant, responsive, and agreeable disposition. Other managed behaviors might include a change in paralinguistic emphasis. Behavioral changes such as these can be seen as clear attempts to manage behavior in an evaluational context.

It is important to note that as the norms or expectancies for specific interactive behavior become more explicit, one may have less confidence in interpreting behavior that is consistent with the norm. That is, if the norm prescribes the type of attentive, pleasant, moderately involved behavior described in the interview example, it becomes more difficult for the decoder to determine if such behavior is representative of the applicant's true disposition or a pattern enacted merely for the period of the interview. Of course, if the applicant acts contrary to the norm, such behavior has high informational value (Jones & Davis, 1965). Thus, the interviewer who meets an unattentive, somber, and noninvolving applicant will probably feel confident in making a negative decision about that person. Whether such an applicant simply does not know how to act in an interview, or really knows what to do but does not care enough to manage his or her behavior, may be unknown. Nevertheless, the negative impression of and decision about the person can be confidently made.

Occasionally, the behaviors prescribed by the norm may be enacted in an exaggerated fashion that contributes to a different kind of negative impression, for example, that the person is not sincere. In this circumstance, the behavior may be seen as an attempt to ingratiate or manipulate the other person in the interaction. An interesting example of such an incident occurred several years ago with respect to a candidate for a position in our department. The critical exchange involved the handshake between the candidate and a department member. The candidate supplemented the usual handshake by raising his left hand and grasping the upper right arm of my colleague. This may not seem to be an extreme move, but nevertheless it was disconcerting to my colleague. In our departmental discussion of the candidate's qualifications, this exchange was described and characterized as representative of a manipulative individual. From the perspective of the individual on the receiving end of that greeting, the arm grasp was clearly inappropriate and insincere between two people just meeting. For the department member, that single behavioral pattern constituted a major component in his negative evaluation of the candidate. When another colleague facetiously questioned the validity of the handshake test of competence, he was met with an icy stare that required little effort to interpret.

In interactions having an important evaluative component, nonverbal involvement may be managed intentionally or in a goal-directed fashion to elicit favorable reactions from another person. Included among the behavioral patterns designed to elicit favorable reactions are both candid and deceitful behaviors. The topic of deception will be discussed more fully in the Chapter 6 analysis of the social control function. Consistent with the earlier discussion, such managed behavior should be described as communicative. Goffman (1959, 1967) uses the analogy of the theatre in discussing and analyzing the self-presentations that are required in the evaluative setting. One's behavioral routine is described as a performance enacted for a particular role. Such performances occur in front regions, or on stage, (as opposed to back regions, or backstage) before other interactants or observers who constitute the audience. Underlying Goffman's dramaturgical perspective is the general assumption that much of our social behavior is under control and managed for deliberate ends. Perhaps, as Shakespeare suggested, all the world is a stage, at least when we are concerned about how others view us.

Relaying Sensitive Judgments

A second circumstance that may promote the initiation of communicative behaviors is the necessity of relaying sensitive judgments to other people. The obvious way of accomplishing this end is through the verbal channel, but that can prove difficult for the individuals involved. Direct verbal statements of rejection, dislike, or even approval and love may be threatening or embarrassing to both the encoder and decoder. Because of their ambiguity, nonverbal cues can be used to communicate the same highly evaluative judgement in a less stressful fashion. The earlier example of my own behavior in trying to dislodge a persistent publisher's sales rep would fall in this category. Because I was reluctant to verbalize my disinterest, I merely acted out those feelings by fidgeting in my chair, checking my watch, and scanning my appointment calendar. Although it may be a rationalization on the encoder's part, it is likely that such an indirect (some might call deceitful) message is face-saving and more comfortable for the decoder. In fact, communicating such a message nonverbally may produce less reactance (Brehm, 1966) in the decoder. That is, because the message is indirect, the decoder will not feel forced to respond in a specific fashion. If the decoder's perceived freedom of choice remains high, then reactance will be minimal. In fact, the decoder might feel quite satisfied in being so perceptive in reading the import of the encoder's behavior.

Because there is no systematic code for translating the meaning of most nonverbal behaviors, specific performances may be enacted intentionally and their meaning rejected later if they turn out badly. That is, the meaning of specific gestures, movements, or postures may be ambiguous enough that a decoder's particular interpretation (though accurate) can be rejected by the encoder. For example, a potential romantic encounter may be initiated by a glance, a gesture, or a touch, without any verbal commitment (Schneider et al., 1979, p. 134). The ambiguity of such an approach provides the encoder with enough latitude subsequently to affirm or deny a romantic intent, and thereby decrease personal risk. The advantage of being able to avoid a clear commitment may prevent possible embarrassment and even legal responsibility.

Another sensitive area open to the effective but ambiguous influence of nonverbal behavior is that of discrimination. Whether it is based on race, age, or sex (see Henley, 1977, for a discussion of sex, status, and nonverbal behavior), discrimination can be deliberately managed through nonverbal channels. At a time when societal norms and legal statutes prohibit explicit discrimination in many areas, the written and spoken word is open to close scrutiny. However, comparable discriminatory messages may be encoded nonverbally with a minimum of legal vulnerability and still achieve their desired end, that is, to prevent equal opportunity for some minority group member. Of course, some, and perhaps even most, nonverbal behaviors reflecting discriminatory reactions simply leak out (Ekman & Friesen, 1974) and are not really managed or intentional. Typically, an individual would not be held as responsible for such spontaneous actions as he or she would be for deliberate (communicative) action. Obviously, however, negative consequences to a minority group member may still result from spontaneous (indicative) behavior. A good example of such an effect is the finding reported by Word, Zanna, and Cooper (1974) in their study of nonverbal behaviors of interviewers toward black and white applicants in a simulated interview. Specifically, the black applicant received a lower level of nonverbal involvement from the interviewer than white applicants, which in turn affected the behavior of the applicants. The result was that white applicants responded more positively in the interview and were judged more favorably.

Amplifying Verbal Reactions

The occasion of amplifying verbal reactions differs from simply relaying sensitive judgments in two ways. First, the nonverbal behaviors involved in amplifying verbal reactions necessarily complement and do not contradict or even replace verbal behavior, as they often do in relaying sensitive judgments. The second difference is that in amplifying verbal reactions, the ambiguity of the message is reduced and the encoder's responsibility for it is increased.

It appears that most often the nonverbal behavior that complements the verbal either coincides with or follows the focal verbal behavior. Affective statements, particularly strong ones, may trigger relatively deliberate changes in involvement behaviors. Thus, statements of love, hate, approval, or rejection may either precede or coincide with behavioral manifestations of those sentiments. For example, in praising my son for being a good boy, I am aware of wanting to emphasize it by also giving him a hug or patting him on the back. Ekman and Friesen (1969b) also describe such behavior as either complementing or accenting verbal behavior. In addition, it is possible that a further statement might follow the hug, but it seems likely that the initial action is the verbal one. Perhaps the verbal behavior occurs first because it is simply faster to initiate the verbal response than to wait for a coordinated movement toward the other person. Of course, that argument would not hold for changes in facial expression (e.g., a smile, a nod, a frowning head shake) that can occur as quickly as most verbalizations.

As the time between the verbal and nonverbal components increases, it is less likely that the nonverbal behavior exercises a simple amplification of the verbal. In other words, the two components are not necessarily part of a single program guided by a common purpose. Let us return to the example of praising my son. This time, however, I make the verbal comment alone. Next, he turns, smiles, and starts to move toward me, and I *spontaneously* react by bending over and giving him a hug. In the latter version of this example, the same behavior (giving him a hug) is not coordinated with the verbal statement of praise, but rather it is actually a spontaneous reaction to my son's approach behavior. In such a case, the latter nonverbal pattern would be indicative rather than communicative.

Expressive Indication

Nonverbal behavior initiated without goal direction can still provide important information to the decoder. In fact, the attributions made from such spontaneous or reactive behaviors are usually trusted more than behaviors that might be purposive (Schneider et al., 1979, p. 125). In the following discussion of expressive indication, two issues will be emphasized: (1) the content of information indicated nonverbally; and (2) the feedback function of expressive behavior in the experience of emotion. The first issue has an interpersonal focus and is therefore directly relevant to nonverbal involvement and exchange. The second issue has an intrapersonal focus, and is less directly relevant to nonverbal involvement and exchange.

Informational Content

Inferences made from nonverbal behavior may relate to (1) temporary affective states, (2) interpersonal evaluations, and (3) enduring traits or dispositions. Although the range of possible inferences is quite extensive, the focus of the discussion in this section will be exclusively on the role of nonverbal behavior in indicating temporary affective states. The relationship of nonverbal behavior to interpersonal evaluations and traits or dispositions will be considered in later discussions of both the intimacy and social control functions.

Most of the research on the expressive value of nonverbal behavior examines the role of such behavior in emotional or affective reactions. Not surprisingly, the face is especially important in the expression of affective reactions. It appears that across cultures there is remarkable uniformity in the way facial expressions are encoded and decoded in emotional reactions (Ekman, 1978). Even when one compares members of preliterate cultures to those of literate cultures, very similar patterns of encoding and decoding reactions are found (Ekman, 1972). Figure 3-1 shows posed emotional responses by an American subject and a subject from the Fore of New Guinea. The high degree of similarity evident in these posed reactions is typical of the uniformity found in emotional expression from a variety of very different cultural groups. Results of studies on the decoding of emotional reactions from facial expression show similar cross-cultural uniformity; however, such universality of emotional expression seems to be limited to the basic emotional reactions of happiness, anger, disgust, sadness, and combined fear and surprise (Ekman & Oster, 1979). When facial reactions become more subtle, or when there are blends or expressions (e.g., happiness and surprise or anger and fear), accuracy in encoding and decoding decreases both between and within cultures.

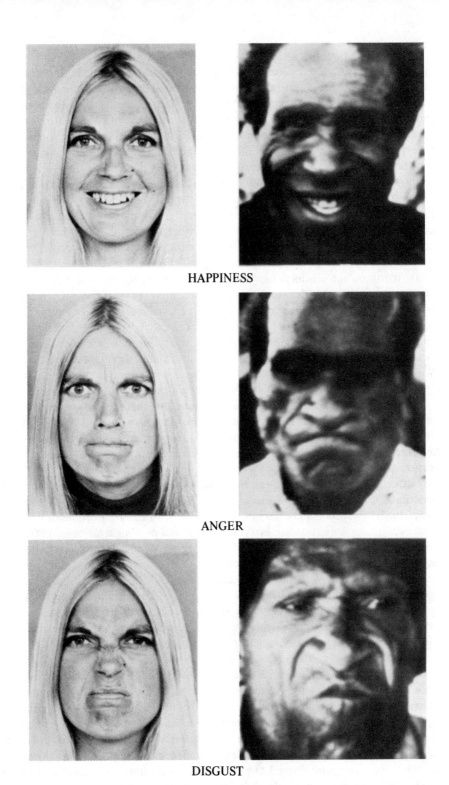

HAPPINESS

ANGER

DISGUST

Fig. 3-1. Emotional responses of American and New Guinea subjects.

Although research indicates that basic emotional states can be encoded and decoded reliably, such a generalization is unwarranted in moving from posed expressions to those present in ongoing interactions. That is, specific facial expressions can be encoded in response to the appropriate stimuli, but often they are modified by display rules operating in a given situation (Ekman, 1972). According to Ekman, an expressive reaction starts with eliciting stimuli (external or internal events) that initiate a facial affect program. This program defines the specific links among the feeling-state, neural impulses, and facial muscle changes. However, display rules determine the reactions that are actually registered facially. Display rules may be a product of individual characteristics and learning, cultural norms, and situational constraints. Display rules typically operate either to dampen the intensity of an emotional reaction or to substitute a contrasting reaction, for example, smiling when one is in fact angry.

In terms of the distinctions made in this chapter, the modification of facial expression by display rules would be communication. That is, there is a definable purpose underlying the initiation of a controlled facial reaction. An example of this can be found in Ekman's (1972) cross-cultural research. Stress-inducing films were shown to college students in the United States and in Japan. When the Japanese and American subjects were seated alone, both groups exhibited very similar expressions. When they were in the presence of the research assistant, however, the Japanese subjects masked their reactions much more than the Americans. The clearly contrasting expressive patterns of the two groups suggests that the masking behavior of the Japanese subjects was motivated by a definable purpose or goal. Specifically, in the presence of others, one should limit the degree of negative affect expressed. For a general review of research on facial expression, see Ekman and Oster's (1979) paper.

Although facial expressions can be a rich source of information about affective reactions (when they are not masked by display rules) other nonverbal behaviors may also be important indicators of affect. The two general categories of behavior that seem most important are body movement and paralinguistic cues. These two categories of behavior seem to be affected by stress and anxiety reactions. For example, a high level of self-manipulations (e.g., grooming, scratching, rubbing hands together) may be indicative of increased arousal (Chapman, 1975) or anxiety (Kleck, 1970). Other research indicates that more frequent self-manipulations are related to increases in covert verbal hostility (Freedman, Blass, Rifkin, & Quitkin, 1973). Other kinds of movements that are not self-directed may be indicative of decreased stress. Specifically, when individuals are seated, an increase in the frequency of rocking, gestures, and leg and foot movements seems to be related to increased relaxation (Mehrabian & Williams, 1969). In contrast, the absence of body movement, reflected in tense and rigid postures, seems to signal increased stress. Anxiety may also be manifested in various paralinguistic cues. Speech errors or speech disruptions in the form of repetition, sentence incompletion, omissions, and unfilled pauses seem to increase with increased stress (Cook, 1969; Feldstein & Jaffe, 1962; Kasl & Mahl, 1965; Mahl, 1956; Siegman & Pope, 1965).

When one compares the relative specificity of information available, it seems quite clear that much more detail in feeling or affect can be transmitted through facial than nonfacial cues. In fact, the degree of variety possible in the face is stag-gering. In developing their comprehensive, anatomically-based system for scoring facial expressions, Ekman and Friesen (1976) reported the enactment and examin-ation of between 4,000 and 5,000 facial movements. The ability to monitor and manipulate our facial reactions in line with specific display rules supplements this remarkable variability in facial expressiveness. Thus, even though facial responses can be especially informative, they can also be controlled and deceptive. At times, we literally cannot take another person's reaction at face value. The issue of decep-tion and the role of facial expressiveness in deception will be discussed at some length in Chapter 6. At this point it is sufficient to note that the management of facial expression is a critical component in deceptive performances. In contrast to the deceptive potential of facial expression, changes in body movement and para-inguistic cues may be relatively reliable indicators of negative affect. In addition, increased lower body movement, decreased gesturing, and higher pitched responses are indicative of deceptive interactions (Ekman & Friesen, 1974; Ekman, Friesen, & Scherer, 1976).

Expressive Behavior and Affective Experience

A consideration of the role of an actor's nonverbal behavior in his or her own affec-tive experience is technically outside the scope of this text. That is, an analysis of the link between what a person does and how he or she feels is an intrapersonal rather than an interpersonal issue. Nevertheless, this is another sense in which behavior can be indicative. Furthermore, through a process of social comparison and modeling, an individual's own behavior may not only become self-informative, but also trigger similar reactions in others (Leventhal, 1974).

All of us appreciate that there must be some link between what is experienced covertly and what is represented or indicated overtly in our behavior. Consistent with this assumption, the earlier discussion of Ekman's research emphasized the apparent universal link between specific facial patterns and several basic emotional states. A common intuitive interpretation of this link is simply that as our feelings develop they are reflected in our overt behavior. But the opposing view, that our expressive behavior determines the nature of our emotional reactions, has generated a great deal of research and controversy. William James (1950/1890, 1968/1884) first described this position in his body reaction theory of emotions. Basically, James proposed that patterns of covert (internal and visceral) and overt (skeletal- and facial-muscular) responses provided explicit neural feedback that identified one's emotional reactions. Thus, it was presumed that the visceral and skeletal-muscular reactions occurred first and in turn precipitated a specific emotional exper-ience. James's theory seemed to emphasize the contribution of the internal, visceral reactions to emotional experience more than the skeletal- and facial-muscular reactions. Because, however, those internal reactions were not found to be critical in defining emotional reactions (Cannon, 1927), the body reaction theory lay dor-mant for many years.

The revival of James's theory, with special emphasis on the feedback from facial expression coincided with the development of self-perception theory (Bem, 1967,

1972). Like the body reaction theory, self-perception theory assumed the primacy of behavior in molding affective and evaluative experiences. In one interesting test of the facial feedback hypothesis, Laird (1974) found that manipulated facial expression had a significant effect on rated mood during standardized slide presentations. Specifically, independent of the content of the slides, subjects whose faces were manipulated into a frown reported feeling more aggressive than those who smiled. The manipulation of a smiling face also produced a nonsignificant increase in rated elation. Although the methodology in Laird's study has been criticized, particularly in terms of demand characteristics, his results have certainly helped to stimulate new interest in the facial feedback hypothesis. Furthermore, the results of another study are consistent with the Laird findings. In this second study, subjects who were given a series of shocks and told to hide their expression of pain actually reported feeling less pain (Lanzetta, Cartwright-Smith, & Kleck, 1976). Presumably, the display of a nonpainful expression informed the subjects that they did not feel much pain.

These results and the conclusions generated by them have not gone unchallenged. Buck (1980), in a critical review of this research, concluded that the nature of the experimental designs (a complicated matter of the validity of between- and within-group designs), demand characteristics, and the artificial nature of the facial expressions manipulated all cast doubt on results apparently supportive of the facial feedback hypothesis. In addition, Buck argued that facial expression simply serves as a controlled readout of central affective processes, that is, facial expressions are the visible product, not the cause, of affective reactions.

One of the more recent empirical studies manipulating facial expression reported results consistent with Buck's analysis. In this study, manipulated facial expressions produced no effect on reported emotional reactions (Tourangeau & Ellsworth, 1979). These results, in turn, have been criticized by other prominent researchers and theorists (Hager & Ekman, 1981; Izard, 1981; Tomkins, 1981). It is interesting to note that these latter criticisms appealed to some of the same issues that Buck identified in criticizing the opposing results of earlier studies, namely, the artificial nature of the manipulations and demand characteristics.

There is substantial evidence that facial expressions can provide detailed information about the affective reactions of others. That is, facial expressions can reliably indicate an actor's emotional experience to observers. Of course, such a generalization must be tempered by an appreciation of the influence of display rules on the extent and form of expression actually presented. The exact role of the actor's own expression on his or her own emotional experience is still unclear, however. It seems likely that facial expressions alone cannot account for the detail and subtlety present in many emotional experiences. On the other hand, it is quite possible that feedback from facial expression can have some effect on the development of emotional experience. If recent research is any indicator, the basic issue of whether facial expression is a cause or effect of emotional experience, or both, is not likely to be settled soon.

Implications of the Communication-Indication Contrast

The classification of any behavioral pattern as informative is, in itself, not a very critical distinction. That is, within the classification system proposed in this chapter almost all behavioral patterns are informative. However, identifying a particular informative pattern as either communicative or indicative is a basic and very important judgment. The description of communication as goal-directed or purposive behavior (MacKay, 1972) is based on an analysis of the apparent motives underlying an encoder's behavior. In general, because communicative behavior is presumed to be goal-directed, it will tend to be managed deliberately. That is, the encoder initiates a performance and then monitors and controls it so that a particular purpose may be achieved.

Communicative behavior is more likely to occur when (1) an individual is being evaluated, (2) sensitive judgments have to be relayed, and (3) verbal reactions have to be amplified. In most cases the encoder tries to create an impression that his or her communicative behavior is really indicative, that is, the encoder tries to appear as though he or she is being spontaneous, even though the opposite is true. There are exceptions to this general rule. Sometimes an individual may enact a flawed performance very deliberately. In other words, the encoder will make it obvious that some reaction is forced and not at all indicative. For example, if you had to meet someone you did not like and wanted this person to appreciate your feelings without being obviously rude, you might give a very slight smile and a weak handshake. In that case, you have technically offered a greeting, but it is one that makes it clear to the other party that you are less than enthusiastic about the honor. In practice, your behavior will almost certainly be seen as forced or deliberate, which in turn reflects a negative attitude. If you were questioned about your behavior, it would be easy to deny any dislike because you did greet the other person and had not made any unfriendly comments. Nevertheless, the intended message has been *communicated.*

Indicative behavior may be described as spontaneous or reactive (Schneider et al., 1979, chap. 6). If an observer judges an actor's behavior as indicative, the observer will not usually attempt purposive attributions about the behavior. The observer's judgments about an actor's behavior probably follow some of the same general principles that apply to any naive attributional analysis. For example, one or more of the following criteria may lead to a judgment that an individual's behavior is communicative: (1) the behavioral pattern is socially desirable or the actor benefits from the behavior; (2) the behavioral pattern is inconsistent with the way the actor usually behaves; and (3) the actor is apprehensive about being evaluated. It seems likely that in interacting with others we do not make explicit indicative or communicative judgments about each behavioral sequence. Rather, it is presumed that most social behavior is indicative, and as long as there is no reason to question this judgment, there is no need to evaluate behavior in any systematic way. But when the circumstances suggest that one or more of the three conditions just mentioned may exist, some relatively explicit evaluation of the potential purpose or meaning of the behavior may be made.

A final consequence of the indication-communication contrast is worth mentioning. If we infer that another person is managing his or her behavior for a purpose (i.e., communicating), we are obviously going to try to determine the true purpose and meaning of the behavior. A more general result of this inference of communication is an increased sensitivity to managing our own behavior. That is, if we assume that our partner is deliberately managing his or her behavior to affect us in some manner, we are more likely to manage our own behavior to maintain control or influence in the situation. This increased concern for managing our own behavior may be stimulated by reactance against the influence attempts of the other person. On the other hand, if the partner's behavioral pattern is seen as indicative, reactance should not occur, and consequently there will be less need to counter the behavior with a purposeful routine.

Summary

This chapter analyzed and discussed the informational function of nonverbal behavior. This function and that of regulating interaction are the two categories proposed for describing molecular or isolated behavior patterns. A distinction between informational behavior that is communicative and that which is indicative was discussed in the context of three distinct perspectives toward defining nonverbal communication. Although it is inappropriate to judge how correct these contrasting views of communication are, each possesses some characteristics consistent with the functional approach. That is, one or more characteristics from each of these three different approaches was stressed in attempting to identify a useful set of assumptions for the present functional approach. These characteristics are the following: (1) an emphasis on the motivation underlying behavior, reflected in purpose or goal direction; (2) the sufficiency of an idiosyncratic code as a vehicle for communication; (3) an emphasis on a multichannel approach in analyzing communication; and (4) a distinction between communication as managed and goal-directed behavior versus indication as spontaneous and nonmanaged behavior. The purposive or goal-oriented definition of communication is one that will be critical in the later discussion of intimacy and social control functions. Three specific circumstances were identified as potential determinants for initiating communicative behavior. These circumstances include the following: (1) the presence of evaluational pressures; (2) relaying sensitive judgments; and (3) amplifying verbal reactions.

The category of indicative behavior was discussed in terms of its role in conveying information, both to others and to oneself. When an actor behaves in a spontaneous indicative fashion, observers are likely to use that information to make inferences about either the actor's dispositional traits or temporary state. For the present analysis, this is the most important sense in which behavior is indicative. However, it is also possible that the actor's own behavior provides neural feedback that contributes to defining his or her own experience of different affective states.

For both the other- and self-informative consequences, facial expression provides the greatest potential for discriminating among varied emotional reactions. One's awareness and control of facial reactions, however, is probably greater than that of other nonverbal behaviors. As a result, facial responses seem to be more easily managed, and consequently more important in attempted deception.

The distinction offered in this chapter between communicative and indicative behaviors is not always an easy one to operationalize. MacKay's suggestion of evaluating the behavioral consequences of a potentially communicative pattern is a useful though fallible criterion. Nevertheless, it is assumed that most people are sensitive to an indicative versus communicative, or spontaneous versus goal-directed, distinction. Furthermore, such a judgment is basic to an interpretation of the other's behavior and to the initiation of an appropriate response to that behavior.

Chapter 4
Regulating Interaction

In the course of comfortable and fluid interactions, our attention is rarely directed to the nonverbal behaviors underlying the smooth give and take in conversation. Nevertheless, there are subtle yet important behavioral patterns related to continuity and sequencing in interaction. The disruption of these patterns often produces noticeable discomfort and increased self-consciousness. The purpose of the present chapter will be to discuss and analyze the behavioral patterns related to the regulation of interaction. The primary emphasis will be on direct verbal encounters, or what Goffman (1963) calls focused interactions.

Goffman (1963) uses the term *focused interaction* to refer to situations in which people are directly communicating, or at least sharing a license to communicate, while excluding others who are physically present. In contrast, the term *unfocused interaction* refers to circumstances in which individuals are not directly communicating, but merely sharing a common presence, for example, isolated individuals seated in a waiting room or people passing on a sidewalk. The discussion of unfocused interactions in this chapter will emphasize the brief encounters that are characteristic of people crossing paths in pedestrian traffic. Even at this minimal level of interaction, the regulation of interpersonal involvement shows some definable patterns. As one examines more extended unfocused interactions such as working or studying, interpersonal involvement may be more a product of the activity than of the need for regulating interaction. Consequently, the analysis of extended unfocused interactions will be covered in the chapter on the service-task function (Chapter 7).

The vast majority of research on the regulation of interaction has examined various issues in sustained focused encounters. Consequently, the discussion and analysis of focused interactions will receive greater emphasis in this chapter. Later in the chapter the discussion will turn to the subtle behavioral patterns regulating passing encounters in unfocused interactions.

Focused Interactions

Arrangement Features

When people initiate focused interactions, they position themselves in an arrangement that facilitates the easy visual access necessary in fluid conversations. There is obvious variability in particular orientations and distances as a function of factors such as (a) the number of people in the group, (b) the characteristics of its members, (c) the task or activity, (d) the nature of the setting, and (e) the amount and shape of the available space. Underlying this potential variability, however, is a basic form or structure common to almost all focused interactions. Kendon (1976, 1977) has analyzed these arrangements and developed a system for describing them. Kendon uses the term *F-formations* (or facing formations) to designate the general form of face-to-face interaction arrangements.

The description of the F-formation can be developed best by identifying first the orientation component contributed by each interactant. A particular space, the individual's *transactional segment,* refers to the area in front of the individual where most of the person's activities take place and where the greatest control of the environment is possible (Ciolek & Kendon, 1980). One's transactional segment varies as a function of the size and positioning of the individual and the specific activity. However, regardless of the particular shape of the transactional segment, individuals will try to maintain exclusive control over it, and usually this control is recognized by others. For example, a man standing and gazing at an item in a store window has a narrow focus of attention and expects to control the foot and a half space between him and the window. Others will typically walk around and not disturb that space. If an intrusion should occur, he would probably feel a little upset even if that intrusion were preceded by an "excuse me."

As individuals move to initiate a face-to-face interaction, they usually position themselves in an arrangement permitting the overlap of their respective transactional segments. The F-formation can be defined as the arrangement of overlapping transactional segments producing a common orientation or *O-space* (Kendon, 1976, 1977). Thus, each person has easy, direct, and equal access to the transactional segment of every other person in the group. Consequently, contrasting arrangements might be expected in focused and unfocused interactions. Batchelor and Goethals (1972) examined such arrangements in groups following instructions designed to facilitate either focused or unfocused interactions. Each subject in both the focused and unfocused interaction conditions brought a chair into the room and placed it wherever he or she wanted. Groups in the focused (collective decision making) condition group not only positioned themselves in physically closer arrangements than did the unfocused (individual decision making) groups, but the focused groups also oriented themselves in more directly facing arrangements. Typical of the unfocused groups were arrangements that approximated a J-shape, that is, six individuals in a straight line and two on the bottom of the J. Typical of the focused group was either a closed circular or C-shape arrangement. Thus, the focused groups initiated the F-formation while the unfocused groups avoided it.

Examples of the F-formation in social groups and the resulting O-space can be seen in Figure 4-1. As the number of interactants increases, the area of the O-space necessarily increases. When a sufficiently large number of people, perhaps 10 or more, occupy a large enough area, the F-formation may become unstable and break down (Scheflen & Ashcraft, 1976, p. 108). The result may be occasional exchanges between adjacent individuals or a dissolution of the original F-formation into several smaller F-formations. This can be seen in Figure 4-1d.

Occasionally, the restrictions of a setting may prevent the easy development of an F-formation. For example, straightline seating arrangements are common in waiting areas of offices, train and bus stations, and airports (Sommer, 1974). Even many living rooms or family rooms are arranged so that several individuals may be required to sit in a row on a sofa or couch. Concern about the constraining effects of certain fixed arrangements prompted us to examine their consequences in the laboratory. Distance (close vs. far) and arrangement (circle vs. L-shape) were manipulated factorially in four-person groups. Although manipulated distance produced no effects, manipulated arrangement did. Specifically, postural adjustments, self-manipulations, and duration of pause time were increased in the L-shape groups compared to the circle groups (Patterson, Kelly, Kondracki, & Wulf, 1979). It seems possible that the nonfacing orientation of the L-shape groups made turn-

(a)   (b)

(c)   (d)

Fig. 4-1. An illustration of changes in F-formations with increasing group size. (Photos courtesy of Ellen Toler.)

taking in conversation more difficult and produced longer pause times. Because the frequency of postural adjustments showed low positive correlations with rated satisfaction in the group, the increased frequency of postural adjustments in the L-shape groups may reflect attempted accommodation to the nonfacing arrangement. In social settings with restrictive arrangements, postural adjustments may permit more direct orientations and can facilitate at least an approximation of the F-formation. Of course, as Sommer (1969, 1974) suggests, it is far more desirable to have the physical environment support, rather than restrict, the desired social behavior.

The environment is important not only in the limits it places on the arrangement of individuals within a group, but also for the manner in which it insulates the group from intrusions. For example, Ciolek and Kendon (1980) suggest that F-formations can function more smoothly in well defined, bounded areas than in open spaces. The presence of furniture, trees, or walls can help to define the boundaries of an F-formation and facilitate a more stable interaction. However, F-formations may create their own psychological boundaries even in the absence of environmental ones. For example, as individuals walk by an interacting group, it is common for the passersby to give wider berth to the group and even lower their head and eyes (Scheflen & Ashcraft, 1976, p. 112). Such adjustments by outsiders signal a recognition of the group and a willingness to avoid intruding.

In concluding this section, it should be emphasized that arrangement characteristics set distinct limits on the development of conversational exchanges. That is, the arrangement or standing features of an interaction remain relatively stable over time and influence the manner in which dynamic features such as gaze, facial expression, and verbal intimacy are initiated in interactions (Argyle & Kendon, 1967). The characteristic arrangement in most interactions is the F-formation. In fact, Ciolek (1978) reported that 98% of two-person, face-to-face, stationary interactions recorded between pairs in outdoor public settings took the form of the F-formation, that is, only 2% arranged themselves so that their transactional segments did not overlap.

Ciolek and Kendon (1980) have proposed five positive consequences of an F-formation. Specifically, it is presumed that the F-formation (1) defines the type and normalcy of an interaction, (2) identifies the number of participants in the interaction, (3) creates a congenial communication network, (4) facilitates equality of participation, and (5) creates an identifiable boundary between the group and the surrounding environment. Thus, the arrangement characteristics of the F-formation can be seen as adaptive adjustments facilitating coordinated and undisturbed interactions. The specific means by which those conversational exchanges proceed in a smooth and orderly fashion is the focus of the next section.

Dynamic Features

If we focus solely on the form or structure of focused interactions, it soon becomes evident that there is considerable order in the manner in which conversations progress. Usually, a speaker can judge when a listener (a) understands him or her, (b) is willing to let the speaker continue, and (c) is anxious to take a speaking turn. In a complementary fashion, a listener can usually judge when the speaker (a) may be more or less certain of a statement, (b) is determined to continue speaking, and (c) is ready to let the listener talk. These regulating functions are substantially determined by the subtle dynamic behaviors that either accompany or supplement speech, including cues such as gaze, facial expression, gestures, postural changes, paralinguistic cues, and nodding.

Functional versus objective perspectives. A concern basic to the present discussion is the issue of defining turn-taking and the related speaker and listener roles in conversation. It might seem that agreement on these basic concepts should be a simple matter, but this is not the case. Two contrasting orientations can be identified and described. One position is concerned with the function of exchanging information in conversation and the role of turn-taking in facilitating the exchange. Representative of this functional orientation is Yngve (1970), who proposed that an individual takes a turn, or holds the floor, in communicating a substantial amount of information. Although this makes some intuitive sense, it is not clear how much information is necessary to constitute a turn (Feldstein & Welkowitz, 1978; Rosenfeld, 1978). For example, Yngve's definition of a turn in terms of a substantial informational unit allows for some verbalizations by the listener or auditor without the listener technically taking a turn and assuming the speaker's role. Thus, a distinction is made between a vocalization and taking a turn. The comments initiated by the listener that support the speaker's maintaining the floor are called back-channel responses (Yngve, 1970). They include verbal responses such as "mm-hmm," "yeah," "I see," and nonverbal agreement in the form of head nodding. Thus, even though the listener initiates a brief comment, it does not signal an interest to take a turn. In fact, Duncan (1972) suggests that the back-channel response can be used by the listener to *avoid* taking a turn even though the speaker may be ready to yield the floor. Other forms of back-channel signals include the following: (a) the listener's completion of the speaker's unfinished sentence; (b) brief requests for clarification; and (c) a brief summary or restatement of the speaker's immediately preceding comments (Duncan, 1972). The difficulties in differentiating speaker-listener roles reliably and the related issue of identifying a turn are obvious problems for this functional view of conversation.

A contrasting orientation to describing and analyzing conversations might be described as an "objective" approach (Feldstein & Welkowitz, 1978). This approach makes no assumptions about the function of a conversation, but merely describes a sequence of sounds and silences identifiable by their source. A turn is simply identified by one participant starting to talk while the other person is silent. The distinction between speaker and listener roles, characteristic of the functional view of conversation, is ignored in favor of operationally defining participants' patterns of talk and silence. The analysis of temporal patterns of talk and silence can be accomplished easily with an electronic system such as the Automatic Vocal Transaction Analyzer, or AVTA (Jaffe & Feldstein, 1970). Through voice relays, AVTA evaluates several times a second the talking or silent state of a conversation. In addition, this system has the capacity to filter the input of each speaker's voice from the other speaker's microphone, and thus provides a reliable identification of each speaker's temporal pattern of talking. As long as an utterance exceeds some pre-determined threshold, matched against normal auditory acuity, then the initiation of a turn is identified. Consequently, the content, duration, and the informational value of an utterance are irrelevant to the identification of a speaker's turn.

The objective approach to analyzing conversational sequences certainly has the advantage of defining talk and silence intervals in a straightforward operational manner. The functional nature of the alternate approach, however, is clearly consistent with the emphasis of this book. In addition, it is convenient to use the functional terminology of *speaker* and *listener* in describing the verbal and nonverbal behavior of interactants.

Speaker behavior. This section focuses specifically on the regularities in speaker behavior that are identifiable both within and across units of speech in conversation. The speech unit of particular importance in describing speaker behavior is that of the phonemic clause. Boomer (1978) describes the phonemic clause as a discernible "segment" of speech from one to seven or eight syllables in length that seems to be spoken as a unit. Boomer identifies the three following characteristics that mark the termination of a phonemic clause: (1) a rising, then falling, pitch for some or all of the last word in the clause; (2) stretching out the last word in the clause; and (3) an increased loudness in the last syllable or word. The convergence of these simultaneous changes in pitch, rhythm, and loudness identifies the primary stress in a phonemic clause. The point at which the characteristics of primary stress level off in preparation for the next phonemic clause is called the terminal juncture (Boomer, 1978). The following sentence can be seen to contain two phonemic clauses (as Boomer notes, the characteristics of a phonemic clause are recognized more easily in speech than in the printed word, so the reader might try saying the sentence aloud).

If we decide to leave/we'll have to start soon/

The three characteristics marking the termination of the phonemic clause should be noticeable in the words "leave" and "soon". In addition, hesitation at the terminal junction following "leave" should be evident.

Both pause and body movement seem to be related to the position within a phonemic clause (Boomer & Dittmann, 1962). In the example, the pause after "leave" and "soon" should be noticeably longer than any pause within each phonemic clause. This may be related to the more complex demands of encoding a plan for a full clause, compared to encoding a single word at a time within the clause. In describing movement here, the reference is generally to nonspecific changes in body position such as adjusting one's posture while seated, shuffling a foot on the floor, or lifting a hand to brush back one's hair.

Although there is agreement about the relative position of body movements in the flow of speech, minor differences in the perceived timing of these movements have a substantial effect in interpreting their function. Specifically, Dittmann and Llewellyn (1969) noted that several researchers (Ekman, 1965; Pittenger, Hockett, & Danehy, 1960; Scheflen, 1964) judged that body movements coincided with words having the greatest vocal emphasis (primary stress). Thus, according to those researchers, it appeared that movement accentuated the primary stress words located at the end of a phonemic clause; that is, the movement emphasized the critical ending word in a phonemic clause. Dittmann and Llewellyn's (1969) data, however, indicated that increased movement occurred not at the end of a given phonemic clause, but primarily at the beginning of the next clause. Depending on the length of the terminal pause at any given time, this probably reflects a difference of less than a second in specifying the position of greatest movement, but this fraction of a second has important implications for understanding the relationship of movement to speech. If Dittmann and Llewellyn are correct, then movement would seem to related more to the demands of encoding a speech unit rather than emphasizing the terminal words of an already encoded speech unit.

A more general issue in the speech-movement link is the causal relationship underlying the link. There is considerable disagreement about this concern. One view emphasizes the primacy of speech in determining movement. In particular, if movements occur more frequently at the start of speech units, they may be the result of the release of increased muscle tension associated with encoding (Boomer, 1963). A second, differing alternative suggests that various movements may facilitate the verbalization of material that was previously outside of consciousness (Mahl, 1968, 1977). Mahl came to this conclusion by analyzing exchanges occurring in psychoanalysis, noting that specific meaningful movements often immediately preceded the verbalization of material not previously accessible to the client. Thus, movement may trigger recall and facilitate specific verbalizations. Obviously, even if Mahl's assessment of these psychoanalytic exchanges is correct, it is not clear that such a process can be generalized to more mundane conversations. A third alternative is that the timing of both speech and movement is constrained by underlying rhythms that have their roots in the human neurological response process (Condon, 1976). Condon claims that both speech and movement follow a regular cyclical pattern of pulses, and that speech may be hurried or slowed to meet the form of the rhythm pattern. For example, if the information to be expressed requires several words, and the end of the rhythm cycle is near, the words will be more rushed.

There are obvious differences of opinion on the function of the speech-movement link for the speaker; however, independent of its function for the speaker, the speech-movement link does seem to have distinct effects on the listener. Specifically, when messages are presented with movement synchronized to the verbal stream, listeners recall the content better and are more influenced by the message than when movement is not synchronized (Woodall & Burgoon, 1981).

There are two additional factors modifying the speech-movement link that should be mentioned. First, it appears that the scope of the movement is related to size of the speech segment. That is, larger shifts in posture or location seem to coincide with larger conversational segments, whereas smaller, briefer movements are related to smaller conversational segments (Scheflen, 1964). The results of a study by Thomas and Bull (1981) seem to support the distinction proposed by Scheflen. Specifically, these authors found that increased postural change was more frequently associated with a statement introducing new information than with questions, answers, or responses elaborating on earlier information. Furthermore, Thomas and Bull speculated that larger postural changes in speech may be analogous to paragraphs in written language by demarcating the introduction of new themes.

The second factor modifying the speech-movement link relates to the type of movement, particularly the classification of hand movement. For example, Ekman (1972) notes that most researchers distinguish between self- or body-focused movements and gestural- or object-focused movements. The former movements, including behaviors such as scratching, rubbing one's hands together, or grooming movements, seem to be related to anxiety, boredom, annoyance, or other forms of negative affect. The latter movements, including emblems, such as raising an open hand to indicate stop, and illustrators, such as pointing toward an object or tracing its shape in the air, seem to illustrate or elaborate on the verbal content of a conversation (Ekman, 1972).

Of course, movement not only marks the breaks and transitions in speech but also describes the means by which other involvement behaviors are managed. For example, changes in the speaker's gaze direction often require head movements or even postural changes. In such cases, movement may be a by-product of the relationship between gaze and speech. In a detailed analysis of gaze patterns, Kendon (1967) found that in beginning a conversational turn (i.e., in moving from a listener to a speaker role), an individual generally looked away from the other person. The points at which gaze was most commonly directed at the listener were (a) during stretches of fluent speech, (b) at the ends of phrases, and (c) at the conclusion of a conversational turn. Direct gaze was usually avoided during both nonfluent speech and hesitations (Kendon, 1967). Presumably, a speaker breaks his or her gaze at the listener during nonfluencies and hesitations in order to concentrate more fully on what is going to be said. That is, avoiding direct gaze becomes a means of managing potential stimulus overload.

Allen and Guy (1977) tested this explanation by examining gaze patterns associated with mental processes and judgmental words versus gaze patterns associated with affirmational words. It was assumed that mental process words such as "think," "hope," "know," or "wonder" imply a process with a potentially doubtful outcome. By extension, judgmental words such as "bad," "good," or "probably" should imply a process of comparison and evaluation. Allen and Guy hypothesized that both the mental process and judgmental words would reflect greater effort and uncertainty. In contrast, affirmations ("yeah," "yes," "un-huh") and negations ("no") should reflect assurances or certainties demanding less mental effort. Consistent with Kendon's results, mental process and judgmental words were associated more frequently with gaze avoidance than with gaze holding patterns. An opposite pattern was found for the affirmation words. Thus, gaze may be related to the evaluative certainty of specific verbal content. On the other hand, because affirmation words are commonly used as back-channel responses, the increased gaze-holding associated with them may simply reflect their feedback function.

The analysis of speaker behavior discussed up to this point suggests that pause, movement, and gaze patterns are reliably related to the structure of speech. In addition, it appears that some facial actions, particularly eyebrow movement, are related to conversation. Ekman (1979) recently commented that, although he knew of no quantitative studies of brow movements in conversations, he felt that some patterns were nevertheless discernible. I will rely on his description in the following discussion. First, it will be necessary to provide illustrations of his basic brow and forehead actions. These action units can be seen in Figure 4-2.

The facial movements represented in action units 1 + 2 and 4 are used to emphasize or stress one or more words. Alternately, action units 1 + 2 and 4 can serve as either a comma in a list of events or as a question mark in delivering an inquiry. Finally, action unit 4, in combination with finger snapping or trying to pluck the word from space, can serve to indicate a word search. Such a movement may also help to maintain the speaker's claim on the floor.

In summary, the dynamic behavior of speakers seems to facilitate different aspects of interaction regulation. Pause, movement, and changing gaze patterns help to demarcate phonemic clauses as specific informational units. Pause and the avoidance of direct gaze seem to be related to the general demands of encoding and the specific problem of resolving uncertainties in speech. The initiation of gaze provides a means by which the speaker can monitor the listener's reaction to a completed statement. Finally, hand movements and facial expressions can serve to emphasize and segment the content of speech.

Listener behavior. Over the course of a conversation, the behavior of the listener usually follows a definable pattern. In general, listener behavior, both verbal and nonverbal, seems to be concentrated between phonemic clauses, that is, during the

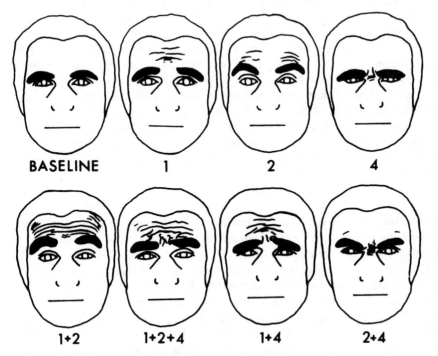

Fig. 4-2. Basic brow and forehead action units. (From Ekman, 1979. Reprinted by permission.)

terminal pause (Dittmann, 1972). For example, in one study, the verbal recognition of agreement ("mm-hmm") and other more extended comments by the listener were 10 times more likely to occur between phonemic clauses than at other times (Dittmann & Llewellyn, 1967).

In a later study, the timing of head nods was found to be even more distinctive than that of verbal responses. Listener head nods were 50 times more likely to occur between phonemic clauses than anywhere else (Dittmann & Llwewllyn, 1968). Specific behaviors of the speaker, however, can precipitate head nods prior to terminal pauses. Rosenfeld (1978) reported that listener head nods are more likely to occur when the speaker initiates one of the following behaviors: (1) a filled hesitation pause (e.g., "ah") in combination with a gesture; (2) a filled pause in combination with a head movement; (3) a phrase whose content repeats that of an earlier comment; and (4) a sociocentric sequence (Duncan, 1972) such as "y'know."

Although speakers may not be aware of listener responses when they occur, their absence can be disruptive. For example, Rosenfeld (1972) described a videotaped exchange in which a listener failed to reciprocate a smile by the speaker on three occasions. After each statement the speaker modified the content of the comment into a less offensive form accompanied by a weaker and briefer smile. When the listener finally responded with a broad smile, the speaker suggested talking about something else. On occasion, if there are no back-channel responses, the speaker may even ask if the listener understood the comment. In addition, if a back-channel response is out of place in the flow of speech, the speaker may conclude that the listener is not really paying attention or is even being facetious in responding. For example, an adolescent listening to some common parental admonition might initiate a series of head nods before his father even finishes his statement. If a series of such nods occurs concurrently with a very bored expression and a "yeah, yeah," one translation might be "I've heard this before; do we have to go through it again?"

Listener behavior not only provides feedback concerning agreement and degree of attention, but also facilitates the ordered sequencing of conversation. The discussion of this issue in the next section requires an examination of coordinated speaker and listener behaviors.

Turn-taking. One of the basic characteristics of verbal interaction is that turns are usually taken in a very smooth and orderly fashion. The fluid operation of turn-taking seems to be the result of distinctly coordinated exchanges between speakers and listeners. Earlier, reference was made to the contrasting gaze patterns of speakers and listeners at change points in conversation. Kendon's (1967) results showed that a speaker, in ending a turn, usually looks directly at the listener, whereas the listener, in moving to the speaker's role, usually avoids direct gaze. The results of two other studies suggest that the patterns described by Kendon are not invariant (Beattie, 1978; Rutter, Stephenson, Ayling, & White, 1978). Kendon (1978) noted that situational differences between his original study and the later ones may account for the differing results, but at the very least the generality of his initial findings must be questioned.

A possible explanation for the failure to replicate Kendon's (1967) results, and one that is consistent with Kendon's (1978) focus on situational differences is offered by Thomas and Bull (1981). They found that head movement immediately preceding the initiation of a speaker's turn was related to the type of speech category that followed. For example, turning one's head toward another person (obviously facilitating direct gaze) was predominantly related to asking questions and less strongly related to making statements and responses. Raising one's head was exclusively related to asking questions, whereas turning one's head away from the other person was exclusively related to answering questions (Thomas & Bull, 1981). Thus, the pattern of asking or answering questions or making statements may determine the probability of initiating gaze at the start of a turn.

The role of other behaviors in turn-taking has been examined in detail by Duncan (1972). He classified six discrete types of behavioral cues that a speaker may initiate in signaling readiness to yield a conversational turn. These cues included two of the three characteristics Boomer (1978) used to mark the termination of a phonemic clause: (1) change in the pitch of the last word in a clause; and (2) drawl or stretching out on the last word or syllable in a clause. In addition, Duncan identified the following cues as signaling speaker readiness to yield a turn: (3) the termination of gestures; (4) sociocentric sequences such as "but uh," "or something," and "you know"; (5) a decrease in pitch or loudness at the end of one of the sociocentric sequences; and (6) the completion of a grammatical clause.

In a detailed analysis of two interactions, Duncan (1972) found strong support for the hypothesized role of these six cues in turn-taking. Specifically, when the speaker did not initiate a signal that suppressed turn yielding (such as continued gesturing with one or both hands), the correlation between the number of turn-yielding cues and the probability of a turn-taking attempt by the listener was $r = .96$. As long as the speaker sustained gesturing, however, the listener almost never attempted to take a turn, regardless of the number of turn-yielding cues displayed with the gesturing. That is, the attempt-suppressing signal by the speaker was almost always successful, even though several turn-yielding cues were also present. It is interesting to note that even when all six turn-yielding cues were present, the probability of a listener attempting a turn was only about .50. Thus, when the clarity of the speaker's readiness to yield a turn was maximized, the listener attemped a turn only half of the time.

In a later study, Duncan and Niederehe (1974) examined the behavior of the listener in an attempt to differentiate the initiation of a speaker turn from a simple back-channel response. That is, the purpose of the study was to determine if listeners behave differently when they initiate a simple back-channel response (listener response) than when they initiate a turn (take the speaker's role). Duncan and Niederehe found that four cues, which they termed a speaker-state signal, discriminated between turn beginnings and back-channel responses. Specifically, turn beginnings were characterized by higher frequencies of the following cues in listeners: (1) shifting the head from a position pointing directly toward the speaker; (2) audible inhalation; (3) initiating a gesture; and (4) overloudness in speech. It might be noted that the head shift cue by the listener immediately before taking a turn is consistent with the gaze changes reported by Kendon (1967).

A consideration of the complementary behaviors of speakers and listeners in turn-taking suggests how a smooth continuity is typically maintained in verbal interaction. Speaker turn-yielding cues signal an opportunity for the listener to take a turn, but that does not ensure that the listener will do so. If the listener initiates the speaker state signal, then the (former) speaker will usually not attempt any further comment. But if the listener does not initiate the speaker state signal, even though some back-channel verbal responses occur, the speaker can determine that he or she still has the turn. This coordination of speaker and listener behavior in verbal interactions is not the only form of behavioral interdependence in interactions. It appears that more general coordination in movement across interactants is also typical. This will be the focus of the next section.

Behavioral synchrony. Various researchers have proposed that the behaviors of interactants are matched or synchronous along several dimensions. Detailed, frame-by-frame analysis of filmed interaction suggests that specific patterns of movement by listeners are linked to the structure of the speaker's speech, just as the speaker's own movement is linked to his or her speech. This coordination between speaker and listener has been called interactional synchrony (Condon & Ogston, 1966). Synchrony is reflected in the initiation of organized listener movement patterned after the flow of different sounds from the speaker (Condon, 1976). Analyzing this synchrony requires segmenting the constituent sounds of each word against a detailed profile of listener behavior. Condon claims that patterned listener movements such as the turning of a wrist or the flexing of a finger may follow distinct speech sounds with as little as a .05 second lag time.

Kendon (1970) notes that interactional synchrony does not require that the listener look at the speaker, but merely attend to the structure of speech. Furthermore, Kendon proposes that the precision of the listener's synchrony with speech probably requires that the listener be able in some way to anticipate what the speaker is going to say. That is, the listener can be described as constructing a running hypothesis about the form of the speaker's next comments. Although such a process would seem to be the result of learning, Condon and Sander (1974) report that neonate movement is synchronous with human voice patterns in the first day of life.

Another form of behavioral synchrony relates to the congruence of postures and movements among interactants. That is, interactants who move or hold body positions in a similar fashion can be described as being congruent. Postural congruence can take the form of either "carbon copies" or "mirror images" (Trout & Rosenfeld, 1980). Scheflen (1963, 1964, 1974) has described postural congruence in psychotherapy exchanges, and has proposed that increased congruence reflects greater rapport between individuals. The results of one recent study provide some support for Scheflen's interpretation. In an evaluation of videotapes of simulated client-therapist interactions, subjects judged that there was greater rapport between a client and therapist when the therapist's seated posture was mirror-image congruent with the client than when it was not (Trout & Rosenfeld, 1980). In that same study, however, forward lean by the therapist produced higher ratings of rapport than did behavioral congruence. Similarly, LaFrance (1979; LaFrance & Broadbent,

1976) found that increased postural mirroring between students and instructors in college seminars was related to higher reported levels of class involvement by the students.

One contrasting set of results merits attention in the light of the apparently clear association between postural congruence and rapport. LaFrance and Ickes (1981) unobtrusively videotaped postural patterns for pairs of strangers left alone for a 5-minute period. They found that increased postural mirroring showed a low negative relationship to perceived rapport and a positive relationship to a perception of the interaction as being forced, awkward, and strained. LaFrance and Ickes suggested that their failure to find a positive relationship between postural mirroring and rapport may be related to the difference between their interactional context and those characteristic of the previous research. Because the subject pairs in their study were just getting acquainted, mirroring may have reflected a concern for developing communality and rapport that was difficult to achieve in such a brief exchange. In the more established relationships typical of therapy (Scheflen, 1964; Trout & Rosenfeld, 1980) and classroom (LaFrance, 1979; LaFrance & Broadbent, 1976) settings, the opportunity was present for individuals to move from a mere concern about rapport to its actual development over time. That is, initial postural mirroring may first reflect a concern about rapport (negatively experienced because of its absence) that facilitates its later development.

A final focus of behavioral synchrony involves the paralinguistic dimensions of loudness and duration of speech. Matching in these dimensions has been termed conversational congruence by Feldstein and Welkowitz (1978). Their brief review of research on conversational congruence indicates that intensity or loudness levels within pairs are moderately correlated (e.g., $.40 \leqslant r \leqslant .60$). The correlations between duration measures within pairs are usually not as high as those between intensity measures, especially early in interactions. There are some results, however, showing that the durations of vocalizations within pairs tend to converge over time (Welkowitz & Feldstein, 1969).

McDowall (1978a, 1978b) has attempted to determine the strength of interactional synchrony by examining the frequency of synchronous behaviors relative to a baseline of chance occurrence. In general, McDowall reported that synchrony was not found above chance levels, and thus he concluded that synchrony was not as important as previously claimed (McDowall, 1978a, 1978b). His results and conclusions have not gone unchallenged. Gatewood and Rosenwein (1981) have criticized McDowall's research because McDowall's attempts to replicate Condon's findings used a different methodology and a different means of operationalizing interactional synchrony from those used by Condon. In this area of research, one that demands highly detailed and time-consuming work, it may be some time before more definitive answers about the range, antecedents, and consequences of behavioral synchrony are available.

Paralinguistic divergence. Although synchrony or convergence has been a common finding in research on behavioral patterning between interactants, there is also some evidence for divergence between interactants. In particular, divergence may be most evident in speech or paralinguistic cues. In their review of the literature, Street and

Giles (1982) note that speech divergence can be manifested in interactants' contrasting changes in accent, rate of speech, latency of speech, and other cues. Such developing divergence may serve to provide information about the differences between the partners. Although divergence may indicate contrasting attitudes and dispositions between the interactants, divergent information can also facilitate the organization of interaction. That is, the partners may be sensitized to those differences between them that might otherwise lead to negative and conflicting attributions. Street and Giles propose that behavioral synchrony (convergence) and divergence can be interpreted in terms of a speech accommodation theory (Giles, 1977) that emphasizes a purposive basis for related speech behaviors. Although convergent and divergent patterns are assumed to be purposive, this does not mean that the interactants are necessarily aware of and deliberately managing their behavior. The suggestion of a purposive basis underlying convergent and divergent behavioral patterns is not only an economical explanation, but also an explanation that may have relevance for the social control function.

Conclusions

Although almost any nonverbal behavior might be described as informative, the patterns discussed up to this point seem to reflect a more specific regulatory function. On most occasions it appears that the regulation of interaction is managed almost automatically and rarely enters an individual's awareness. But awareness of and deliberation in regulating interaction probably increases as the individual anticipates: (1) an unusual interaction (e.g., an interaction with someone who cannot speak the language well); (2) a highly evaluative interaction (i.e., interaction in which the costs of social gaffes and other breakdowns in the flow of interaction may be high); or (3) an increasing discrepancy from normal regulatory patterns.

In general, the arrangement features of an interaction in the forms of interpersonal distance, orientation, and posture constrain the level of involvement possible between individuals. In focused interactions, as individuals are closer, more directly oriented, and more open in posture, greater involvement through dynamic behaviors is possible. For example, close, directly confronting arrangements provide an opportunity for touch, and greater involvement ensures a smoother regulation of interaction. In fact, involvement patterns that are discrepant from the situational norm can disrupt a smooth process of exchange, for example, touching a high status person in a formal interaction to get his or her attention may cause more problems than it solves. Hall's (1966) discussion of interpersonal distance zones appropriate to different types of interaction stresses this point.

In spite of the constraints introduced by relational and situational norms, some important generalizations can be made. In particular, the extensive research on the dynamic features of focused interactions has uncovered some interesting patterns in the regulation of interaction. Subtle but predictable changes in gaze, paralinguistic cues, gestures, and posture are related both to sustaining speaker and listener roles and to the initiation of speaker turns.

Finally, specifying the role of nonverbal involvement in regulating interaction facilitates our understanding of other functions of nonverbal exchange. That is, we can consider some minimal range of nonverbal involvement as necessary for the comfortable management of interaction. Our confidence in classifying such behaviors as regulatory increases to the extent that they are consistent across interactions, particularly (1) at the start and end of a conversation, (2) at speaker turn points, or (3) when there is ambiguity about the meaning of some comments. To the extent that we can identify a mutual pattern of gazing, smiling, nodding, and paralinguistic cues as regulating interaction, these behaviors become less salient as means to fulfill other purposes such as intimacy, social control, or service-task functions. These latter functions may be characterized in terms of different motivational bases that are presumed to underlie patterns of nonverbal exchange over the course of an interaction. In the next chapter, the discussion will focus on the first of those motive-based functions—intimacy.

Unfocused Interactions—Passing Encounters

In the previous section, patterns of regulating extended focused interactions were described and analyzed. In unfocused interactions, although there is no explicit verbal agenda, there is a need for regulating the level of involvement with others present. This section will deal specifically with the regulation of brief encounters typical of people passing one another on sidewalks or in hallways. More extended unfocused interactions involving activities such as working or studying in the presence of others will be treated in the chapter describing the service-task function of nonverbal behaviors (Chapter 7). Although such longer unfocused encounters might be analyzed in terms of the regulating function, the nature of the particular activities is probably more important in determining sustained involvement patterns. Thus, the longer unfocused interactions may be more effectively analyzed in terms of the service-task function. The analysis of brief unfocused encounters required in both pedestrian navigation and passing and greeting others will be considered next.

Pedestrian Navigation

A situation in which most of us find ourselves several times a day is that of simply crossing paths with others. This situation may involve walking to the bus stop or store and passing others coming from the opposite direction. At work, we may encounter others in the hallway, either individually or in small groups. In any such instance, we are only momentarily in the presence of one or more other(s), but even in such brief passing encounters, consistencies in the regulation of interaction can be found.

In terms of movement alone, it is clear that a kind of subtle but effective choreography is involved in our passing by others. Of course, most of us, at least in the United States, follow the rule of the road—stay on the right side. There are numerous exceptions to this rule which can make for occasional (though rarely serious) collisions, but in fact, they occur quite infrequently. Goffman (1972, pp. 5-18) discusses the topic of pedestrian traffic and suggests some regularities in this subtle exchange between pedestrians. First, he describes a narrow oval-shaped scanning zone in front of the individual as the focal area for checking out those who approach us. In this scanning range, extending perhaps 15 or 20 feet forward, mutual recognition of the other's presence usually ensures that each will comfortably pass the other. When that recognition is not mutual, the check must be repeated or one's course must be accentuated until the other shows some sign of appreciating the common navigational decision. Occasionally, in very crowded circumstances, approaching pedestrians will have to turn sideways and slide past one another, thus ensuring that both can be accommodated in a space smaller than their combined shoulder width. Alternately, one might lightly touch or guide another by placing a hand on that person's back or shoulder to facilitate movement in a congested area. This type of touching in a crowded setting is usually interpreted in a benign fashion by the recipient, although that may not be the case in an uncrowded setting.

Other patterns of nonverbal exchange are identifiable in crossings in low density traffic. From my own observations and reports of colleagues and students, there seems to be some regularity in the gazing patterns of approaching strangers. It seems that a first glance toward the approaching other is frequently made at a relatively great distance, well beyond the scanning range suggested by Goffman. In an open area outdoors this distance might be a 100 feet or more, depending on the setting and the amount of traffic. Of course, the distance of this first glance is also dependent on the individual's not being otherwise occupied in looking at surrounding sights or in talking to a walkmate. This first glance might be described as simply a noticing look. As the individuals get closer, somewhere within Goffman's scanning range, there is often a subsequent glance that is facially focused, which might be termed a recognition gaze. Between the noticing and the recognition there is often avoidance of additional looking as the other person approaches. A continuous stare from the time of first noticing the other person would be conspicuous and potentially threatening. Consequently, gaze avoidance in that zone probably facilitates mutual comfort.

Even when walkways are uncrowded and the initiation of gaze is unnecessary for traffic control, regularities in the recognition glance are identifiable. Goffman (1963, p. 84) proposes that the rule of civil inattention structures gaze patterns when unacquainted people pass one another on the street. According to Goffman, civil inattention permits glancing at the other person up to about eight feet, followed by gaze withdrawal as people approach closer and pass. The initial gaze in the pattern of civil inattention demonstrates an important recognition of the other person's presence. The subsequent withdrawal of gaze seems to indicate that the other individual is not considered a curious or threatening person.

Cary (1978) notes that although the concept of civil inattention has received wide acceptance, very little empirical research has been initiated to examine its viability. In fact, in a series of studies on college students passing one another on campus, Cary found little support for the concept of civil attention. In particular, two filmed studies of pedestrian behavior found no evidence for people lowering their heads or eyes or using less direct gaze when passing another person. In another study in that series, Cary found that decreased gaze toward a staring confederate who walked past the subject occurred only when the confederate was male and the subject was female.

Cary admits that the failure to support the concept of civil inattention could be due to differences between the subjects and settings that he and Goffman sampled in coming to their contrasting conclusions. Thus, it is possible that the gazing patterns characteristic of civil inattention are specific to certain groups or settings. Such an after-the-fact explanation in defense of civil inattention is obviously less convincing than supportive empirical results. But it might be noted that to the extent college students on their own college campus represent a homogeneous group on a "home territory," some of the motivation for civil inattention suggested by Goffman may be irrelevant. That is, looking away to demonstrate that another student is neither feared nor the object of curiosity may be generally unnecessary because these motives are less salient between students on their own campus.

Distinctive behavioral patterns in pedestrian traffic are not limited to the approach of isolated others. Not only do we avoid bumping into individuals, but we also seem sensitive to the existence of a kind of group space. For example, individuals are less likely to pass between two persons who seem to be a pair than between two objects, such as trash cans, placed at comparable distances (Knowles, 1973). This avoidance of group space seems to increase with increasing group size (Knowles, 1973), but this effect may be moderated by the configuration and activity of the group (Knowles & Bassett, 1976; Knowles, Kreuser, Haas, Hyde, & Schuchrat, 1976).

Although individuals will almost always try to avoid intruding on an interacting group, occasionally a group (usually a pair) will position itself so that an approaching individual will have to split the group. For example, two people might be talking to one another as they stand on each side of a doorway. Someone coming through the doorway has no choice but to walk between them. Nevertheless, the person walking through the doorway probably feels uncomfortable and may feel pressured to say "excuse me" as he or she goes through the pair. Such an apology may be replaced or supplemented by the person's averting his or her eyes downward and increasing his or her pace while passing the pair. Thus, even though the intruder has no option, that person acts as if he or she were at fault.

Passing and Greeting

The behavior of acquainted individuals who cross one another's path is usually different from the behavior of unacquainted people in a similar encounter. Although a verbalization is often involved, it is usually a perfunctory greeting. Given this minimal verbal exchange, it is appropriate to consider such encounters between acquainted individuals as a category of brief unfocused interactions. Goffman (1981, p. 47) observes that a brief verbal greeting, such as "hello" or "how are you?" initiated by one person and repeated by the other, does not really represent a statement and reply that are typical of verbal interactions. Instead, the greetings of both people are reactive responses produced by their accidental shared presence. In fact, "the point of performing these little rituals is not to solicit a reply or reply to a solicitation but to enact an emotion that attests to the pleasure produced by the contact" (Goffman, 1981, p. 47). There is little research on the specific details of these passing encounters between acquaintances, but nevertheless some regularities can be suggested. Again, this discussion will *not* focus on those occasions in which acquaintances stop to talk. Such occasions would obviously qualify as focused interactions.

If acquainted individuals anticipate nothing more than a brief greeting as they approach and pass one another, then the noticing look described in the previous section is especially critical. From my own unsystematic observations, it appears that the distant noticing glance usually permits easy identification of the other person. But initiating a verbal greeting at 100, 50, or even 30 feet is awkward if nothing more than a greeting is intended. If a verbal greeting is made at too great a distance, some further exchange will be required as the parties approach and pass. That makes it difficult to limit the intended exchange to "hi," "how are you?" or "good morning." Because mutual gaze usually precedes a verbal greeting, gaze avoidance becomes the means for ensuring that a premature greeting will not be required. When the mutual glance is initiated at a 10 to 20-foot distance, there is usually just enough time for a brief balanced verbal exchange before the parties pass one another. In this way, the delayed initiation of mutual gaze ensures that the verbal greeting is held to a comfortable minimum. Finally, some aspects of the accompanying nonverbal routine seem to transcend cultural differences. Specifically, Eibl-Eibesfeldt (1972) notes that the eyebrow flash and smile are common components across culture in greeting exchanges between good friends.

Repeated crossing of paths over a relatively short interval presents an interesting and often uncomfortable situation for people. This sort of occurrence may be common for those who work near one another and have to use the same hallways in the course of their daily routines. The location and arrangement of offices in my own department presents a good example of this kind of setting. Faculty offices are located on the outside corridors of three floors of our building. The main office of the department is in a more central location. Because most faculty members make several trips a day to the main office, go to and return from classes or lunch, and initiate various other trips, the likelihood of passing others repeatedly is fairly high.

The first crossing in a setting like this presents no problem because the individuals can share a brief greeting of some sort. This first exchange may simply be a "good morning," but once it has been said, it can't be said again—at least, not on the same day. If the first exchange were a "hi" or "hello," that might be used again, but probably not for some time. Goffman (1972, p. 78) describes an analogous situation from an unpublished paper by Cook (Note 3). The study contained a description of a formalized way of managing repeated encounters between officers and enlisted men on board small ships. Apparently, an enlisted man had to salute an officer (other than the captain) only on the first occasion of seeing him each day.

What happens when repeated crossings occur over a short interval? Although I am not aware of any data on this particular problem, it seems from my own experience that some regularities can be suggested. One option when you pass a person a second time is simply smiling and nodding. This involves some recognition of that person's presence, but relieves an individual from having to repeat the greeting made 15 minutes earlier. Another strategy is to avoid steadfastly recognition of the other's presence by looking down or to the opposite side. This latter tactic is probably easier to accomplish in wider and/or busier hallways than in those that are narrow and lightly used. Again, in my own situation, the office hallway is just wide enough for two people to cross without touching. Under such circumstances, it is extremely difficult to avoid giving some recognition to the other person because you have to look at that person in order to pass without bumping. In fact, the attention that is required toward the oncoming individual is often sufficient to precipitate a verbal greeting or nod and smile even from strangers. In contrast, the main hallway is over twice as wide, and passing an approaching person does not require attending to that individual's movements. Consequently, repeated passings may be more conveniently managed by avoiding recognition of the other person.

Of course, when passings occur only a few times throughout the day, separated by several hours, verbal greetings may be repeated without the individuals feeling uncomfortable. My guess is that as the duration between repeated crossings increases, the probability of a verbal greeting also increases. There may also be more pressure on the lower status member to be ready to initiate a greeting toward the higher status person than vice versa.

Conclusions

The brief shared-presence experiences of individuals passing in pedestrian traffic provide an opportunity for examining how people manage a situation of minimal social contact. Goffman (1963) suggests that a pattern of civil inattention in such settings permits a glance toward the other person as each approaches in the 10 to 20-foot range. Gaze is then withdrawn as each nears and passes the other. However, observation of college student pedestrian traffic showed no support for the gaze patterns described by Goffman (Cary, 1978). Nevertheless, it is probably premature to assess the viability of the civil inattention construct until a wider range of subjects in various settings can be observed.

When the circumstance of crossing paths involves acquaintances rather than strangers, the pressure for initiating some sort of greeting increases. The management of gaze in approaching acquaintances can help to ensure that any verbal exchange is limited to a brief, balanced greeting. For example, once the approaching acquaintance is visually identified at a distance, gaze avoidance may often occur up to the range of 10 to 20 feet. At that point, a mutual gaze usually precedes a brief, reciprocated verbal greeting just before the individuals pass one another. Repeated crossings over the course of a day can make repeated similar greetings awkward. In that case, either a nod and smile or a more active avoidance of the recognition gaze can replace a verbal greeting.

Summary

The regulation of sustained verbal interaction is usually accomplished so smoothly that the process seems to be an automatic one. In spite of this apparent simplicity, there are many factors contributing to the complex, yet subtle, management of interaction. First, individuals usually arrange themselves in a relatively facing orientation or F-formation (Kendon, 1976, 1977). Such arrangements facilitate easy communication within the group and provide a boundary between the group and the environment. Whereas the F-formation provides a relatively fixed general arrangement promoting interaction, a number of dynamically changing behaviors guides the specific form of give-and-take within the interaction. For example, speaker movement seems most common either at the start of or between the small segments of conversation called phonemic clauses. In a complementary fashion, listener responses, both verbal and nonverbal, also seem to be concentrated between phonemic clauses. Listener back-channel responses, such as a head nod, "mm-hmm," or "yeah," signal agreement with the speaker and a willingness to let the speaker continue.

Coordinated turn-taking in interactions is related to the speaker's cessation of gesturing and the initiation of one or more turn-yielding cues. Generally, as more turn-yielding cues are initiated, the probability of a listener taking a turn increases. Finally, coordinated, interdependent behavioral patterns in an interaction do more than simply regulate the give-and-take of verbal interaction. Behavioral synchrony, in the form of postural or paralinguistic congruence, may serve as an index of rapport between interactants. Behavioral divergence in the same behavioral cues may also facilitate interaction by specifying and emphasizing critical differences between the interactants.

Research on the management of passing encounters also suggests some regularity in the way these encounters are managed. The initiation of gaze between individuals who approach and pass one another permits the identification of the other person and provides an opportunity, if necessary, to signal one's pathway. Goffman (1972) suggests that gaze avoidance is characteristic of encounters between strangers as they approach closely and pass one another. The gaze patterns of acquainted individuals who approach and pass one another is slightly different because of the likelihood of some verbal greeting between them. In particular, a distant noticing glance (i.e., at 25-100 ft.) is usually followed by gaze avoidance until the parties are close enough to glance up again (i.e., at 10-20 ft.) and offer a brief verbal greeting. Repeated passings between acquaintances may present some pressure to initiate either an alternate form of greeting with a shared gaze or gaze avoidance.

Chapter 5
Intimacy

Much of the research on nonverbal behavior in social interaction has been analyzed in terms of intimacy exchange. This emphasis is largely the result of the direction provided by Argyle and Dean (1965) in their intimacy-equilibrium model. Because the intimacy-equilibrium model has been discussed in Chapter 2, it is unnecessary to review its substance. It is appropriate, however, to consider the construct of intimacy more closely and examine its place in the present functional analysis of nonverbal behavior.

In this chapter, I will not be attempting to review the extensive research on parent-child or caretaker-infant relationships. It is evident that the parent-child bond is an intensively intimate one, probably the most intimate in any human relationship. This bond is characterized by very frequent high levels of mutual tactile involvement, especially in the early years. Bowlby's (1969) discussion of the parent-child relationship emphasizes the critical importance of bonding for normal development. It should be noted that even young infants seem to take a very active role in managing their interactions with adults (Lamb, 1976). Contrary to the traditional view, the infant's social role is not a passive one. In fact, Cappella's (1981) review provides considerable evidence that infants use compensatory and reciprocal adjustments in nonverbal behavior to maintain an optimal level of stimulation.

In their discussion of the equilibrium model, Argyle and Dean (1965) used the term intimacy to refer both to an affiliative-like function of nonverbal behavior and to the set of behaviors manifesting that function. At the same time they acknowledged that intimacy behaviors can serve functions other than expressing intimacy—a theme emphasized in this book. Even though the multiple functions served by intimacy behaviors have been noted, such a dual usage of the term intimacy is misleading. Of course, this misleading usage has been continued by others, including myself (Patterson, 1976). That circumstance, however, prompted me to propose the term involvement in Chapter 1 to refer specifically to the overt behavioral description of an interaction. In contrast, the functions underlying the nonverbal behavior are higher order constructs designated by different terms. Thus, the term intimacy in this book identifies one of several functions of nonverbal involvement. The first concern of this chapter will be a closer look at the intimacy construct.

The Construct of Intimacy

In their intimacy-equilibrium model, Argyle and Dean (1965) propose that the dynamics underlying the management of involvement include both approach and avoidance forces. In terms of intimacy per se, the relevant concern is the degree to which affiliative needs are fulfilled. Thus, as there is less fulfillment of the affiliative need, approach or greater involvement will be attempted. If the actual involvement level exceeds the desired affiliative need, avoidance or decreased involvement will be attempted. Of course, Argyle and Dean make it clear that other motives also influence nonverbal involvement, notably the desire to seek information and to regulate interaction. For Argyle and Dean, however, the intimacy motive can be essentially equated with the management of affiliative needs.

Another view of intimacy is characterized by its contrast with affiliation. Recently, McAdams (McAdams, 1980; McAdams & Powers, 1981) proposed a clear conceptual distinction between the two constructs. Furthermore, he has developed a reliable projective test measure for the assessment of the intimacy motive. McAdams notes that notions of affiliative motivation have been modeled after achievement motivation. That is, the affiliative motive, like the achievement motive, is manifested in striving for a desired goal. In the case of the affiliative motive this is reflected in attempts to initiate, maintain, or restore positive relationships with others. In contrast, intimacy as a motive shifts the focus from striving to achieve a desired relationship to an evaluation of the experience and quality of the relationship (McAdams & Powers, 1981). The definition of the intimacy motive offered by these authors is as follows: "a recurrent conscious and/or unconscious preference or readiness for a particular quality of interpersonal experience, an experience of warm, close, and communicative exchange with another or with others" (p. 574).

A similar contrast between affiliation and intimacy provided the basis for a study of sex differences in interactive motives (Mark & Alper, 1980). In this study, females developed more intimacy-related themes on a projective test than did males. Thus, it is possible that individual differences exist in the frequency or intensity of intimacy motivation. It is noteworthy that this particular sex difference is consistent with the general pattern of females preferring greater nonverbal involvement with one another than males do.

McAdams and Powers note that this conception of intimacy is consistent with the works of Maslow (1954, 1968), Bakan (1966), Buber (1965, 1970), and Sullivan (1953). Representative of these works are descriptions of intimacy that identify an exchange characterized by (a) openness, (b) receptivity, (c) harmony, (d) concern for the other person, and (e) a surrender of manipulative control over the other person (McAdams & Powers, 1981). The surrender of manipulative control is especially salient for the distinction proposed between intimacy and social control in the present functional analysis. Specifically, when nonverbal involvement is the product of the intimacy function, reactions should be a spontaneous consequence of some affective evaluation of either the other person or the relationship. Thus, manipulative control is absent in the manifestation of the intimacy function. In contrast, when nonverbal involvement is the product of the social control function, reactions should be more deliberate attempts to change, impress, or otherwise influence the other person, that is, manipulative control is characteristic of such encounters.

McAdams and Powers's description of intimacy involves a rich and intense interpersonal experience that is probably not characteristic of most of our interactions. In contrast, the broader-based conception of intimacy linked to affiliative motivation is undoubtedly a more common factor in interaction. For the purpose of the present functional analysis, the communalities between these two views are more important than their differences. These communalities are reflected in an affective and evaluative reaction toward either the other person or the relationship. Practically, this would mean affection, love, interest in and concern for the other person, or possibly some commitment either to the other person or to the relationship. That affective reaction is, in turn, manifested through the relatively spontaneous display of nonverbal involvement. Although the examples discussed here have involved positive affective reactions, such as liking or loving, the intimacy function should be recognized as representing a continuum. Thus, negative affective and evaluation reactions toward others, characterized by a disliking, can be seen as opposite the liking or loving end of the continuum.

In order to appreciate the variable influences of intimacy across different relationships, it is useful first to provide a system for classifying and analyzing relationships. An approach that seems well suited to this purpose is the stage analysis of social penetration theory (Altman & Taylor, 1973). In the next section, the discussion of social penetration theory will provide a structure for the analysis of intimacy and nonverbal involvement.

Social Penetration Theory

The basic assumption of social penetration theory is that relationships develop (and deteriorate) through a series of predictable stages. The process of social penetration refers to the extent to which individuals in a relationship are mutually engaged in sharing aspects of the self. Altman and Taylor (1973) liken the development of the penetration process to the peeling of layers from an onion skin to uncover the core. In the case of social penetration, the onion would be an individual's personality structure. Increased social penetration is represented by successively more fundamental layers the closer one gets to the core. An individual's openness to another person in this process can be described in terms of its breadth and depth. Breadth refers to the range of accessibility in a given topical area, whereas depth refers to the degree of centrality represented by a topic.

The depth dimension of personality is particularly important in understanding the development of intimacy exchange over time. Altman and Taylor identify a number of properties of the depth dimension that are relevant for social penetration. The first property concerns the general contrast in content of the different layers of personality. As one moves from peripheral to intermediate to core layers of the personality, there is a shift of focus from issues dealing with simple biographical information through specific attitudes and opinions to basic values and self-concepts. Second, the more central the issue, the more it is assumed to influence an increasing number of specific, peripheral issues. For example, basic personal values have an impact on specific political attitudes or reactions to various social programs. Third, the more central layers reflect more unique and less visible aspects of the personality. Fourth, because the more central layers of the personality are assumed to include unique and more socially undesirable content, an individual's vulnerability is increased by disclosing their content (Altman & Taylor, 1973, pp. 17-18).

As individuals initiate and develop a relationship, they gradually move toward deeper levels of each other's personality. The direction and rate of development in a relationship may be different for each individual. It is assumed, however, that changes in the course of a relationship are a product of (1) the rewards and costs associated with the relationship, (2) the influence of individual differences, and (3) the pressure of situational constraints. Altman and Taylor's stage analysis of the development of relationships is an especially useful means for describing changing patterns of intimacy between people.

Stage Analysis

Stage 1: Orientation. In the initial phases of a relationship, particularly in the first few interactions, individuals usually make only limited, peripheral aspects of their personalities accessible to others. There is usually less variability in behavior than there is in later stages. A great deal of effort is often invested in trying to ensure that exchanges are pleasant. Although impressions may be formed quickly, open evaluations, particularly negative ones, are usually not initiated by the interactants. If negative reactions do develop, they must be handled subtly, perhaps by attempting to change the conversation or by simply excusing oneself. A verbal challenge or an explicit frown and head shake would be too direct and uncomfortable at this stage of a relationship. This would probably be the case even if one decided never to see that person again. Because the content of exchanges at this stage are often limited to the outer, more public, areas of the personality, the development of these exchanges tends to be rather stereotyped.

Stage 2: Exploratory affective exchange. Representative of relationships at the second stage are those between casual acquaintances. In such relationships, there is an increase in the breadth of public areas of the personality accessible to each party. Complementing this variety and detail is increased understanding and efficiency in communication. Specific phrases, glances, or facial expressions can develop precise, shared meanings. Furthermore, interactions are assumed to be more synchronized and predictable. In other words, the regulation of interaction proceeds more smoothly. Although there is greater spontaneity at this stage, exchange is still focused around the more superficial levels of the personality. Relationships at this stage are characterized generally as being friendly, relaxed, and casual (Altman & Taylor, pp. 138-139). Even though such relationships may have a distinctly positive quality, interpersonal commitments are often limited. As a result, many of these relationships may not develop beyond this stage, for example, relationships between neighbors or coworkers.

Stage 3: Affective exchange. As individuals get to know one another well, the opportunity exists for developing affective exchange. At this stage, interactions are characterized by spontaneous and broad exchanges, especially at outer layers of the personality. In addition, there is an increase in communication in intermediate and central areas of personality. Exchange focusing on core issues of personality may still be somewhat tentative or guarded. Because one's vulnerability increases as the core areas are made accessible to the partner, this stage can be critical in determining the future of the relationship. Altman and Taylor (p. 140) suggest that because the blending of personalities in a love relationship is a demanding and extensive task, long-term courtship may have developed as a means of facilitating this process. It is important to appreciate that this stage is characterized not just by the increasingly intimate content of exchanges. Interactions are also different in the manner in which they transpire. For example, the regulation of interaction should show increased synchrony over that typical of earlier stages. Furthermore, Altman and Taylor suggest that switching from one mode of response to another is easily managed. That is, a glance and a smile or a pat on the back can easily be substituted for a pleasant comment.

Stage 4: Stable exchange. Relatively few relationships achieve a level of stability that permits open and spontaneous exchanges in the core and the intermediate areas of the personality. When this stability is attained, verbal and nonverbal messages reflect each partner's interest in and concern for sharing more private feelings and experiences. Attainment of this stage or any of the preceding ones is not like reaching a static plateau. A relationship may develop or deteriorate at variable rates over time, and attainment of a stable exchange does not ensure the permanence of a relationship (Altman & Taylor, p. 141).

Relationship Intimacy and Nonverbal Involvement

The stage analysis of social penetration theory describes the graduated progression of intimacy in relationships. In general, the theory proposes that as the intimacy of a relationship (i.e., in the sense of liking or love for another person, or interest in or commitment to that person) increases, the mutual sharing of central or core aspects of personality also increases. One could argue about the causal link here. That is, does some relatively independent evaluation of the relationship lead to an appropriate level of sharing? Such a causal sequence would assume the primacy of the cognitive-affective state in determining the behavioral sharing. Conversely, does the behavioral sharing evolve rather subtly and later reflection on such sharing behavior determine the evaluation of the relationship? This causal sequence might be described as a self-attribution perspective (e.g., Bem, 1972) that stresses the primacy of behavior. Of course, the safe, middle road (which probably provides the more accurate option) is to suggest that both processes affect the link between the relationship stage and its characteristic behavioral pattern.

In the next section of this chapter, the focus of the discussion will be on the patterns of nonverbal involvement typical of relationships at different stages or levels of intimacy. Unfortunately, the existing research on intimacy and nonverbal involvement is not distributed in a representative fashion across Altman and Taylor's four stages. For the practical reason of conducting research on readily accessible populations, much of the work is based on college students who are meeting for a first time. In effect, such studies are focusing on the orientation stage. An alternate strategy involves focusing on patterns of nonverbal involvement in established relationships. Thus, pairs of couples in a developed relationship are recruited and their interactions are observed. In many cases, the subject pairs probably have relationships classified at either the affective or stable exchange stage. But such a judgment usually cannot be made with much confidence. Given the nature of this research, it seems most reasonable to develop the following analysis in terms of a simple contrast between initial and developed relationships.

Initial Relationships

In beginning relationships, individuals often are concerned about trying to maintain a pleasant and comfortable interaction. In some of these interactions, evaluative pressures run high and individuals may be managing their involvement to achieve a specific effect. A good example is the employment interview. Sensitive applicants are probably aware that it is important to look attentive, seem interested, and occasionally nod approval when the interviewer talks. Some individuals may even "program" themselves to adopt high levels of gaze, a moderate amount of smiling, and occasional head nods. When early exchanges are clearly guided by such strong evaluative concerns, the social control function, rather than the intimacy function, may be primary in determining nonverbal involvement.

Although some evaluative pressures are probably present in most initial exchanges, the intimacy function may still be very important. To the extent that liking (or disliking) of another person is present, nonverbal involvement can be in the service of the intimacy function. In fact, it might be suggested that initial liking or attraction, in the most general sense, is a necessary antecedent to the development of intimacy in a relationship. The link between first impressions and nonverbal involvement in initial relationships is the next concern in this discussion.

Impressions and nonverbal involvement: Early research. Interest in the relationship between nonverbal behavior and attraction or liking accelerated in the 1960s. Although a substantial number of studies of impressions and nonverbal involvement accumulated in these years, much of this research might be questioned on grounds of external validity or representativeness. For example, many studies of interaction distance employed figure placement tasks instead of live interactions. In these studies, a subject would be required to arrange a pair of miniature cutout figures on a standard background in response to some instructional manipulation. The manipulation might be a contrast between friend versus stranger pairs or between same-sex versus opposite-sex pairs. There is considerable disagreement over the validity of such figure placement tasks (e.g., Greenberg, Strube, & Myers, 1980; Knowles, 1980; Knowles & Johnsen, 1974; Patterson, 1978b; Sundstrom & Altman, 1976). At the very least, however, one should be cautious in assuming that differences on a reactive figure placement task reflect comparable differences in the spontaneous selection of actual interaction distance.

A second general procedure employed in much of the early research on attraction required subjects to role-play a particular impression toward another person, that is, the subject encoded the impression in a specific pattern of nonverbal involvement. The other person might be the experimenter, a confederate, an imaginary other, or a svelte, firmly-built coat rack. The use of this role-playing technique or the figure-placement task may tell us how an individual *thinks* a specific behavioral reaction should be encoded, but it does not mean that a similar pattern would occur spontaneously in an ongoing interaction. Of course, such information is important because it relates to stereotypes about nonverbal behavior. It is my judgment, however, that if one wants to study the relationship between impressions and nonverbal behavior, one should focus on the dynamic exchange between individuals in an ongoing interaction.

On the other hand, the assessment of nonverbal behavior in an ongoing interaction does not ensure that observed patterns are representative of real-life behavior. But the use of either an engaging interaction task or a convincing cover story can maximize experimental realism even though the mundane realism of the setting may be low (Aronson & Carlsmith, 1968). Alternatively, subjects may be led to believe that they are not yet in the experiment. For example, Ickes and Barnes (1977) employed a storage room as an impromptu waiting area for subjects who were told that the experiment would start in a few minutes. In fact, the storage room contained a hidden camera that permitted the unobtrusive videotaping of the subjects' spontaneous interactions. Still another approach would be the observation or videotaping of interactions in natural settings. Obviously, the unobtrusive recording of subjects in a natural setting should eliminate any concerns about reactivity and increase the mundane realism of the results. In place of these concerns, the researcher would have to contend with the logistics of such a study and the associated ethical issues (e.g., consent and invasion of privacy).

This is not the place to discuss in detail the methodological problems in nonverbal research. The issues addressed here, however, are important in evaluating the research on impressions and nonverbal involvement. Mehrabian's (1969a) review seems to mark something of a turning point in the sophistication of this research. Specifically, much of the research reviewed by Mehrabian seemed open to question on the grounds of external validity. There were, however, important exceptions to such a judgment of the early research. Especially notable was a number of studies on gaze in ongoing interactions (e.g., Efran, 1968; Efran & Broughton, 1966; Ellsworth & Carlsmith, 1968; Exline, 1963; Exline, Gray, & Schuette, 1965; Exline & Winters, 1965; Exline & Eldridge, Note 4).

The development of the present discussion may be facilitated by summarizing Mehrabian's (1969a) general conclusions and then moving on to the more recent research. It is easiest to consider the trends in Mehrabian's review by focusing on the three behaviors he judged most relevant to liking: (1) interpersonal distance; (2) gaze; and (3) body orientation. Mehrabian concluded that interpersonal distance was negatively correlated with liking—up to the point where distances were too close to be appropriate. For example, the manipulation of close interpersonal distances in spatial invasion studies typically produced some form of negative reaction in the person approached (e.g., Felipe & Sommer, 1966; Garfinkel, 1964). In general, gaze was found to increase toward others as a function of increased liking (e.g., Exline, 1963; Exline & Winters, 1965; Mehrabian & Friar, 1969). Finally, Mehrabian reported a curvilinear relationship between orientation and liking. Orientation was least direct for intensely disliked others, most direct for those judged as neutral, less direct again for those intensely liked. The decrease in directness of orientation for those liked may be a result of the closer approaches typical in such pairs. That is, a minimal approach distance usually results in people assuming a side-by-side orientation (Mehrabian, 1969a).

The following discussion of the more recent research on impressions and nonverbal involvement will emphasize studies employing live interactions. A useful means of organizing this discussion is in terms of an encoding versus decoding methodology. When a given impression either already exists or is manipulated in the research, that impression may be encoded by the subject into a specific pattern of nonverbal involvement. In contrast, another person's pattern of nonverbal involvement might be manipulated and then decoded by the subject. In the former circumstance, it is assumed that the subject encodes or expresses an impression in nonverbal channels. In the later circumstance, the subject forms an impression from the nonverbal involvement of another person.

Impressions encoded. Are initial impressions of liking or disliking encoded nonverbally? In order to pursue such a question, these impressions must be known and their effects on the nonverbal behavior of the interactants must be observed. The most common procedures for varying such initial impressions in some reliable manner include one or more of the following: (1) manipulating feedback regarding similarity in attitudes; (2) selecting or manipulating physical attractiveness; and (3) providing some specific interpersonal expectancy. The first two alternatives are indirect means of manipulating impressions. Perceived similarity in attitudes is a major determinant of initial attraction toward others (Byrne, 1971). Similarly, increased physical attractiveness produces increased liking and a more positive general evaluation (Berscheid & Walster, 1978). Thus, manipulating either of these factors predictably influences early impressions of others.

A few studies have examined nonverbal involvement as a function of initial liking in opposite-sex interactions. In one study, liking was manipulated by bogus feedback regarding attitude similarity. Both male and female subjects sat closer to a liked than to a disliked opposite-sex confederate (Allgeier & Byrne, 1973). Factual feedback about attitude similarity was used in a study of computer-dating matches (Byrne, Ervin, & Lamberth, 1970). College students matched on the basis of high or low similarity of attitude responses were introduced and asked to spend 30 minutes together on a "Coke date." When the pair returned to receive their final instructions from the experimenter, the distance between them was unobtrusively recorded. For both males and females, increased attraction to the partner was predictive of closer interpersonal distances. Proximity was related to the rated physical attractiveness of females, but not of males. Thus, interpersonal distance may have been more under the control of the male than the female in each pair (Byrne et al., 1970).

This last finding is especially interesting because the correlation of rated attraction toward the partner and physical attractiveness was higher for females ($r = .60$) than it was for males ($r = .39$). At the same time, more males judged physical attractiveness as the most important factor in responding to the partner, whereas more females judged attitudes as most important. These two contrasting results are puzzling. If attitudes are, in fact, more important to females than is physical attractiveness, then it is not surprising that proximity is not affected by the males' attractiveness. If physical attractiveness, however, is as important for females as it is for males in determining attraction, then the behavior of females (at least in the Byrne et al. study) may be more controlled than that of males. That is, females may be more attracted to the physically attractive males, but that attraction is not manifested nonverbally. If this were the case, such restraint of involvement might be classified as a social control function.

The influence of both attitudinal similarity and physical attractiveness was examined in a study by Kleck and Rubenstein (1975). Male subjects interacted with a female confederate in a structured interview exchange and in a brief postinterview session. For the period in which they were interviewed, male subjects spent more time looking and smiling at the attractive than the unattractive confederate. No effect from the confederate's physical attractiveness was found on seating distance chosen in the postinterview session. Over 75% of the subjects chose a chair one position removed from the confederate. The similarity manipulation had no effect on rated attraction toward the confederate. Consequently, it is not surprising that the similarity manipulation did not affect any of the nonverbal measures.

Even when an interaction is unfocused (i.e., individuals sharing a common presence, but not talking), nonverbal measures may reflect attraction toward, or at least interest in, another person. For example, Coutts and Schneider (1975) observed gaze patterns in mixed-sex dyads required to wait together in the same room. For both male and female subjects, increased gaze was related to higher ratings of another's physical attractiveness.

Research on involvement patterns as a function of initial impressions in same-sex groups is generally consistent with the cross-sex trends. In a study of the effect of attitude similarity on attraction and proximity in female pairs, liking was negatively correlated with distance and response latency (Tesch, Huston, & Indenbaum, 1973). Specifically, female subjects approached a female confederate more closely and initiated a comment more quickly the higher the rated liking of the confederate. In another experiment, male and female subjects sat closer to same-sex confederates who were described as having similar attitudes than to those who were described as having dissimilar attitudes (Byrne, Baskett, & Hodges, 1971). In a second experiment, the authors found that males and females differed in seating preferences when they were given a choice between adjacent and opposite positions relative to both a similar and dissimilar confederate. The attitude similarity manipulation was supported again by greater attraction toward the similar stranger for both males and females. But only the males showed a consistent pattern of seating preference— across from the similar stranger and closer, but adjacent, to the dissimilar stranger (Byrne et al., 1971). Practically, it is difficult to interpret the meaning of the seating patterns in this last experiment because distance and orientation were confounded in the seating choices. That is, the closer adjacent chair was less directly oriented toward the confederate than the farther opposing chair.

Explicitly negative experiences or expectancies may precipitate decreased involvement, just as positive experiences and expectancies can precipitate increased involvement. For example, subjects who were told to expect a hostile group discussion chose more distant seating arrangements than those who were told to expect a friendly group discussion (Barrios & Giesen, 1977). Similarly, comfortable interpersonal distance may increase following an insult (O'Neal, Brunault, Carifio, Troutwine, & Epstein, 1980). This effect was greater when the experimenter who made the insult also initiated the approach. However, compared to a no-insult control, interpersonal distances were also greater when an assistant made the approach.

The general pattern in research on encoded impressions is quite clear. People who have either more positive initial impressions or receive favorable expectancies about others initiate higher levels of nonverbal involvement than those with negative impressions or expectancies. Thus, consistency is demonstrated between the impressions and the behavioral outcome. That is, in terms of the intimacy function, the underlying affective reaction to another person is spontaneously manifested in differential nonverbal involvement.

Such consistency between impressions or affective judgments and nonverbal behavior is not always the case. In Chapter 6, on the social control function, some important exceptions will be analyzed. At this point, it can be suggested that nonverbal involvement is more likely to reflect the intimacy function when the following circumstances are present: (1) there is a strong and clear evaluative impression of the other person; (2) the particular expression of nonverbal involvement is socially appropriate; and (3) other interpersonal or task goals are not adversely affected by that expression of nonverbal involvement.

When these three circumstances are present, the differential intimacy felt toward others as a function of initial impressions is usually manifested nonverbally. Are those nonverbal patterns interpreted or decoded in a manner consistent with their encoding? This is the issue under consideration in the next section.

Decoding nonverbal involvement. In order to understand the relationship between the initiation of nonverbal involvement and subsequent reactions to it, one must appreciate the constraining roles of cultural and social norms regarding nonverbal behavior. Hall's (1966) classification of four distance zones in social settings was an early recognition of the different levels of involvement appropriate on different occasions. Although Hall's system was based on physical distance, he was also interested in detailing related behavioral consequences of distance. For example, in Hall's intimate zone (0-18 inches) the following consequences may be noted: (1) touching is easily accomplished; (2) some perception of the other person's body heat is possible; (3) body odors, perfume, or shaving lotion may be noticed; and (4) the visual image of the other person can be distorted. In general, the more intimate a relationship, the less formal the setting, and the less public the circumstance, the more appropriate is closer proximity.

Sundstrom and Altman (1976) have developed a similar theme, relating interpersonal distance to perceived comfort of the individual as a function of relationship and expectation of interaction. Figure 5-1 contains the descriptive predictions of their model. The curvilinear relationship between distance and comfort makes it clear that, even for an interaction between friends, there is an optimum level of involvement. When that level is exceeded, discomfort increases rapidly.

It is important to understand the issue of appropriate or normative levels of involvement in making the transition from encoding impressions to decoding nonverbal involvement. The variable levels of involvement reported in the research on encoding impressions are a product not only of the impressions but also of the social or situational constraints. Within the normative constraints of people meeting in structured, experimental settings, increased liking is reflected in increased involvement—up to a point. In contrast, when the effects of nonverbal involvement on impressions are manipulated, that point can be exceeded, and the result is often negative. The considerable literature on spatial intrusions (e.g., Felipe & Sommer, 1966; Fisher & Byrne, 1975; Patterson, Mullens, & Romano, 1971) describes consistent negative reactions, in the form of behavioral compensation, when a stranger approaches too closely. Such reactions also include negative impressions about the intruder (Fisher & Byrne, 1975).

The research on spatial invasions and staring (e.g., Ellsworth, Carlsmith, & Henson, 1972) is important in determining how extreme levels of nonverbal involvement are managed in unfocused interactions. Because these intrusive manipulations, however, are almost always studied in unfocused interactions, they are less relevant to the issue of developing intimacy in initial relationships and, consequently, will not be discussed further in this section.

The manipulation of nonverbal involvement in initial encounters has been accomplished with different procedures. Most of this research employs an interview format or emphasizes impression formation in various get-acquainted exercises or in other shared activities.

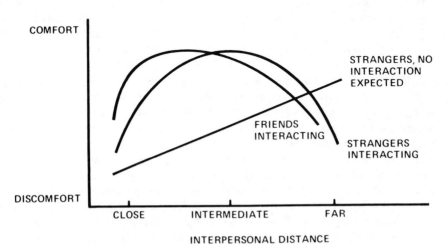

Fig. 5-1. A theoretical model of personal space as a function of interpersonal relationships and expectation of interaction. (From Sundstrom & Altman, 1976. Reprinted by permission.)

Interview studies. The general pattern of results from the interview studies shows that the manipulated involvement of confederates is a major determinant of impressions. In two different studies, subjects interviewed a confederate whose involvement behaviors were varied. In the first study (Patterson & Sechrest, 1970), which manipulated confederate distance (2, 4, 6, 8 ft.), and in the second study (Wiemann, Note 5), which manipulated confederate gaze (100%, 75%, 25%, 0%), the results were similar. Specifically, increased proximity of seating choice and increased gaze by the confederate both showed a curvilinear relationship to rated friendliness of the confederate. As proximity increased up to 4 feet, rated friendliness increased, but then decreased at 2 feet (Patterson & Sechrest, 1970). The same curvilinear pattern of rated friendliness was present as gaze increased from 0% to 100% in the Wiemann (Note 5) study. It is possible that the high involvement signaled by very close proximity and constant gaze in these studies is outside the normative range for involvement and produces more negative reactions.

The effects of interviewer or counselor nonverbal involvement on subject or client reactions are more complicated. Pattison (1973) found that the initiation of touch in a female counselor-female patient dyad produced increased self-disclosure by the client, but did not affect an evaluation of the counseling experience. The absence of a touch effect on evaluative judgments was clarified by a later study in which the sex composition of counselor-client dyads was examined. Touch by the counselor produced a more favorable judgment of the counseling experience, but that effect was qualified by the sex composition of the dyad (Alagna, Whitcher, Fisher, & Wicas, 1979). Specifically, the positive effect of touch was found only in cross-sex counseling dyads.

Programmed changes in interviewer gaze can also affect subjects' impressions. At the very least, it seems likely that increased gaze signals increased attentiveness (Kleinke, Staneski, & Berger, 1975). Increased gaze by an interviewer has also been related to higher ratings of attractiveness and persuasiveness (LaCrosse, 1975). However, evaluations of an interviewer who maintains a high level of gaze may be considerably affected by the nature of the verbal exchange and even the sex composition of the dyad. For example, Ellsworth and Carlsmith (1968) reported an interaction of gaze level and valence of verbal feedback on rated liking of the confederate. In the positive verbal feedback condition, higher gaze produced increased liking, whereas in the negative verbal feedback condition, lower gaze produced increased liking. Moreover, if the content of the interviewer's feedback is too personal in nature, even though it may be positive, rated liking of the interviewer may decrease (Scherwitz & Helmreich, 1973).

A consistent pattern in the effect of increased involvement is discernible across these interview studies. In these encounters, a moderately high level of nonverbal involvement seems to produce the most favorable impressions. Excessive involvement in the form of a too-close approach or constant gaze can have an adverse effect on impressions. Furthermore, even if nonverbal involvement is high but not excessive, the additive effects of negative and/or personal *verbal* feedback can also produce more negative impressions. This latter circumstance should serve as a reminder that the verbal content of interactions can obviously qualify generalizations about nonverbal exchange.

Impression formation studies. In the get-acquainted or impression formation tasks, instructions may focus on (a) getting to know the other person, (b) forming impressions, or (c) cooperating on some task or activity. A particularly important factor in most of this research is the sex composition of the dyad. The effect of manipulated nonverbal involvement seems to be greater in opposite-sex than in same-sex interactions. For example, in one study, an overall effect of close versus far seating on rated liking was magnified in opposite-sex interactions (Kahn & McGaughey, 1977). In particular, male subjects gave the highest liking ratings for female confederates who sat close, whereas female subjects gave the lowest liking ratings for male confederates who sat in the more distant position. Initial impressions were studied in another experiment by manipulating the extent of touch (head nod only, firm handshake, firm handshake plus a squeeze on the subject's arm) used by a confederate in being introduced to a subject (Silverthorne, Micklewright, O'Donnell, & Gibson, 1976). Increased touch produced more positive impressions in all of the dyads except the female confederate-male subject pairs. As the degree of touch initiated by the female confederate toward the male subject increased, the female was viewed less positively. Additional rating items on dating preference, evaluation as a marriage partner, and attraction (included for opposite-sex pairs only) provided an interesting contrast. In general, on these items, female subjects' impressions of the male confederate became more positive as he initiated more touch, whereas male subjects' impressions of the female confederate became more negative as she initiated more touch.

The specific effect of varied involvement in initial opposite-sex exchanges may also be influenced by the physical attractiveness of the individuals. In one study, gaze level and physical attractiveness interacted significantly in affecting male subjects' impressions of female confederates. Although males rated the more attractive confederate more favorably than the less attractive confederate, this pattern was moderated by the gaze level (90% vs. 10%) initiated by the confederate (Kleinke, Staneski, & Pipp, 1975). Specifically, the more attractive females were judged more favorably when they gazed less at the subjects, but the less attractive females were judged more favorably when they gazed more at the subjects.

In initial encounters involving same-sex pairs, there is evidence that high involvement is viewed more favorably by females than by males. Ellsworth and Ross (1975) found that females not only liked a gazing partner better than a nongazing partner, but also disclosed more personal information to the gazing partner. The opposite pattern was found in exchanges between males. However, males may respond favorably to high levels of involvement initiated by other males if there is reason to believe that the other male is friendly or has similar attitudes (Patterson, Jordan, Hogan, & Frerker, 1981; Storms & Thomas, 1977). Finally, it appears that even a casual, often unnoticed, touch in a brief exchange may produce different reactions in males and females. Fisher, Rytting, and Heslin (1976) manipulated hand touching by library clerks as they checked out books for library patrons. When touch was initiated, females not only rated the clerk more favorably but also judged the environment more favorably. The response of males to the touch was more ambivalent.

From the research on various tasks requiring impression formation, three generalizations might be offered. First, consistent with the results of the interview studies, a moderately high level of involvement seems to lead to more positive impressions. Extremely high involvement levels in initial encounters usually produce negative reactions. Second, the effects of increased involvement seem to be magnified in opposite-sex interactions. Female recipients of high involvement from males consistently respond more favorably, whereas male recipients of high involvement from females may respond either positively or negatively, depending perhaps on their expectations about the behavior of the female. Finally, the two trends just described may be qualified by the general tendency for females to prefer higher levels of involvement than males do.

Developed Relationships

The category of initial relationships discussed in the last section was a relatively easy one to describe: such relationships were simply defined as the first encounters between individuals. In contrast, the developed relationships discussed in this section represent a wide range of pairings, from mere acquaintances to family members and lovers. Unfortunately, existing research has not provided much information about changing patterns of nonverbal exchange as a function of the more subtle differences in relationship intimacy suggested by Altman and Taylor (1973). My first concern in this section will be a rather broad description of patterns of nonverbal involvement across different types of developed relationships. Then I will move to a prominent focus of this research—nonverbal involvement in romantic (heterosexual) relationships.

General Trends

There are some comforting regularities in the way involvment is managed as a function of the level of relationship. Specifically, interactions among friends are usually characterized by higher levels of nonverbal involvement than are those among strangers. Heshka and Nelson (1972) have reported such a difference in initial speaking distances in pairs observed on London streets, that is, acquaintance, good friend, or related pairs stood closer than stranger pairs did. Complementing this difference were the results of two studies in which standing interaction distances were manipulated and affective reactions to these distances measured. In both these studies, pairs of opposite-sex friends reported more comfort at closer distances (30 cm-60 cm) and less comfort at farther distances (165 cm-300 cm) than did strangers (Ashton, Shaw, & Worsham, 1980; Baker & Shaw, 1980). The results for the stranger pairs in both of these studies support Sundstrom and Altman's (1976) predictions of a curvilinear relationship between distance and comfort (see Figure 5-1). However, the absence of a clear curvilinear trend for friends, even when a highly intimate topic of conversation was initiated (Baker & Shaw, 1980), is not consistent with Sundstrom and Altman's model. In defense of Sundstrom and Altman's predictions, it should be noted that opposite-sex college student friends might be intimate enough that much closer (i.e., closer than 30 cm or 12 inches) distances would be required to produce much discomfort.

The manner and frequency of touch between individuals may be an important indicator of the intimacy of their relationship. Heslin and Boss (1980) observed and classified the degree of touch initiated in departure and arrival exchanges at an airport. Their scale of tactile involvement included the following scored levels:

0. No touch.
1. A handshake or a touch on the head, arm, or back.
2. A light hug, holding hands, or a kiss on the cheek.
3. A solid hug or a kiss on the mouth.
4. An extended embrace.
5. An extended kiss.

A combination of elements from lower categories could result in the total rating being higher, for example, a kiss on the mouth and a solid hug would be rated 4, or equivalent to an extended embrace. Heslin and Boss found a clear increase in the level of tactile involvement as a function of increased intimacy in a relationship ($\rho = .54$).

In both the Heslin and Boss study and a very similar study by Greenbaum and Rosenfeld (1980)—also on greeting patterns at airports—comparable effects for dyadic sex composition were observed. Specifically, male-male pairs commonly initiated a handshake in the greeting or farewell, whereas male-female and female-female pairs commonly initiated higher tactile involvement in a variety of ways. The contrast in the observed use of the handshake was an extreme one in the Greenbaum and Rosenfeld study. They observed a handshake in 78% of all male-male encounters, but in only 7% of the female-male and female-female encounters.

The influence of relationship variables on nonverbal involvement is not limited to interactions among adults. King (1966) found that unfriendly acts by aggressive children in kindergarten resulted in the recipients of the unfriendly behavior maintaining greater interpersonal distances from the aggressors in later free play. Aiello and Cooper (1972) examined the interaction distances in pairs of 8th-grade students matched on the basis of sociometric choices. In an informal standing exchange, pairs who reciprocated positive choices stood closer together than did pairs who reciprocated negative choices. A comprehensive study of patterns of nonverbal involvement in children investigated the reactions of friend and stranger pairs as they viewed a comedy film (Foot, Chapman, & Smith, 1977). The subjects were 7- and 8-year-old children assigned to boy-boy, girl-girl, or boy-girl pairs. Across sex pairing, friends showed uniformly higher involvement than strangers, manifested by more laughing, smiling, looking, talking, and touching. Some sex differences were evident even at this early age level. Boys laughed and looked significantly more with friends than with strangers of either sex. Girls showed similar though nonsignificant patterns of looking and laughing, but they also smiled and touched significantly more with friends than with strangers of either sex.

The expected pattern of higher involvement in developed relationships than in initial relationships (i.e., the observed or selected stranger pairs) is well supported by empirical research. Furthermore, the results of the Heslin and Boss (1980) study reveal a moderately strong correlation between relationship intimacy and the level of tactile involvement shown. A number of factors, however, apparently interact with the intimacy of relationships to determine specific involvement levels. For example, in comparably intimate same-sex relationships, males demonstrate less nonverbal involvement than do females (Foot, Chapman, & Smith, 1977; Greenbaum & Rosenfeld, 1980; Heshka & Nelson, 1972; Heslin & Boss, 1980). Age may also be an important qualifying variable. Research by Willis and his colleagues shows that the rate of touch in children declines steadily with age (Willis & Hoffman, 1975; Willis & Reeves, 1976; Willis, Reeves, & Buchanan, 1976). In addition, norms associated with culture, race, or ethnicity may facilitate or prohibit specific forms of expressive involvement (Baxter, 1970; Hall, 1966; Watson & Graves, 1966). These variables will be considered in greater detail in the later discussion of antecedent factors influencing nonverbal involvement. At this point, it is probably sufficient to note that the general pattern of increasing involvement as a function of relationship intimacy is one that can be affected by personal and situational variables.

Romantic Relationships

The highly intimate and affectively positive nature of romantic relationships makes their study useful for understanding the mutual exchange of high levels of nonverbal involvement. Although cultural norms regarding such relationships vary considerably, most western societies permit situationally appropriate high levels of involvement in romantic pairs, for example, holding hands or sharing a brief kiss or embrace. Of course, more extreme forms of involvement, particularly of a sexual nature, are proscribed in public settings. Because romantic relationships are highly intimate, the behaviors typically examined in this research have been those that are especially critical in signaling high involvement—gaze and touch.

Common descriptions of exchanges between lovers, characteristic of passages from poetry, songs, and literature, often emphasize patterns of sustained mutual gaze. Although the popular notion is centuries old, the first empirical test of the love-gaze hypothesis was Rubin's (1970) study. In this study, couples were selected on the basis of their scores on a paper and pencil love scale. Strong-love and weak-love subjects were observed either in their interactions within the dating pair or in interactions with opposite-sex strangers. The results clearly showed that strong-love couples displayed more mutual gaze than the weak-love couples. A follow-up of the Rubin study examined the possibility that gaze differences may have been the result of differences in time spent in conversation. That is, because mutual gaze is likely to increase with increased conversation, the presence of longer conversations in strong-love than in weak-love couples might explain the gaze difference. In fact, evidence was found for longer conversations between lovers than between strangers (Goldstein, Kilroy, Van de Voort, 1976). But lovers also spent more time in mutual gaze during periods of silence, consistent with Rubin's results.

A complementary strategy for examining the same issue is the use of observer ratings of staged interactions in pairs. That is, standardized exchanges between individuals are filmed and observers make judgments about the underlying relationships. Thayer and Schiff (1977) used this technique in studying attributions of sexual involvement. In general, longer, reciprocated gazes in pairs were judged to reflect higher levels of sexual involvement. The same technique of presenting standardized videotaped interactions was used in a study requiring observers to evaluate engaged couples (Kleinke, Meeker, & LaFong, 1974). High levels of mutual gaze, compared to no mutual gaze, resulted in stronger attributions of mutual liking in the dyad and more favorable general impressions of the couple.

There is no doubt that sustained mutual gaze can signal an intense romantic relationship. The discrete behavior of touching another person, however, depending on the location and form of the touch, may be even more important in signaling the intensity of romantic relationships. Because touching can be such an intimate behavior, and one that can also be sexual in nature, much of our knowledge of the more intimate aspects of touching is based on self-report. One of the first questionnaire studies was Jourard's (1966) investigation of the frequency and location of touch as a function of the type of relationship. Jourard found that his college subjects generally reported higher levels of touch from opposite-sex friends than from their mothers, fathers, and same-sex friends. Females reported more touching from fathers than did males, whereas both males and females reported comparable levels of touching from their mothers. Not surprisingly, the difference in the reported rate of touching between opposite-sex friends and either parents or same-sex friends was maximized in body locations that could have sexual meaning, for example, hip, thigh, chest. Ten years later, Rosenfeld, Kartus, and Ray (1976) replicated the Jourard study. They found that the reported frequency of sexually relevant touching increased noticeably in opposite-sex pairs. Compared to Jourard's sample, that difference may reflect a real change in sexual behavior, or it may simply reflect a change in the norms about *reporting* such behavior. That is, perhaps the reported increased frequency of opposite-sex touch may be due in part to increased candor in responding to the surveys.

Although these two survey studies provided important information about the frequency of touch as a function of body area and type relationship, the issue of the *meaning* of the touch was not addressed. Two related studies (Nguyen, Heslin, & Nguyen, 1975; Nguyen, Heslin, & Nguyen, 1976) have focused specifically on the meaning of touch in opposite-sex relationships. In the first study, male and female undergraduates answered a questionnaire regarding the meaning of touch as a function of both the location of the touch and the type of touch initiated (Nguyen et al., 1975). Subjects were given the diagram shown in Figure 5-2, and asked to judge the personal meaning of the touch when an opposite-sex friend (steady date, fiancé) touched them in the areas listed on the survey. The subjects were to evaluate the personal meaning only and not the intention of the friend. The 11 areas of the body shown in Figure 5-2 were combined with four modes of touch—pat, squeeze, stroke, and (accidental) brush. Each Location X Mode of Touch was rated on the dimensions of (1) playfulness, (2) warmth/love, (3) friendship/fellowship, (4) sexual desire, and (5) pleasantness. The results indicated that the meaning of touch was dependent upon both the location and mode of touch. For example, a stroke was judged especially salient for love and sexual desire. This generalization, however, was qualified by the location of the touch. Touching hands was related to playfulness, love, and friendship, and touching the genital area was related to sexual desire —independent of the mode of touch. Sex differences had a major effect on the

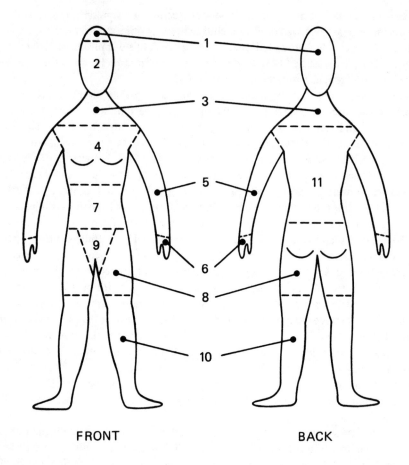

FRONT   BACK

Fig. 5-2. Diagram of the human body employed by Nguyen, Heslin, and Nguyen (1975) and Nguyen, Heslin, and Nguyen (1976). (From Nguyen et al., 1975. Reprinted by permission.)

meaning attributed to touch. Generally, females made finer discriminations among body areas touched, whereas males made finer discriminations among the modes of touch. Furthermore, males viewed sexually related touch as pleasant and warm, but females perceived sexually related touch as neither pleasant nor warm.

In a second study by the same researchers, a similar survey was given to groups of married and unmarried male and female undergraduates (Nguyen et al., 1976). Unfortunately, the results of this second study were not analyzed in the same fashion as those in the first. A further qualification of the sex differences found in the first study seemed warranted, however. Specifically, perceptions of touch by male and female married subjects were generally opposite those of unmarried subjects. Married males' judgments of sexually related touches were more negative, whereas married females' judgments of sexually related touches were more positive, relative to the patterns of comparable unmarried subjects. That is, the correlations of rated sexual desire with rated playfulness, love, and friendship were relatively low for married males, but relatively high for married females.

It is probably not surprising that males and females differ in their perceptions of sexually related touch. If, however, these perceptions do change as a function of marriage, as the results of the last two studies suggest, this would stimulate some interesting questions. For example, does the commitment and stability associated with marriage facilitate a more positive view of sexual involvement among females? If females become more likely to initiate sexual touch in marriage, do males become more threatened and consequently more negative, as the results of the second study indicate? Ideally, more comprehensive longitudinal studies will address these questions, but even such longitudinal studies will have to recognize the variety in motivation for sexual behavior. Sexual behavior might be viewed in terms of one or more of the following purposes: (1) pleasure or sexual release; (2) love or affection; (3) achieving pregnancy; and (4) exercising control or influence over the partner. Furthermore, Hollender (1970) notes that some small percentage of women (and perhaps men too) have a strong desire for body contact and being held that is independent of sexual desire and perhaps even independent of love. Such contact may serve to comfort a person and provide a feeling of protection. In many cases, the women subjects whom Hollender interviewed reported that they felt indifferent or perhaps even negative toward sexual intercourse, but very positive about being held. In such cases, intercourse simply became the means by which they could satisfy their need to be held.

Even though touch of a sexual nature is often emphasized in these survey studies, it is obvious that most instances of touching, even in romantic pairs, are not of a directly sexual nature. If this is the case with touch, it is even more clearly the case with other forms of nonverbal involvement, such as gaze, smiling, body orientation, and interpersonal distance. What does the form and incidence of nonverbal involvement that is not of a sexual nature tell us about the quality of romantic relationships?

There is some evidence that couples in conflict express nonverbal involvement differently from those who are in agreement. Beier and Sternberg (1977) interviewed newlywed couples (married 3 to 6 months) who varied in level of agreement/disagreement with one another. They found that couples who reported the least disagreement manifested greater nonverbal involvement in the interview by (1) sitting closer together, (2) looking at one another more and for longer periods of time, (3) touching each other more often, (4) touching themselves less (probably indicative of less stress or anxiety), and (5) holding their legs in a more open position, than did couples who reported the highest level of disagreement. Such behavioral patterns can inform the partner about specific interpersonal sentiments at any point in time without resorting to words. Although there may be greater ambiguity in such behavioral expressions, this same ambiguity may also provide the partners some safety in verbal expressions of interpersonal judgments, particular those of a negative slant:

Husband: "I didn't *say* I was upset with you" (I'm furious).
Wife: "You didn't have to. You haven't looked at me all night" (You creep).

Husband: "I guess I've just got a headache" (I've got a pain alright, but it's not in the head).

Wife: "Well, why don't you take a couple of aspirins and go to bed" (In the family room).

Such verbal pleasantries may mask the underlying conflict that is nevertheless leaked nonverbally. Relatively subtle cues (e.g., a slight decrease in gaze or a failure to kiss goodbye in the morning) may be especially informative when such patterns are otherwise quite predictable in the relationship. Finally, it seems clear that extreme differences in nonverbal involvement lead to contrasting evaluations of couples and their relationships (Kleinke, Meeker, & LaFong, 1974). We do not have to know the subtle interactive patterns of couples to judge that a complete absence of gaze or touch suggests a relatively tense relationship.

As the intimacy of the relationship increases in romantic relationships, greater involvement is typically expressed in a variety of behaviors. However, mutual gaze and touch are particularly important in facilitating a high level of involvement. As the self-reported love between individuals increases, their mutual gaze increases. Furthermore, observers accurately use a behavior like gaze to make inferences about a couple's relationship. The research on touch reveals increased involvement in romantic relationships compared to other close relationships involving family members or friends. In romantic relationships sexually related touching becomes frequent, but it occurs in the context of a more general increase in tactile involvement. Finally, the quality or stability of romantic relationships may also be signaled by the patterns of nonverbal involvement. That is, tension or conflict in such relationships may be reflected by lower levels of nonverbal involvement.

Assessing the Intimacy Function

General Issues

In the context of the intimacy function classification, nonverbal expression of intimacy is the manifestation of an affectively based reaction toward another person. This affective reaction comprises liking, love, interest in, or concern for another person. Nonverbal involvement in the service of the intimacy function (as opposed to involvement in the service of a social function) should be a relatively spontaneous product of intimacy and should not require a self-conscious, managed behavioral routine. It should also be emphasized that intimacy is represented as a continuum with the negative pole reflecting intense dislike or even hate. Consequently, the spontaneous avoidance of a disliked other reflects the intimacy function just as the spontaneous approach to a loved one does. It is expected that intimacy plays a greater role in determining involvement as interactions become less structured and less evaluative in nature. Casual and informal interactions with acquaintances, gatherings around the water cooler at work, or exchanges at home with family members are examples of situations that may facilitate the intimacy function.

Although some theoretical speculations can be offered about the types of settings and relationships that may activate the intimacy function, in practice some of these distinctions are not so clear. For example, it is obviously not the case that exchanges between intimates (lovers, family members, good friends) are necessarily representative of the intimacy function. The spontaneous expression of intimacy may be common, but it does not exclude the manifestation of other functions. If one member of a pair wants to change the other person's point of view, make the other person feel guilty, or simply isolate himself or herself to complete a task, the social control or service-task functions may determine patterns of nonverbal involvement.

Similarly, in some situations, distinctions between the intimacy and social control functions may be very difficult to make; in fact, intimacy and social control functions may be simultaneously present. For example, I may stand close to, gaze at, and embrace a loved one because of my "feelings toward her" (intimacy). I may, however, also accentuate some of these behaviors (e.g., a little extra hug or a kiss), both because I want her to know that I love her and because I want her to reciprocate that involvement (social control). In terms of the intimacy function, my nonverbal behavior indicates love. In addition, however, to the behaviorally expressed sentiment is the exaggerated and accentuated level of involvement that consciously *communicates* my feelings in the hope of leading her to reciprocate that affection. In other words, the elaboration or intensification of my involvement is purposeful.

The research reviewed in this chapter focused on the relationship differences that seem to be especially relevant for the intimacy function. In initial or beginning relationships, the obvious physical attractiveness of another person (especially in opposite-sex pairs) and the more subtle concern of perceived similarity typically lead to increased liking. Usually, increased liking in turn promotes increased nonverbal involvement. Such involvement may often be representative of the intimacy function. However, the situation of meeting another person who may be a potential friend, or even a potential mate, is likely to be a highly evaluative one. To the extent that one is *managing* his or her nonverbal involvement for the purpose of creating a good impression and/or getting the other person to respond more favorably, social control, not intimacy, may be the dominant function.

In developed relationships, there may be less chronic concern about being evaluated by the other person, but various mutual endeavors present opportunities (or pitfalls) that lead to behavioral strategies reflecting the social control function. For example, one might purposefully show appreciation for a partner's help by a hug or a pat on the back. In contrast, the lack of expected help from a friend or mate may lead to a purposeful avoidance of that person. Again, as the earlier discussion emphasized, the fact that people have an intimate relationship does not mean that all (or even most) of their interactions are guided by the intimacy function. The importance of this last statement is evident in a closer analysis of one aspect of romantic relationships—sexual behavior.

Sexual Behavior and Intimacy

Sexual encounters are obviously intense and highly charged exchanges. In one sense, the sexual side of romantic relationships might be judged the most intimate form of relating to a partner. My choice of the term *intimate* and not *involving* is quite deliberate. That is, such a statement reflects the judgment that the most intense expression of romantic love is manifested sexually. An alternate view, and one that is consistent with this chapter's description of intimacy, requires some analysis of the motivation for sexual behavior. That is, does sexual behavior develop primarily from love and concern for the partner? A characteristic of intimacy described by McAdams and Powers (1981) was the surrender of manipulative control (social control, in the terminology of this chapter). From that perspective, it seems likely that many sexual encounters are not manifestations of an intimacy function. In such cases, sex might be initiated primarily for reasons of pleasure, releasing tension, or exerting influence and control over another person.

A type of naive functional analysis may underlie some of the contrasting evaluations reported in the two studies on the meaning of touch (Nguyen et al., 1975; Nguyen et al., 1976). The results of interest here are the reported sex differences in evaluating sexual touching. These results were not completely consistent. In general, however, they indicated that to the extent that single women (compared to single men) reported touch as stimulating sexual desire, they were less likely to judge it as indicative of love. That pattern was reversed in a comparison between the married women and married men. These results suggest that men and women make different functional attributions of sexual touch depending on their marital status. Perhaps, in spite of our apparently changing sexual mores, women may be more inclined to view sexual contact as indicative of love (intimacy) when there is a marital commitment than when there is not.

Regardless of the sex of the individual, or marital status for that matter, some evaluation of a partner's motivation in initiating sexual behavior is undoubtedly a frequent occurrence. A commonly expressed evaluation might be in terms of whether the partner "really loves me" or is merely "using me." This simple, yet critical, dichotomy is representative of the contrasting intimacy and social control functions. Finally, such a functional evaluation is important not only in describing and analyzing the relevant encounters, but also in predicting subsequent reactions to sexual overtures. Generally, it might be predicted that as the perceived social control motivation of the partner increases there will be a greater ambivalence about future sexual encounters with that person.

Normative Constraints and Intimacy

The importance of normative constraints on the initiation of nonverbal involvement was first mentioned in the section on decoding nonverbal involvement in initial relationships. This issue deserves further elaboration and emphasis. It is generally assumed that when the intimacy function mediates nonverbal involvement, there is a direct correspondence between the quality and intensity of intimacy affect and the extent of nonverbal involvement. This assumption is reasonable as long as we recognize that situational norms and preexisting role relationships set some broad limits for appropriate levels of nonverbal involvement. For example, there will probably be less variability in levels of involvement at a church's ice cream social than there would be at a typical New Year's Eve party. In the latter case, nonverbal involvement might reflect relative intimacy differences between couples better than in the former case.

Situational norms may also interact with role relationships in differentially limiting the influence of intimacy in nonverbal involvement. A specific limited range of involvement may be prescribed in employer-employee relationships in the work setting. Out on the golf course or at a party, differential intimacy may be manifested nonverbally because individuals are away from the structure of the work setting. Of course, because such situations away from the job may still be highly evaluative ones, differential involvement might also be a product of ingratiation, a social control motive. A "diplomatic" employee might even purposely play a poorer round of golf than his less talented employer.

Finally, both situational norms and role-relational influences almost certainly interact with cultural differences. In the United States and some other western nations, a moderate level of involvement is permitted between heterosexual couples in public, for example, holding hands or a brief kiss. In those same countries, traditional norms lead to the expectation that male-male pairs limit their nonverbal involvement considerably. Touch between males, except in gay subcultures, is generally proscribed. Of course, there are the obvious exceptions (e.g., fanny patting on the athletic fields following successful plays). In some countries of the Middle East, particularly those with a fundamental Islamic orientation, the pattern seems to be exactly reversed. Touching and hugging between males (not of a sexual nature) in public is appropriate, but comparable behavior in opposite-sex pairs is clearly inappropriate.

There will be an extended and more detailed discussion of the influence of the situation, role relationships, and cultural differences in nonverbal involvement in Chapter 8. For the immediate concerns of this chapter, it should be emphasized that these three factors contribute to important normative constraints that limit the range of spontaneous nonverbal expression of intimacy.

Summary

This chapter's discussion dealt with an analysis of the intimacy function in nonverbal exchange. In this context, intimacy was defined as liking, love, interest in, or concern for another person. The role of this affective motivation in determining nonverbal involvement was examined in the context of initial and developed relationships. The contrast between initial and developed relationships represents a simplification of Altman and Taylor's (1973) four-stage classification of relationship intimacy described in their social penetration theory. To the extent that initial or beginning relationships are relatively free of evaluational concerns, increased liking generally results in increased nonverbal involvement. The norms relating to initial encounters, however, limit the amount of nonverbal involvement that is usually expressed. Extensive touching and prolonged mutual gazes are not usually appropriate in initial exchanges though they may be typical of developed romantic relationships.

Sex differences are common in both initial and developed relationships. In same-sex interactions, females are usually more comfortable with higher levels of involvement than males are. In fact, it seems that social norms permit greater freedom for females than for males in demonstrating their relative intimacy with a same-sex partner.

In developed relationships, especially those of a romantic nature, high levels of nonverbal involvement are common. Although these high levels of nonverbal involvement are indicative of stronger, more positive relationships, they are not always judged positively in romantic relationships. For example, touch of a sexual nature may be experienced negatively in some circumstances. This may be the result of perceiving the touch as reflecting selfish social control motives more than intimacy motives.

The contrast between intimacy and social-control functions is one that is basic in understanding most social exchanges. Situations that are less structured and formal and appeal less to evaluative concerns should promote the relatively spontaneous behavioral manifestation of the intimacy function. In contrast, situations that are more structured and formal and appeal more to evaluative concerns should promote a more managed and purposeful behavioral routine representative of the social control function. This latter function will be the focus of the analysis in the next chapter.

Chapter 6
Social Control

The discussion in the last chapter focused on intimacy as a determinant of nonverbal involvement. In general, it was assumed that basic evaluative judgments of others tend to be represented nonverbally in a relatively spontaneous fashion. Of course, individual differences and specific situational norms may qualify the form and intensity of involvement manifested. At the same time, it is clear that nonverbal involvement may be managed by an actor to achieve a specific interpersonal goal. The purpose of the present chapter is to describe and analyze this social control function in determining patterns of nonverbal involvement.

In general, the social control function may be described as involving some motive for attempting to influence or change the behavior of another person. Furthermore, it is assumed that this influence attempt is directed at reactions that would not occur without such influence. In comparison to an intimacy pattern, a social control pattern involves a clearer cognitive awareness of purpose and deliberation in behavior. Thus, an intimacy pattern would be characterized by little or no cognitive awareness of the motive-behavior link, whereas a social control pattern would be characterized by some cognitive awareness of the motive-behavior link. Finally, an intimacy pattern necessarily involves consistency between affect and behavior, whereas this is not the case with a social control pattern. Specifically, a social pattern may often involve inconsistency or independence between a social control motive and behavior. For example, a person may manifest a high level of involvement toward a disliked other (i.e., act friendly) in order to win that person's support.

There has been little in the way of organized and integrated discussion of the social control function in nonverbal research (see Henley, 1977, for an exception). But there is a considerable amount of empirical research that can be interpreted within a social control framework. In particular, several distinct social processes seem to be characterized by social control motives, including the following: (1) power and dominance; (2) persuasion; (3) feedback and reinforcement; (4) deception; and (5) impression management. (The present discussion of these social control processes revises and extends an earlier paper by Edinger and Patterson, 1983.)

Power and Dominance

Encoded Power and Dominance

In general, power may be considered the ability to influence others in some fashion. Dominance refers either to one's relative position in a power hierarchy or to the specific outcome of a power conflict. Status usually denotes one's social dominance, that is, it reflects one's relative position in a social hierarchy. All three terms are relevant to the vertical hierarchy that exists in social relationships (Schlenker, 1980, p. 239). In the present discussion, for the sake of consistency, status will be considered the preexisting position in a social hierarchy that contributes to specific instances of power or dominance.

Several studies have examined the relationship between status and nonverbal involvement with others. The prior selection or classification of status differences provides a means for determining how power and dominance may be encoded nonverbally. That is, nonverbal involvement can be examined as a function of the power and dominance that are attributed to differential status. Although this research is only correlational, it does complement other research that focuses either on manipulated or perceived motives and nonverbal involvement. For example, Exline and his colleagues (Exline, 1972; Exline, Ellyson, & Long, 1975) have examined gaze patterns in dyads as a function of power (status) differences. In general, they found that the low status person gazed more at the high status person than vice versa. This effect was qualified as a function of listener versus speaker roles, however. Specifically, the low status person looked much more while listening, whereas the high status person looked more while talking. Apparently, greater looking while talking and less looking while listening may be indicators of higher status.

The initiation of nonreciprocal touch (e.g., placing a hand on another person's shoulder or arm) seems to be a privilege of higher status people. Goffman's (1967, pp. 73-74) description of exchanges in hospital wards emphasized the norm that doctors could initiate touching other staff, but the staff could not initiate touching the doctors. Similarly, Henley (1973) found that other dimensions related to status, such as being (a) male, (b) older, and/or (c) of higher socioeconomic status, were predictive of a greater frequency in the initiation of touch.

Status differences may also affect the amount of facial expressiveness initiated. Hottenstein (1978) found sociometrically high ranked individuals were comparably expressive to recipients of either similar or lower rank; however, lower ranked individuals were most expressive to those ranked higher than themselves. In this instance, expressiveness may be a means for the lower status person to gain recognition or approval from the higher status person. In fact, Rosenfeld (1966a, 1966b) has found that smiling and head nods are important cues that can be used to induce approval from others. Presumably, a high status person has enough confidence, esteem, or power that he or she does not have to employ such behaviors in the service of approval-seeking.

Finally, it appears that relative status differences in an interaction may be related to behavioral indices of relaxation. Although the relaxation cues of arm and leg asymmetry, sideways lean, and hand and neck relaxation are not included in the construct of nonverbal involvement, the differences in behavioral relaxation are still worth noting. In general, relaxation seems to decrease linearly as a function of increased status of the partner (Mehrabian, 1969b).

The pattern of findings related to encoded power and dominance suggests that high status individuals have greater flexibility in the instrumental use of nonverbal involvement than low status individuals. Thus, a high status person can typically relate to others with variable involvement and not risk the censure or the disapproval a low status person would.

Decoded Power and Dominance

In the decoding approach, various levels of nonverbal involvement are either selected or manipulated, and attributions of power and dominance are inferred from these involvement levels. In some cases, the patterns evident with the decoding strategy are not analogous to those found with the encoding strategy. For example, both Thayer (1969) and Zimmerman (1977) found that confederates who gazed more at others were rated more dominant or potent than those who gazed less. This result seems to be in conflict with Exline's (Exline, 1972; Exline, Ellyson, & Long, 1975) findings that low status individuals generally gaze more at high status individuals than vice versa. This latter result, however, seems to be characteristic of occasions when the low status person is talking. This circumstance and other constraints (e.g., the lower status person being evaluated by the higher status person) may cause the lower status individual to gaze more at the higher status individual than vice versa. Finally, deliberately ignoring another individual necessarily leads to a lower level of gaze toward that person. Such a reaction is more clearly the prerogative of the higher status person, and thus provides another opportunity for the higher status person to gaze less at others than the lower status person does (Geller, Goodstein, Silver, & Sternberg, 1974).

The attribution of power and dominance seems to be affected by nonreciprocal touching. Summerhayes and Suchner's (1978) results showed that subjects who rated photos of nonreciprocal touch in male-female dyads perceived the recipients of touch as less dominant than the no-touch controls; however, the dominance of the touchers was not increased relative to the control pairs. Because the effect of touch was present only in the unequal status condition, Summerhayes and Suchner proposed that touch was only a status reminder and not a status indicator. That is, the initiation of touch, in itself, did not lead to differential inferences about status, but given already existing status differences, touch could serve to reinforce these differences.

The results of a similar study by Major and Heslin (1982) suggest that nonreciprocal touch can affect attributions of dominance when there are no status-relevant cues present. Specifically, Major and Heslin found that the toucher was seen as more aggressive, more confident, and more independent, whereas the recipient was seen as less aggressive, less confident, and less independent following the touch. Furthermore, some perceptions of touching were affected by the sex of the observer-subjects. In particular, females rated actors as more attractive when they touched than when they were not touching, but males showed the opposite pattern.

Facial expressions may also be managed to produce differential attributions of dominance. In a study of posed facial expressions, subjects judged the relative dominance of photographed models. The results indicated that lowered brows and non-smiling mouths contributed to higher rated dominance than did the contrasting conditions (Keating, Mazur, & Segall, 1977).

The overall pattern in decoding research suggests that gaze, touch, and facial expression can be powerful determinants of dominance and power attributions. A definite limitation of much of this research, especially that using posed photographs, is that these exchanges are often highly artificial. Major and Heslin (1982) note that the effect of touch in particular may not be as extreme in everyday interactions in which various contextual and relationship cues also determine impressions. On the other hand, because this research has consistently involved the manipulation of a single behavior at a time, inferences about power and dominance may be even more extreme in everyday interactions when a particular behavioral pattern involves a number of coordinated cues.

Persuasion

The circumstance of trying to persuade or convince another person on a particular matter is likely to sensitize an individual to the management of his or her behavior in the pursuit of this goal. It is likely that the more important the issue and the greater an individual's potential role in influencing others, the more concerned the individual is about managing his or her behavior effectively. Some distinct behavioral strategies related to persuasion can be identified.

For example, Mehrabian and Williams (1969) found that when subjects were instructed to be more persuasive, a number of behavioral changes occurred, including the following: (a) increased gaze; (b) head nodding; (c) more frequent gesturing; (d) increased facial activity; and (e) increased speech volume and rate. A similar set of behaviors, including (a) 80% gaze level, (b) smiling, (c) positive head nods, (d) gestures, and (e) a directly facing body orientation, was judged more persuasive in counseling interactions than was a less involving set of behaviors (LaCrosse, 1973). In another experiment in the Mehrabian and Williams article (1969), subjects rated the persuasiveness of contrasting patterns of nonverbal behavior. Although Mehrabian and Williams found that perceived persuasiveness increased with decreased interpersonal distance, sex differences qualified the generalizations about the most effective behavioral presentations. Males were perceived as more persuasive when they approached at closer interpersonal distances and maintained a less direct body orientation, whereas females were perceived as more persuasive when they increased their gaze, remained at a greater distance, and had a lower level of body relaxation.

Although the research on perceived persuasiveness identifies some effective behavioral strategies, it is important to note that perceived persuasiveness and actual persuasion may be very different. In fact, when Albert and Dabbs (1970) examined actual attitude change, their results provided a contrast to the Mehrabian and Williams findings. Although Albert and Dabbs found that the *perceived* expertise of the speaker was greater at a moderate distance (4-5 ft.) than at either a close (1-2 ft.)

or far (14-15 ft.) distance, actual attitude change increased directly as a function of distance. Albert and Dabbs suggested that greater attitude change at the farthest distance may have been facilitated by a lowering of the subject's defenses about the topic; that is, closer approaches, especially at 1-2 feet, may make subjects very defensive and less open to change.

The tactic of maximizing involvement to produce stress seems to be one that is effectively used in police interrogations. Often, a suspect may be questioned by an officer who sits close and directly opposite the individual. During the course of questioning, the officer may move his chair closer and try to align one of his knees in between the suspect's knees (Heslin & Patterson, 1982, p. 58). (This scenario typically involves a male officer and a male suspect. It is not clear that a similar tactic would be successful, or even tried, in a different sex pairing.) Presumably, increased stress from high involvement makes the suspect more likely to confess. In any case, however, a suspect's common manifestation of nonverbal discomfort by avoiding gaze, turning sideways, and decreasing either postural openness or relaxation is often taken as evidence of guilt (Baxter & Rozelle, 1975). Because comparable reactions might be anticipated from anyone who is approached so closely in a frontal arrangement, the validity of these cues as indicators of guilt or innocence is questionable.

Close approaches and the initiation of touch may be especially effective when the influence attempt is focused on a fairly straightforward and simple request. Baron and Bell (1976) found that a closer approach produced greater compliance to a request for volunteering time in answering a survey. Similarly, Kleinke (1977, 1980) found that touching a subject on the arm before requesting him or her to return money (left in a phone booth) resulted in greater compliance. The conflict apparent in the effectiveness of high involvement in these studies and the Albert and Dabbs study may be related to the complexity of the change or compliance demanded in the influence attempt. If a high level of involvement does produce increased stress, the tactic may be most effective when the focus of change requires a minimum of cognitive processing, for example, agreeing to volunteer time or simply returning the money left in a phone booth. (The relationship between increased nonverbal involvement and arousal was discussed in Chapter 2. Stress may be viewed as one form that increased arousal may take under circumstances of high involvement.) If the influence attempt involves attitude change, then the greater cognitive processing required may be negatively affected by stress.

Paralinguistic cues may also be managed in a distinct fashion when individuals are attempting to persuade others. For example, Hall (1980) instructed subjects in telephone surveys to elicit greater willingness to participate in psychological research. The subjects who attempted to be more persuasive had voices that were judged as (a) more expressive, (b) more natural, (c) warmer, (d) calmer, and (e) more pleasant. In this study, the persuasive condition resulted in greater volunteering only with subject-respondents who were identified as skilled decoders. That effect was reversed for the subject-respondents who were less skilled decoders. This kind of interaction effect of the Involvement Level X Subject Type should remind us that general principles that summarize the effect of specific behavioral presentations may be valid only for particular types of subjects.

One explanation for the effects of specific patterns of nonverbal behavior on persuasion emphasizes the mediating role of persuader credibility. That is, the effectiveness of specific nonverbal presentations is mediated by the degree of credibility inferred from the nonverbal behavior. London (1973) found that paralinguistic confidence and doubt indices discriminated between individuals who became either the persuader or persuadee in verbal exchanges. Scherer, London, and Wolf (1973) identified faster and louder speech and speech with shorter pauses as expressing more confidence and less doubt. If, however, pitch and volume are too divergent from normal, the speaker may be evaluated more negatively (Apple, Streeter, & Krauss, 1979). There is also evidence showing that when subjects attempted to argue a position with either confidence or doubt, hand movements changed. Specifically, gesturing was very frequent in the confident condition and very infrequent in the doubtful condition (Timney & London, 1973). Furthermore, self-manipulations tended to be more frequent in the doubtful than in the confident condition. The most discriminating behavioral difference was in gaze direction. Confident speakers maintained almost continuous direct gaze and doubtful ones rarely held direct gaze. The effect of increased gaze on both greater perceived confidence of the communicator and greater eventual attitude change has also been noted elsewhere (Argyle, 1967, p. 108; Scherer, 1978).

An examination of the research on nonverbal involvement and persuasion suggests two relatively distinct processes that may promote increased persuasion through increased nonverbal involvement. First, high levels of involvement, characterized by a very close approach, touch, or sustained gaze, can produce increased arousal that may commonly take the form of stress. Of course, an alternate attribution for involvement-induced arousal might be liking or attraction, and this too could facilitate the influence process. The latter alternative will be discussed in more detail later. Related to the stress reaction, perhaps in a causal fashion or simply as an epiphenomenon, may be a feeling of being intimidated and/or losing control. In this circumstance, a simple direct request, especially one involving minimal effort or expense (e.g., signing a petition, returning the dime left in the phone booth) will probably lead to greater compliance under conditions of high involvement. Quick compliance with such a request also terminates the stressful exchange. That is, if one agrees to the request, the exchange is ended and further stress can be avoided. If the influence attempt focuses on the more complex issue of changing an attitude, then increased stress may interfere with the efficient cognitive processing necessary for this change. The contrasting results reported in the Baron and Bell (1976) and Kleinke (1977, 1980) studies versus the Albert and Dabbs (1970) study are consistent with this explanation, and more generally with the curvilinear relationship between arousal and performance proposed by Yerkes and Dodson (1908). Thus, as the focus of the influence attempt is increasingly complex, lower levels of nonverbal involvement may be more effective in producing change.

A second explanation for the link between involvement and influence relates to the effect of involvement on attributions about the communicator. Research reviewed in this section suggests that credibility may be one of the critical dimensions mediating persuasiveness. Paralinguistic cues such as faster speech rate, increased loudness, and shorter pauses are related to increased credibility. In addition, more frequent gestures, an absence of self-manipulations, and a high level of gaze also increase a communicator's credibility.

The attribution of credibility is one inference about a communicator that determines the degree of influence, but other types of attributions can also affect the influence process. A very general one is the attribution of liking or attraction. Not surprisingly, when the communicator is better liked, the greater is his or her influence over an audience (McGuire, 1969). A considerable amount of research reviewed in Chapter 5 suggests that an actor's initiation of moderately high levels of involvement produces the most positive impressions in interactions, especially in initial encounters. Thus, depending on both the situation and relationship between the individuals, a communicator would probably create a more favorable impression by initiating moderately high involvement with the other person, and that in turn would facilitate the influence process. Very close approaches, touch, or constant gaze may be too extreme and diminsh liking, especially in initial encounters.

Feedback and Reinforcement

Performance Effects

The initiation of specific involvement cues can provide a subtle means for exerting influence over the behavior of others. Existing research shows that a diverse range of behaviors on various performance tasks can be affected by discrete patterns of involvement behaviors. Even performance on tasks as simple as digit coding may be improved by having the experimenter engage in higher levels of gaze when reading the instructions (Fry & Smith, 1975).

More general effects on classroom behavior and test-taking have also been observed. Kazdin and Klock (1973) found that when a teacher initiated contingent smiling and touching, retarded elementary-school children became more attentive in classroom activities. Nonverbal warmth in the form of close interpersonal distance, frequent smiling, and touch, compared to a neutral condition, has been effective in improving both intelligence test scores (Kleinfeld, 1973) and classroom learning (Kleinfeld, 1974) in Indian and Eskimo children. It is interesting to note that gaze was not included as part of the complex of warm behaviors in the Kleinfeld studies because, apparently, direct gaze in Indian and Eskimo cultures can signify anger. Kleinfeld's (1973) results showed that noncontingent nonverbal warmth can improve intelligence test scores, but contingent nonverbal warmth may also increase intelligence test scores (Isenberg & Bass, 1974; Sheckart & Bass, 1976).

A few studies have examined the effect of nonverbal involvement on various types of verbal responses. In one of the classic studies, Reece and Whitman (1962) showed that the combination of an interviewer's verbal ("mm-hmm") and nonverbal warmth (gaze, smile, and direct body orientation) increased the total amount of talking by a subject. More specific dimensions of speech may also be affected by contingent nonverbal reinforcement. Stewart and Patterson (1973) found that contingent direct gaze at the farther of two distances (6 ft. v. 3 ft.) increased the number of thematic responses given over five cards of a Thematic Apperception Test

(TAT) presentation. But gaze at the closer distance and body lean were not effective reinforcers. In a similar study, subjects were differentially reinforced for the use of specific pronouns with verbal and nonverbal cues (Banks, 1974). In this study, gaze, head nods, forward lean, and a verbal utterance all increased the frequency of the target pronouns.

The positive effect of nonverbal warmth on various performance measures seems to take two forms. First, cues such as a distinct gaze, a smile, a head nod, a touch, or forward lean can serve as discrete contingent reinforcers for very specific behaviors. In other words, singly or in combination, these involvement behaviors become defined as positive reinforcers when the behavior they contingently follow increases in frequency. The other way in which increased nonverbal involvement may improve performance is in a noncontingent fashion. In this case, high involvement in the form of a close and direct seating arrangement, a generally high level of gaze, and a smiling or positive facial expression provides a broad, warm behavioral context in which performance tends to improve. The specific mediating mechanism producing improved performance as a result of the noncontingent increase in nonverbal warmth might be one or more of the following processes: (a) a reduction of debilitating anxiety; (b) a feeling of approval or acceptance from the examiner (therapist, teacher); and (c) increased liking for the examiner (therapist, teacher) that, in turn, increases the motivation to do well for him or her.

Counseling and Employment Interviews

Several studies have examined the effectiveness of specific forms of nonverbal involvement in the context of counseling and employment interviews. Bourget (1977) found that a counselor who smiled, held gaze, and had a pleasant tone of voice enhanced the effectiveness of simple verbal reinforcement. Specifically, those in the high involvement condition were more likely to report that the session had not only improved their feelings about themselves, but had also increased their interest in relating better to others. In addition, in a follow-up questionnaire a week later, the high involvement subjects tended both to rate the counselor's comments as more sensitive and informative and to recall more of the feedback received than did participants in the low involvement conditions.

In another experiment, the relative effect of positive versus neutral verbal feedback by a counselor was examined at either a "personal" or "social" distance from the client (Greene, 1977). The results showed that physical proximity strengthened adherence to a counselor's recommendations when positive verbal feedback was offered and lowered adherance when neutral verbal feedback was offered. Greene suggested that the Feedback Valence X Distance interaction was a result of differential consistency in the communication of evaluative feedback. That is, positive verbal feedback at a close distance is consistent, but neutral verbal feedback at a close distance is not. In the latter condition, the client's suspicions about the meaning of the counselor's behavior may lessen the counselor's influence.

The use of reinforcement within the counseling setting has also been applied to the training of counselors. In one study a confederate/client reinforced each of a counselor trainee's reflection-of-feeling statements in one of three conditions: (a) a verbal response condition, (b) a verbal and nonverbal condition, and (c) a noncontingent control condition consisting of a verbal plus nonverbal response (Lee, Hallberg, Hassard, & Haase, 1979). Both contingent reinforcement conditions increased the frequency of feeling statements relative to the noncontingent control, but the verbal plus nonverbal condition was not significantly more effective than the verbal only. This represents at least one case in which nonverbal feedback did not increase the effectiveness of verbal feedback. Of course, this particular situation is the reverse of the usual direction of effect in counseling interviews.

In an employment interview, the interviewer's nonverbal demeanor can be a critical determinant of the applicant's behavior. In one experiment, candidates were differentially reinforced with either nonverbal approval or disapproval from the interviewer (Keenan, 1976). Observer-subjects who were blind to the conditions rated candidates in the approval condition as more relaxed, more comfortable, and more at ease than candidates in the disapproval condition. The approval condition candidates were also seen as being more friendly toward the interviewer, more talkative, and more successful in creating a good impression. In a study using a simulated interview format, similar results were found. Specifically, a high level of interviewer nonverbal enthusiasm (gaze, gestures, and smiles) resulted in the job applicant being judged more favorably than applicants who received a low level of interviewer enthusiasm (Washburn & Hakel, 1973).

It seems clear that differential involvement by an interviewer can contribute to differential performance by a client or job applicant. Differential involvement may be mediated by existing or newly developed expectancies about the other person. Such expectancies can become self-fulfilling prophecies (Merton, 1948), in that they lead to those particular behavior patterns that are likely to draw out the anticipated behavior from the other person. For example, if an interviewer anticipates that a candidate will not be qualified, the interviewer will probably act in such a way (less gaze, fewer smiles, low general interest) as to facilitate a poor performance by the candidate. This type of effect has been demonstrated in white interviewers' lower level of involvement with black than with white applicants (Word, Zanna, & Cooper, 1974). The results of the Word et al. study, consistent with those of other studies in this section, showed that black applicants were judged less favorably. When a similar low level of involvement was manipulated in interviews with white applicants, their performance was comparable to the black applicants who were similarly treated (Word et al., 1974). Even when these critical evaluative expectancies are absent at the start of an interview, a clear judgmental impression may be formed quickly, in perhaps as little as 4 minutes (McGovern, 1977). Zajonc (1980) suggests that the latency of impression formation may be much shorter. He claims that basic evaluative judgments (good vs. bad) can be made in *a fraction of a second*—presumably on the basis of nonverbal cues available in an initial encounter.

The research reviewed in this section provides clear support for the role of nonverbal involvement in affecting a variety of task-specific outcomes, whether the task is an abstract problem or a complex interpersonal assessment. Discrete cues, such as a smile, a nod of approval, or the initiation of gaze, may serve as contingent reinforcers for a partner's correct or desirable responses. In addition, a more sustained level of moderately high involvement may provide an interaction context in which the partner can feel comfortable and experience acceptance or approval. Such a general positive reaction should facilitate performance on a variety of personal and impersonal tasks.

Deception

The topic of deception has received considerable attention in nonverbal research in recent years. The recognition of the potential role that nonverbal behavior plays in deception has been known for many years, however. Representative of such recognition is Freud's (1925/1959) often quoted observation: "He that has eyes to see and ears to hear may convince himself that no mortal can keep a secret. If his lips are silent, he chatters with his finger-tips; betrayal oozes out of him at every pore" (p. 94). Betrayal may not ooze quite as profusely as Freud suggested, but recent research does document that deception can be reliably identified under at least some circumstances.

My primary interest in the present discussion is not in the determinants that affect the accurate decoding of deceptive performances, but in analyzing the management of various nonverbal behaviors in deception. Ekman and Friesen (1969a) propose that, in general, people in Western cultures are more aware of managing their facial behavior than their body behavior because they are held more accountable and receive more reinforcement for facial behavior than for body behavior. The lessened vigilance regarding body behavior results in both leakage cues and deception cues being expressed with the body. Leakage cues are behaviors that reveal the message that was being concealed, while deception cues simply reveal that deception was attempted, but do not reveal the content of the concealed message. Presumably, an individual has some sensitivity to the behaviors he or she successfully manages in deception. An individual is less likely to be aware of behaviors that provide leakage or deception cues. An alternate interpretation is that an individual may be aware of leakage and deception cues, but is for some reason unable to control these behaviors.

Research suggests that the two most important behaviors managed in deception are smiling and gaze. Unfortunately, the results from various studies are not completely consistent, but some cautious, qualified generalizations can be offered. First, there is some support for the hypothesis that deceivers smile more than those who are truthful (Ekman, Friesen, & Scherer, 1976; Mehrabian, 1971). Mehrabian (1971) suggests that greater facial pleasantness may serve to relieve some of the tension felt by the speaker when he or she is attempting deception. But an individual who smiles more at an interaction partner will also tend to be better liked and thereby have greater influence over the partner. In the case of deception, such influence should serve to reduce the partner's potential suspicion about deceptive comments. The common assumption that liars are less able to look others in the eye has not received consistent support in the research (e.g., Exline, Thibaut, Hickey, & Gumpert, 1970; Knapp, Hart, & Dennis, 1974; Mehrabian, 1971). Just as individuals sometimes increase smiling when they are deceptive, so they can also increase gaze.

Individual difference factors may contribute to different expressive styles during deception. For example, Mehrabian's (1971) results, over a series of three experiments, suggested that an individual's habitual level of anxiety interacts with the deceitfulness of a communication in determining the nonverbal behavior enacted. Specifically, high anxious deceivers seem to smile less when they are attempting deception, whereas low anxious subjects smile more. Presumably, the less skilled or the more anxious one is in social situations, the greater the level of negative affect expressed during deception. Thus, low anxious individuals or those high in social skills are able to manage their smiling better during deception than are high anxious individuals or those low in social skills.

Gaze during deception may also be affected by individual difference variables. In one study, subjects who scored high on Machiavellianism responded with increased gaze when they tried to cover their cheating, compared to those scoring low on Machiavellianism. Furthermore, deceivers paired with opposite-sex confederates have been found to gaze more at their partners when they are lying than when they are telling the truth.

In general, it might be suggested that frequency of attempting deception probably increases to the extent that deception is a salient personal strategy (e.g., a high Machiavellian individual) and the consequences of deception are increasingly important. Individual differences in anxiety or social skills, however, may limit the success that subjects actually have in being deceptive. That is, subjects high in anxiety or low in social skills may be less able to perform deceptive behaviors successfully. Thus, the indirect effects of anxiety or a real deficit in social skills may contribute to an inadequate deceptive performance (e.g., failure to either smile or gaze enough at the partner).

Just as actors (encoders) attend more carefully to the management of facial cues than body cues when they are being deceptive, so do perceivers (decoders) attend more closely to facial cues than body cues of the actors. The result is that the body cues of deceivers that might be informative tend to be ignored in favor of the facial cues that can be more easily managed, and therefore less informative. In fact, when attention to body versus facial cues is manipulated, facial cues are less useful in discriminating honest from dishonest replies (Littlepage & Pineault, 1978, 1979). The cues that appear to be most reliable in discriminating between honest and deceptive performances are lower body movement (Ekman & Friesen, 1974) and vocal pitch (Ekman, Friesen, & Scherer, 1976; Streeter, Krauss, Geller, Olson, & Apple, 1977). That is, increased lower body movement and higher pitch are both characteristic of deceptive performances. Again, however, the fact that such cues are apparently present during deception does not mean that these cues are routinely used by observers. Consequently, the actor's typical emphasis on managing facial cues would still seem to be the best strategy for successful deception, even though body and vocal cues may be reliable deception cues.

Impression Management

There is no doubt that people in social situations attend to others and form impressions from what they see and hear. This impression formation process is an active one that involves selectivity in attending to and interpreting the cues that are available from others. There are a variety of characteristics that are potentially informative. Some of these characteristics are relatively unchanging, especially physical characteristics, such as gender, height, weight, and skin color, whereas as other characteristics, especially behavioral cues such as elements of verbal and nonverbal behavior, are more variable over time.

Nonverbal cues are particularly interesting not only because they are potentially so variable, but also because they are usually judged to be spontaneous and unintentional reactions. If such behaviors are spontaneous and unintentional, then it is usually assumed that they accurately reflect some personal disposition. Thus, we are typically more likely to trust the accuracy of nonverbal behaviors than verbal behaviors in reflecting some personal disposition. Schneider et al. (1979, chap. 6) use the term *reactive attributions* to describe inferences made from behaviors judged to be spontaneous and unintentional. Reactive attributions usually focus on dispositional factors such as personality traits. When behaviors are identified as precipitating some specific consequence intended by the actor, the resulting inferences are termed *purposive attributions.*

Although it may be commonly assumed that nonverbal behavior is spontaneous and unintentional, the theme of the present chapter is that nonverbal involvement may be frequently managed to achieve desirable ends. In this particular section, the role of nonverbal behavior in the development of favorable impressions will be analyzed. That is, it is assumed that nonverbal involvement can be managed to promote the development of favorable impressions. In a general sense, all of the topics reviewed so far in this chapter involve impression management. In the earlier discussions of power and dominance, persuasion, feedback and reinforcement, and deception, however, nonverbal involvement was managed for specific ends and its effect on impressions was secondary.

In this section, the discussion will focus first on two particular settings—counseling interactions and employment interviews. In these two settings, the creation of favorable impressions is usually a major factor in a successful exchange. The last topic in this section is the role of interaction strategies in determining nonverbal involvement. Finally, the evidence regarding interaction strategies and nonverbal involvement will be reviewed and analyzed.

Counseling Interactions

It is obvious that a counseling exchange is a situation of interpersonal influence. Although the assumptions and techniques of different schools of counseling may vary considerably, the counselor's impression on the client is always critical in the influence process. Most of the research on counseling interactions indirectly examines the influence process by focusing on the client's perceptions of the counselor's expertise and warmth. Presumably, the more favorable the judgment of the counselor in these two dimensions, the greater the influence on the client.

A few studies have examined the relative impact of nonverbal cues versus other cues on the counselor's perceived expertise. In one study, the relative influence of objective evidence of expertise, defined as the presence of diplomas and state licensure certificates, was compared with the nonverbal evidence of expertise, defined as increased gaze, forward body lean, and hand gestures directed toward the client

(Siegel & Sell, 1978). The nonverbal manipulation was consistently more effective in determining subjects' perceptions than was objective evidence. The authors proposed that visible diplomas and certificates can enhance the client's perception of the counselor, but only when the counselor has already demonstrated his expertise nonverbally. A later, similar study by Siegel (1980) found an interaction of Nonverbal Expertise X Objective Expertise on the rated expertise of the counselor, with the most favorable ratings in the nonverbal-objective expert condition.

The effects of the counselor's nonverbal responsiveness (paralinguistic cues, facial expressiveness, head nodding, gaze, and gestures) and mode of verbal intervention (interpretation vs. restatement) were examined in a study by Claiborn (1979a). Increased responsiveness resulted in the counselor being rated significantly more expert, trustworthy, and attractive. This main effect, however, was qualified by a significant interaction of Nonverbal Responsiveness X Mode of Verbal Intervention, with the responsive-interpretation condition having higher ratings of expertness and trustworthiness than any of the other three conditions. The interaction of the verbal and nonverbal cues in this study is similar to the interaction of objective and nonverbal cues in the Siegel (1980) study. Both sets of results suggest that objective or verbal cues may have an influence only when the nonverbal involvement of the counselor is already sufficiently high.

The client's perception of the counselor's warmth is also substantially affected by the counselor's nonverbal behavior. For example, counselors who were more active in changing facial expression, gaze, and posture, and initiated more gestures, were judged to be more casual, warm, agreeable, and energetic than were counselors who reduced the frequency of their nonverbal movements to a minimum (Strong, Taylor, Bratton, & Loper, 1971). Although the more active counselors were generally seen as more friendly, they were also seen as less serious, orderly, and controlled. Consequently, the authors proposed that the friendly-attractive dimension may be somewhat incompatible with the dimension of intellectual potency in counselor behavior. Nonsignificant trends in support of Strong et al.'s (1971) results on counselor movement and perceived warmth were reported in a study by Smith-Hanen (1977).

Perceived counselor warmth was affected by a number of verbal and nonverbal behaviors in a study by Sobelman (1974). Although a high level of verbal warmth produced the greatest effect on rated counselor warmth, nonverbal warmth, defined as gaze, head nodding, open hand movements, and a direct body orientation, also led to higher ratings of perceived counselor warmth. It is not surprising that the quality of the counselor's verbal comments can have an effect on the client's perception of the counselor, but the quantity of such comments can also be a critical factor. For example, Kleinke and Tully (1979) found that counselors who talked less were liked best, whereas those who talked more were evaluated as more dominant and potent.

The research on counselor behavior and client perceptions clearly indicates that a counselor's nonverbal behavior is critical in determining the client's evaluative judgments. Such a conclusion is consistent with the recommendation that effective training of counselors must prepare them in specific verbal *and* nonverbal skills (Alagna, Whitcher, Fisher, & Wicas, 1979). Although such a conclusion seems warranted, some caution should be exercised in making such generalizations from existing research. Specifically, almost all of the results in this area (and in other research on nonverbal behavior and impression formation) are based on first impressions of the counselor. Thus, although the counselor's nonverbal behavior may be critical in the first few sessions it is possible that the influence of nonverbal behavior decreases over time (Claiborn, 1979b).

My own judgment on this issue is that nonverbal behavior continues to be very important over sustained interpersonal contact, both in the counseling setting and across most relationships. In general, the research on nonverbal behavior and impression formation shows that early behavioral patterns are major determinants of impressions. Later samples of nonverbal behavior may tend to be less carefully evaluated and/or actually consistent with the earlier patterns. The latter condition may be the product of either the actor's own intraindividual stability over time or the result of self-fulfilling expectancies generated by the other person on the basis of the first encounter.

Even though early patterns of nonverbal behavior seem to have a disproportionate effect on impression formation, this does not mean that later patterns of nonverbal behavior are less important for the interactants and their relationship. Rather, the importance of the nonverbal behavior is focused on issues other than just impression formation. In particular, because the early patterns of behavior establish some expectancy, later behavior can take on a special meaning and thus provide the opportunity for initiating directing feedback and reinforcement. For example, if a counselor is almost always smiling and gazing at the client, continued smiling and gazing is not very informative. However, a sustained look away from the client, accompanied by a frown, may be very informative. In this instance, the *change* in gaze direction and expression would probably not lead to a changed impression of the counselor, but rather to a careful evaluation of the comments leading up to the counselor's change in behavior.

Employment Interviews

The setting of the employment interview presents an interesting context for examining the utility of managing one's nonverbal behavior. It is generally assumed that an applicant's nonverbal behavior can have a significant impact on his or her perceived effectiveness (Hatfield & Gatewood, 1978). Interviewers may be especially sensitive to an applicant's nonverbal behavior because: (a) it is highly useful in gathering accurate information about the applicant; and (b) it is assumed that such information (especially the negative information) is not likely to be expressed verbally (Schlenker, 1980, p. 237). In such a highly evaluative setting, serious applicants will be trying to appear as desirable as possible. At the same time, interviewers will be carefully monitoring the applicant's nonverbal behavior. In this way, potential inconsistencies between what is said and what is done may be identified as indicative of true feelings. Consequently, this analysis of employment interviews will focus on how the applicant's behavior may reflect a social control motive.

Several studies have examined the effect that applicant nonverbal behavior has on impressions and hiring decisions. In these studies, the involvement levels of confederate-applicants were manipulated and subjects had to evaluate the applicants in a variety of different dimensions. McGovern (1977) used personnel representatives from business and industry as subjects in a study in which applicant nonverbal involvement was manipulated. High involvement, characterized by a high level of gaze, high energy level, and a combination of desirable paralinguistic cues produced much more favorable ratings of the applicant than did low involvement. Furthermore, 89% of the subjects who saw the high involvement applicant would have invited that person back for a follow-up interview, whereas 100% of the subjects who saw the low involvement applicant would *not* have invited that person back for an interview. Similar distinctly favorable hiring judgments were found in another study in which applicants initiated a high level of gaze, head movement, and frequent smiling. Specifically, these three behaviors accounted for almost all of the variance on a deserve-the-job rating (Young & Beier, 1977).

Apparently the effects of applicant behavior on judges' general impressions and specific evaluations of job qualifications are not affected by the modality of the input. Imada and Hakel (1977) found no differences in subjects' impressions and evaluations as a function of their conducting a live interview, being a live observer, or simply viewing the interview on videotape. Across all modalities the pattern was similar to that found in the earlier research: high involvement applicants are not only liked better but also judged as more competent, more qualified, more motivated, and more successful than low involvement applicants.

Analyses of the relationship between applicant behavior and hiring decisions in actual job interviews compliments the experimental research just discussed. For example, Forbes and Jackson (1980) analyzed the nonverbal behavior of applicants for trainee positions in engineering-related jobs. A four-member panel classified each applicant into one of three categories: (1) accept; (2) hold on reserve; or (3) reject. The behaviors characteristic of the successful or accept applicants were (a) high level of direct gaze, (b) frequent smiling, and (c) frequent head movement. Contrary to predictions, a more forward lean was not typical of the accept group. In a study similar to the Forbes and Jackson study, a variety of applicant behaviors was examined as potential predictors of hiring decisions made by campus recruiters (Hollandsworth, Kazelkis, Stevens, & Dressel, 1979). The results showed that the verbal content of the applicants' replies was the best predictor, followed by speech fluency, and then composure. Gaze, posture, voice loudness, and personal appearance were significant but weaker predictors of hiring decision. In this last study, the verbal factor, rather than any nonverbal factor, was the most important element in hiring decisions.

The pattern of results from a number of studies on employment interviews suggests that increased gaze, smiling, gestures, and head nods by an applicant seem to produce generally favorable impressions and favorable hiring decisions. At least two qualifying factors about these trends should be considered, however. First, results from a study by Tessler and Sushelsky (1978) suggest that the effects of applicant nonverbal involvement may interact with the status of the applicant. For example, Tessler and Sushelsky found that a lack of interviewer-directed gaze by the applicant was evaluated more negatively with a high status applicant than with a low status applicant. The authors suggested that the absence of direct gaze by the high status applicant was clearly more inappropriate than it was for the low status applicant. Such counternormative behavior may reflect a lack of confidence by the high status person and thereby lead to a more negative evaluation. To the extent that decreased involvement by a high status person on other behaviors is seen as inappropriate, similar negative judgments might be expected.

The other factor limiting the generalizability of the results discussed here was addressed by Forbes and Jackson (1980). Specifically, because candidates are often screened prior to an interview by means of tests or resumés, the final sample is often relatively homogeneous in aptitude or intelligence dimensions. Thus, the nonverbal behavior of the candidates may be a salient way of discriminating among them. In contrast, when the candidates are highly variable in aptitude, their nonverbal behavior may be overlooked, because decisions are relatively easily made on the basis of other distinct characteristics. Such a tendency may account for the occasional result showing that verbal measures predict impressions and decisions better than nonverbal measures.

Interaction Strategies

A final area of impression management that is relevant to a social control function is one that applies to a variety of interaction contexts. This area focuses on the activation of interaction strategies that guide a person's nonverbal involvement. In general, an interaction strategy describes a plan of variable specificity for managing one's involvement for some interpersonal purpose or advantage. Interaction strategies might include some of the dynamics discussed in the sections on counseling interactions and employment interviews, but interaction strategies are not simply a product of expectancies about settings. In fact, the role of *interpersonal expectancies* in determining interaction strategies is the central concern of current research.

Research on interpersonal expectancies and social behavior has emphasized the importance of the self-fulfilling prophecy (Merton, 1948; Rosenthal, 1966), or behavioral confirmation process (Snyder & Swann, 1978; Snyder, Tanke, & Berscheid, 1977). The self-fulfilling prophecy, or behavioral confirmation process, refers to the causal influence of prior interpersonal expectancies on later interactive behavior and interpersonal judgments. Specifically, it is assumed that the existence of an interpersonal expectancy causes an individual to act toward another person in a manner consistent with the expectancy. In turn, the first person's behavior toward the other person tends to elicit the very behavior that was expected. In this way, the original expectancy is confirmed and related evaluations are strengthened. For example, if you hear that your new neighbor is a cold, disinterested person, your first encounter with her might lead to your being considerably reserved (e.g., standing farther away than usual, maintaining a low level of gaze, and controlling your expressiveness). Whether the expectancy is technically correct or not, your behavior will tend to produce the behavior you expected from her. That is, in response to your reserve, she too will be reserved. Thus, you would probably come away from the interaction with the judgment that your source was correct in describing her as a "cold fish."

The self-fulfilling prophecy/behavioral confirmation process has been broadly supported in a variety of studies since Kelley's (1950) classic demonstration of the effect of such expectancies. In this study, Kelley found that groups of subjects who were given contrasting warm or cold expectancies not only developed later judgments in line with these expectancies, but also behaved differently in class; that is, the cold expectancy subjects initiated less discussion than the warm expectancy subjects. The underlying strategy characteristic of this self-fulfilling prophecy might be described as one of *reciprocity* (Ickes, Patterson, Rajecki, & Tanford, 1982). That is, the actor reciprocates the behaviors that are *anticipated* from the other person, not the actual behaviors emitted. As the interaction develops, however, the other person may also reciprocate the actor's initial behavior. It is important to appreciate that the reciprocity strategy describes the actor's behavior as a function of what he or she anticipates from an interaction partner.

There is also evidence that some interpersonal expectancies can produce an alternate interaction strategy characterized by *compensation,* not reciprocity. (The terms reciprocity and compensation were used in a slightly different manner in Chapter 2. There, reciprocity referred to a behavioral adjustment of matching the other person's behavior, whereas compensation referred to a behavioral adjustment that was, in effect, opposite the involvement change initiated by the partner.) A compensatory strategy describes a behavioral plan in which the actor behaves in opposition to the expectancy about the other person, that is, the actor tries to overcome the other's anticipated behavior by initiating an opposing pattern of behavior. For example, Bond (1972) manipulated "warm" versus "cold" expectancies about the subject's interaction partner (confederate). The behaviors of the subject and target person were rated on overall warmth by independent judges. The results showed that the subjects given the cold expectancy acted more *warmly* with their partner than did those subjects who were given the warm expectancy. Furthermore, the cold expectancy subjects actually induced the target person to act more warmly in return. Apparently, the cold expectancy subjects initiated the contrasting warm behavioral strategy in an attempt to avert, or at least minimize, the anticipated unpleasantness with their partners. In turn, that strategy led to the confederate's increased warmth in the interaction. In this case, even though the partner was a confederate, the compensatory strategy seems to have been successful.

A second relevant study is the Coutts, Schneider, and Montgomery (1980) study that was discussed first in Chapter 2. The details of that experiment will not be repeated here, but the results should be reemphasized. Contrary to the experimenters' hypothesis, subjects who received negative feedback and increased involvement from the confederate *reciprocated* the increased invovement. One interpretation of this finding, mentioned in Chapter 2, was that the increased confederate involvement that followed that inital feedback may have signaled an increase in the confederate's attraction toward the subject. In turn, the subject could have increased his or her liking of the confederate and reciprocated the higher involvement. But in the negative feedback-increased involvement condition, the subject's rated liking of the confederate was not correlated with the amount of increased involvement. Thus, this explanation, one that may be representative of an intimacy function, is not well supported by the results. However, Coutts et al. suggest an alternate interpretation for these results that clearly describes a social control function: "Under these circumstances, the negative condition subjects may have viewed the accomplice's subsequent increase in immediacy as a return to a more appropriate level of intimacy and thus *exaggerated their own nonverbal immediacy to encourage it*" (Coutts et al., 1980, p. 588, italics mine).

The results from two experiments in the Ickes et al. (1982) study shed additional light on the relationship between expectancies and the social control function. The two experiments were conducted independently at about the same time, but they developed from different interests and differing methodologies. Ickes, Rajecki, and Tanford were primarily interested in the behavioral consequences of contrasting interpersonal expectancies, whereas I was interested in testing my intimacy-arousal model. In my case, the expectancy manipulation was merely a convenient means for providing contrasting information that might be used to label a hypothesized arousal mediator. Ickes, Rajecki, and Tanford were far better at anticipating their results than I was. My theory-derived hypotheses were generally not supported; nevertheless, I did find some interesting expectancy effects. When Ickes and I began discussing and comparing the results of the two experiments we were surprised at the degree of similarity and decided to report them in a single manuscript.

In Experiment I (Ickes, Rajecki, and Tanford), friendly *and* unfriendly preinteraction expectancies led subjects to initiate greater nonverbal involvement compared to a no-expectancy control. Most striking was a higher level of smiling in the unfriendly condition relative to both the control and friendly conditions. The pattern of increased smiling in the unfriendly condition suggests that a compensatory strategy may be operating. This interpretation was supported by a clear difference in rated impressions as a function of the expectancy. That is, the contrasting ratings given to the partners in the friendly and unfriendly conditions suggest that differing underlying strategies may be operating. In the friendly condition, the positive ratings suggest a high level of attraction. Such a pattern seems to describe an intimacy function. In the unfriendly condition, however, the overall pattern of ratings was not only less favorable, but specific ratings showed a distrust of the partner's seemingly friendly behavior. This pattern seems to describe a social control motive, that is, a high level of involvement presumably masking or compensating for negative feelings about the partner.

In the second experiment (Patterson) of the study, expectancy was manipulated in terms of bogus similarity or dissimilarity in a set of personality measures taken in a previous session. As in Experiment I, subjects in the dissimilar condition smiled more, and at the same time, rated their partners more negatively than subjects in the similar condition. Nonsignificant trends on the remaining involvement measures—gaze, duration of talking, and body orientation—also indicated greater involvement for the dissimilar subjects. Finally, subjects in the dissimilar condition showed increased arousal on an electrodermal measure of physiological activity taken immediately after the expectancy instructions. This result is consistent with the functional model's prediction of arousal change following unusual or discrepant information about an interaction partner.

Across the two experiments, unfriendly or negative expectancies produced as high or higher involvement (i.e., smiling) than did friendly or positive expectancies. At the same time, attraction to the partner was predictably very different as a function of the expectancy. The pattern present in the positive expectancy conditions is consistent with an attraction-mediated, or intimacy, function, whereas the pattern in the negative expectancy condition is consistent with a social control function. In the former case, the intimacy motive leads to a pattern of reciprocity, whereas in the latter case, the social control motive leads to a pattern of compensation. In both of these cases, the outward behaviors may be highly positive and similar, but the underlying dynamics are very different.

The results from these studies suggest that nonverbal involvement may be managed to facilitate a more pleasant interaction. Specifically, the anticipation of an uncomfortable interaction may stimulate a behavioral strategy designed to counteract it. At the same time, the impression of the other person and the interaction may remain very negative. When one's expectancies about another person are negative, increased smiling seems to be a critical component in the behavioral strategy. This management strategy of increased smiling is similar to that found in attempted deception (Ekman & Friesen, 1974). In fact, one might judge such interaction strategies as deceptive or, at least, Machiavellian. The appropriateness of such a judgment is debatable, but nevertheless it is probably accurate to conclude that successful interaction strategies, like successful deception, may provide the actor with a means of reducing discomfort in a difficult interaction.

Comparing Intimacy and Social Control Functions

The discussion of the intimacy function in the last chapter and the social control function in this chapter provide a contrast in two basic motive systems that relate to interpersonal behavior. Nonverbal involvement in the service of the intimacy function is assumed to reflect interpersonal affect toward another person. Thus, within the normative constraints of a given setting, nonverbal involvement toward another person should be proportionate to the degree of perceived positive intimacy toward that person. Furthermore, it is assumed that the nonverbal expression of intimacy is a relatively spontaneous, indicative pattern. Schneider, Hastorf, and Ellsworth (1979, chap. 6) describe such nonverbal behavior as reactive. That is, the individual reacts spontaneously to the relevant stimulus. Furthermore, Schneider et al. note that an observer who judges a behavioral pattern to be reactive assumes that such a response is sincere and accurately represents some internal disposition. Very simply, reactive behavior can be trusted.

When a social control motive underlies a patten of nonverbal behavior, it is assumed that such behavior is a managed, communicative pattern designed to influence the other person in some specific fashion. That is, the communicative description refers to the purposive nature of the behavior (MacKay, 1972). In fact, Schneider et al. use the term purposive to describe behaviors that contrast with the reactive behaviors. When an observer or interaction partner judges a particular pattern to be purposive, this clearly implies that the behavior was initiated to achieve a specific effect. Obviously, in this case, the observer would not assume that such behavior was representative of a dispositional characteristic, unless the characteristic were Machiavellianism.

From the actor's perspective, there is often some attempt to make the purposive social control behavior appear to be spontaneous and indicative. That is, the actor often wants to be viewed as spontaneous, candid, and sincere when the opposite is true. This is certainly the case with the deception and impression management aspects of social control, and perhaps also with persuasion and feedback/reinforcement. Deception and impression management necessarily involve a false, or at least exaggerated, behavioral representation of an internal state. Thus, successful deception and successful impression management require that the actor's performance is convincing enough (or the observer insensitive enough, or both) to avoid detection. That is, the observer would infer that the behavior is a candid representation of an internal state.

Although the abstract distinction between intimacy and social control can be easily made, classifying everyday exchanges is more difficult. For example, one might judge that most nonverbal exchanges between friends, lovers, or family members typically reflect the intimacy function. It is one thing, however, to describe relationships as being based on an intimacy motive, but it is quite another to expect that all of the specific encounters reflect that motive. We all know that even in the closest and most unselfish relationships, individuals subtly, and sometimes not so subtly, seek to influence the other person. Increased involvement in the form of a hug or a gentle touch may be deliberately used with a loved one in the context of asking for a favor or seeking help. A deliberate decrease in involvement, manifested by remaining more distant from and initiating less gaze toward a loved one, may have the purpose of letting that person know that we are upset with him or her. Such a behavioral strategy may also be designed to extract an apology, reassurance of continued love, or perhaps the acknowledgment of some personal debt (the old "I'll make it up to you" defense).

If a partner is frequently judged to be acting out of selfish social control motives, the relationship will probably suffer. In effect, the perceiver is judging that the partner's warmth is not a sincere and spontaneous demonstration of love and concern, but an act designed for other purposes. If the loved one initiated a pattern of high involvement only when he or she appears to want something, there may be additional effects beyond a perception of that person as selfish or manipulative. Specifically, the recipient of such performances may develop considerable reactance to the partner's apparent purpose (Brehm, 1966). One example involves the perception of a social control motive in the initiation of a sexual encounter. If the only time the partner initiates a warm, high-involvement pattern is when he or she wants to have intercourse, it is likely that such overtures will be judged as selfish and manipulative. It may then be easy for the recipient to have a feeling of being used. In fact, doubt about such behavior might be verbally described in terms of whether the other person "really loves me or is just using me." The former judgment would describe an underlying intimacy function, whereas the latter would describe an underlying social control function. The judgment of feeling used may even go beyond reactance to a specific encounter to a more general doubt about the partner and the relationship.

In all this discussion of functions, it is assumed that there is some utility in being able to discriminate between intimacy and social control presentations. Because we react not only to what someone does, but also to our judgment of that person's motive, it is important to be as accurate as possible in these inferences. How do we go about making these judgments?

One approach simply involves an application of the general principles involved in making attributions. If a person acts in a normative or socially desirable fashion, it provides less information about dispositional bases for behavior than if he or she acts in a counternormative or socially undesirable fashion (Jones & Davis, 1965). Thus, the friendly, agreeable behavioral pattern initiated by a job applicant toward an interviewer in a highly evaluative setting tells us little about whether such behavior represents a social control or intimacy function. In this case, one should at least be skeptical about assuming that such behavior reflects intimacy or liking. On the other hand, if a vulnerable employee acts unfriendly and uninvolved with his superior, it suggests that the employee's dislike is so great that it overcomes the normative pressures for being friendly and pleasant.

Another approach stresses the utility of identifying deception cues (Ekman & Friesen, 1974) present in a social control performance. That is, to the extent that a social control pattern represents a managed presentation inconsistent with an internal state (e.g., acting friendly toward a disliked superior), some behavioral cues may signal such inconsistency. The research on deception suggests that the body cues may be more informative than the facial cues. In fact, it was noted earlier that the management of facial expression in smiling seems characteristic of both deception and interaction strategies. Facial cues may, however, still provide some clue to a managed performance. For example, a detailed videotape analysis of spontaneous and deliberate facial expressions showed that deliberate smiles were characterized by greater asymmetry in facial expression than were spontaneous smiles (Ekman, Hager, & Friesen, 1981). Whether or not such asymmetries can be identified in ongoing interactions is another issue. Ekman et al. (1981) doubt that such subtle changes in facial expression may be noticed in conversations, but this question is open to study. In addition, it is possible that some insincere expressions may be held longer than the analogous spontaneous expression. This may be seen in forced smiles that continue well beyond the time a spontaneous smile would fade.

In this discussion of social control, it should be emphasized that social control motives and performances are not necessarily negative or selfish. On many occasions we *choose* to express our satisfaction or pleasure with others in the form of a hug, kiss, or embrace. Such reinforcers are often dispensed in a deliberate fashion by parents after a child has accomplished something noteworthy. For children and adults, the awareness that a high involvement response from others is, in some sense, deliberate does not detract from their appreciation of the response.

Finally, it should be obvious that many interactions may reflect a mixture of intimacy and social control motives. In such cases, the perception of both the relative strengths of the motives and the underlying self-interest should contribute to the valence of the cognitive, affective, and behavioral responses to the partner.

Conclusions

In this chapter, the role of the social control function has been discussed and analyzed. It was proposed that the influence of the social control function on nonverbal involvement can be seen in the following processes: (1) power and dominance; (2) persuasion; (3) feedback and reinforcement; (4) deception; and (5) impression management. Any one of these processes can be facilitated in an interaction by a deliberate and managed pattern of nonverbal involvement. Such a purposive pattern would be classified as communicative, in contrast to the indicative classification that identifies the spontaneous pattern determined by the intimacy function.

A general issue of importance in all of the social control processes discussed here is the identification of specific mediators that might link the nonverbal behavior to social influence. In most cases, existing research does not adequately address this concern, but some speculations can be offered. First, there is considerable research showing that an actor's increased nonverbal involvement with a perceiver usually produces more favorable impressions (see reviews by Heslin & Patterson, 1982, chap. 2; Mehrabian, 1969b). As this involvement becomes too high, however, impressions become more negative and the perceiver may avoid the actor (Felipe & Sommer, 1966; Fisher & Byrne, 1975). Thus, liking or attractiveness can be an important mediator of the effects of managed nonverbal involvement. In particular, if high involvement initiated by an actor signals increased liking of the other person, this in turn, makes the actor more attractive. In general, the more the actor is liked, the greater is his or her influence on the other person.

An alternate, complementary explanation for the dynamics linking nonverbal involvement and social control focuses on the communicator's credibility. Some of the research on persuasion suggested that increased involvement produced a higher level of judged credibility. In this case, it might be suggested that only those who are very capable are confident enough to initiate high levels of nonverbal involvement. That is, the less capable and less confident show greater interpersonal reserve. Again, it should be noted that attributions of both attraction and credibility should increase up to moderately high levels of nonverbal involvment.

A third explanation is that high nonverbal involvement may simply be intimidating. This explanation is consistent with Henley's (1977) theme regarding the use of touch in unequal status relationships. A very close approach, a long stare, or a nonreciprocated touch may well be more intense than the optimum for producing increased liking. But one who can closely approach, stare at, or touch another may be judged dominant or powerful enough to violate the common norm of an appropriate involvement level. It is important to appreciate that intimidation is likely to be a factor only at an extremely high level of involvement. At this point the positive effect of involvement on attraction is likely to be minimized. That is, attraction is probably maximized at a moderate level of involvement, whereas intimidation is maximized at an extremely high level of involvement. In addition, attempted intimidation runs the risk of developing reactance and a loss of real influence (Brehm, 1966). Even here, however, one should consider whether the real purpose is simply behavioral compliance or a change in attitudes and beliefs. If the goal is simply behavioral compliance, intimidation may be the most effective strategy. If, however, the purpose of the exchange is attitude change, this end will probably be better served by the attraction or credibility mediators. In an analogous fashion, if the specific influence attempt is directed at a simple, reflexive, or overlearned behavior, the higher arousal produced by the extreme level of involvement (and intimidation) should be most effective. At the same time, if the goal is the learning of, or a change in, a complex network of cognitions, high arousal may well produce a decrement in learning.

For the most part, the research on power and dominance, persuasion, and feedback and reinforcement simply shows nonverbal correlates of various influence attempts. Such results do not offer direct evidence that the pattern of nonverbal involvement is enacted to accomplish the social influence. Fortunately, more direct evidence of purpose is available in research on deception and managing interaction strategies. In both situations, instructional or expectancy manipulations produce clearly contrasting patterns of involvement and/or affective reactions. It is interesting to note that, for both deception and interaction strategies, the management of facial expression may be a common behavioral component. For example, in attempting deception (Ekman & Friesen, 1974) and in responding to negative interpersonal expectancies (Ickes et al., 1982), smiling seems to increase. In both of these situations, positive facial expression seems to be used to mask an opposing internal disposition. Such inconsistency between behavior and cognitions is obviously at the very core of deception. The presence of the same kind of inconsistency in interaction strategies (e.g., Ickes et al., 1982), however, emphasizes the broad instrumental nature of subtle changes in nonverbal involvement.

Some speculation can be made about the circumstances likely to precipitate a particular interaction strategy. Ickes et al. (1982) suggest that a compensatory interaction strategy may be attempted when another person's anticipated behavior is viewed as undesirable, yet potentially modifiable by the actor. That is, the actor may initiate a contrasting pattern (e.g., smiling) to change the anticipated undesirable (e.g., unfriendly) behavior of the other person. Presumably such a compensatory strategy is designed to make the interaction more comfortable by drawing out a more friendly response from the other person. If, however, the anticipated negative behavior of the other person is viewed as unmodifiable, there may be no reason to attempt such a strategy. In this case, the outcome will likely be the uncomfortable interaction the actor anticipates. That is, the actor will probably initiate a reciprocal strategy, reflecting the self-fulfilling prophecy, or behavioral confirmation process. To date, there are only a few studies that provide evidence supporting interaction strategies as the link between expectancies and patterns of nonverbal involvement. In the last chapter, suggestions for more detailed research on interaction strategies will be discussed.

Summary

This chapter's discussion of the social control function emphasized an instrumental perspective on nonverbal behavior. This perspective was discussed in the context of processes such as power, persuasion, feedback, deception, and impression management, all of which share a focus on interpersonal influence. When we are involved in these influence processes, there is a greater likelihood that we will monitor and manage our nonverbal behavior so as to maximize that influence on others. In such circumstances, it may often be the case that our behavioral involvement is relatively independent of our affective reaction toward another person. That is, the emphasis on interpersonal influence can override the manifestation of interpersonal affect (positive or negative) toward the other person. Although the emphasis in research up to now has been on the expressive side of nonverbal behavior, this discussion and analysis of social control should make it clear that the instrumental uses of nonverbal behavior are common, yet efficient, means for influencing other people.

Chapter 7

The Service-Task Function

In the earlier discussions of the intimacy and social control functions, the focus was on the role of contrasting motive systems in determining nonverbal involvement. Thus, there was an attempt to identify and analyze the link between internal cognitive-affective states and nonverbal behavior in interactions. Specifically, the intimacy function described the role of interpersonal affect in determining the relatively spontaneous expression of nonverbal involvement. In contrast, the social control function was described as the purposeful management of nonverbal involvement designed to influence others.

For both the intimacy and social control functions, the motives underlying the actor's behavior are primarily, if not exclusively, interpersonal in orientation. That is, these specific motives reflect some quality of affect toward the other person. Obviously, the interactions themselves occur in a variety of situations and settings and these factors may influence the specific form of the exchange, but the primary determinant is the interpersonal motive. In contrast, the service-task function identifies determinants of nonverbal involvement that are generally independent of the quality of interpersonal relationships, that is, the patterns of nonverbal involvement reflect primarily a service or task relationship. To the extent that the service or task relationship is well specified, the behavior of both interactants may follow the predictable sequential steps of a script (Abelson, 1981). Furthermore, because the behavior of the interactants is primarily a product of the service or task norms, dispositional attributions about the other person's service- or task-related behavior may be inappropriate.

At this point, it may be useful to consider the differences between the service and task components of this function. The service component refers to interactions determined by a service relationship between individuals, for example, a physician-patient interaction. These exchanges between people would be unlikely to occur if one person did not need the service and the other person did not have the expertise and availability to provide the service. Thus, the interactants relate to one another essentially on an impersonal basis. It is presumed that service exchanges require some explicit interaction, and consequently the service function usually takes the form of a focused interaction.

The task function identifies interactions, focused or unfocused, that require each person to relate to one or more others through a particular task or activity. In the case of a focused interaction, two people might be cooperating on the completion of a common job, for example, a construction job that literally requires two or more people to finish a specific task. The activity may require two or three people to share in exactly the same task, for example, lifting a heavy frame or partition, or each person may be responsible for separate sequences, as in assembly line work. The necessity for variable involvement in these task-oriented focused interactions seems relatively straightforward. More interesting, and perhaps less automatic, are unfocused interactions in which people share a common presence, but are independently absorbed in the particular task or activity, for example, two clerks sharing a common work area, but engaged in separate and independent tasks.

In this chapter, the emphasis will be on the service component in focused interactions and the task component in unfocused interactions. These two functional themes differ in an interesting and consistent fashion. Specifically, the demands of the service function often require involvement levels that are more intense than those characteristic of casual social interactions. In contrast, the demands of the task function (in unfocused interaction) require involvement levels that are usually less intense than those characteristic of casual social interactions, and sometimes even less intense than those characteristic of most unfocused interactions.

Service Relationships in Focused Interaction

Most people have occasional interpersonal contacts that are based on some service requirements. In these interactions, the behavioral norms are naturally based on the constraints of the particular service. Heslin (Note 1) used the term functional-professional to describe a category of service relationships that require touch between people. Heslin's classification is essentially identical to the service component in the service-task function. In fact, the initiation of touch is a critical factor in many service careers. Heslin notes that although the participants may deny it, the relationship is essentially one between the manipulator (actor) and the receiver as object.

An Overview

In service or professional relationships the critical direction of behavior is usually from the professional to the client (patient or customer). Whether it is a physician-patient, golf professional-student, or barber-customer exchange, the professional takes the initiative in acting on the subject or client. To the extent that the client or recipient is considered an object, the exchange becomes more imbalanced and determined by the professional. That is, unlike other interactions, the client's or customer's behavioral reaction may be irrelevant to the continued administration of the service. In fact, in many cases, it is assumed that the client or customer should be very passive in response to the high level of involvement initiated by the professional. Furthermore, in those service-professional contacts that require very intimate touch, the procedure is often conducted in a very formal, "cold" fashion. Heslin suggests that such constraints are important cues that help to define the exact meaning and relevance of the touch.

A good example is the obstetrician's pelvic exam. The formalities in this procedure are probably most closely observed when the physician is a male. Critical elements may include draping a sheet over the lower half of the woman's body, having a female nurse present during the exam, and pulling sterile gloves on in a distinct and overplayed manner. In addition, the obstetrician who conducts such exams may be more careful to wear his white coat as a signal of his legitimate status than would other kinds of specialists, for example, an allergist. The latter specialist also touches patients, but in less intimate areas of the body. Consequently, he or she does not have to be so formal in constructing a setting that legitimizes the professional service.

There are a number of other service relationships that require tactile involvement of varying degrees. Barbers, hairdressers, tailors, and dentists all have to touch their clients extensively in the course of performing their service. The tactile involvement of a barber or a hairdresser does not generally seem to be very intense. In contrast, when a dentist probes into a patient's mouth and hovers close to his or her face, the result can be stressful. I recall from my recent dental checkup that it was much more comfortable to close my eyes during the cleaning and examination. Glancing up to see a face just inches from mine was a little disconcerting. From the dentist's perspective, it is also probably more comfortable when the face in front of him or her is not staring back.

In a few special occupations, great care has to be taken in describing the services and distinguishing them from less legitimate enterprises. One such vocation is that of masseur or masseuse. The professional masseuse may have to overplay her credentials and legitimacy in order to avoid male clients who want to "get rubbed the wrong way." In some locations, massage parlors have often been convenient covers for prostitution. In such areas, the masseuse may either have to avoid advertising under the label "massage" or be very clear in specifying her legitimacy. In our local yellow pages, there are no obvious ads for the services of a masseuse, under "massage," "masseuse," or any other related term. Of course, I am making the assumption that establishments with names like *Let the Good Times Roll* do not specialize in basic therapeutic massage.

If one chooses to ignore the "legitimate" occupations, prostitution can also be considered a service-based occupation. The tactile relevance for this service relationship is obvious, but the accompanying elements of the prostitute's performance are often designed to make this strictly business transaction appear to be something other than it really is. That is, the enterprising prostitute might act as if the sexual encounter really reflected love, or at least intense sexual desire for the client (Goffman, 1959, pp. 232-233). In terms of the functional orientation of this book, such a strategy can be seen as an attempt to redefine the sexual encounter in terms of an intimacy function rather than a service function. Obviously, such a motive is much more flattering to the naive client, and may increase the likelihood of return business.

Nonverbal Involvement in Health Care

In recent years there has generally been increased interest in the sensitivity that physicians show to their patients (Hall, Roter, & Rand, 1981). One contributing factor may simply be that physicians are not held in quite so much awe as they were previously. Thus, physicians may be less able to structure the doctor-patient relationship solely on the basis of their status and expertise. If this is the case, the desired relationships (and continued business) may be more influenced by the manner in which they interact with their patients. (Obviously, many poorer patients, especially those on some kind of public assistance, may have little choice in selecting a physician. Under such circumstances, physician sensitivity to special patient concerns may be even more important, although at the same time, there may be little incentive for the physician to exert such an effort.)

The importance of the physican's nonverbal behavior can also be seen in terms of the feedback it gives the patient. Friedman (1979) notes that because some health problem brings the patient to the physician, the patient is usually fearful or anxious about his or her physical condition. Under these circumstances there will be a considerable need for information and support from the physician. Furthermore, reluctance to ask questions of the physician may force the patient to rely on the physician's subtle nonverbal cues. Thus, the patient may easily overinterpret very subtle cues from the physician and come to inaccurate judgments.

Of course, the patient's nonverbal behavior may be very useful and informative to the physican (Friedman, 1979). The patient's nonverbal responses (especially facial expressions) to diagnostic tests or probes may reveal something about the intensity of a problem. In addition, the consistency between the patient's verbal report and nonverbal behavior may indicate something about the patient's insight into or ability to deal with the health problem itself. The 50-year-old male with a cardiac problem who claims he is optimistic and relaxed, but projects an image of depression and stress, is likely to be lying or is showing very little insight into his feelings.

Another aspect of the physician-patient relationship that may be reflected in nonverbal cues is the evaluation of the doctor's bedside manner, a common label for the physician's typical way of relating (primarily nonverbally) to patients. Most people seem able to distinguish this dimension of physician evaluation from that of medical expertise. Nevertheless, a specific global evaluation of a physician might be relatively negative because of a poor bedside manner, even though the physician was a highly skilled "technician."

Related to this last point is the judgment that a high level of involvement from the physician, typically in the form of touch, may have actual therapeutic value. It is clear that those who are distressed can be comforted by a touch or an embrace. In fact, the results of the Whitcher and Fisher (1979) study, discussed earlier in the book, show that a nurse's touch of a female patient produced positive affective and behavioral responses. The contrasting negative effect with male patients clearly shows, however, that a beneficial effect of high involvement may be limited by the gender of the interactants.

The involvement pattern initiated by the physician as a direct consequence of diagnosing or treating a patient's medical problem is obviously characteristic of the service function. In spite of the apparent intimacy characteristic of many physician-patient relationships, however, criticism is occasionally directed at the cold, uncaring nature of medical treatment. In many instances, it appears that the physician does relate to the patient as an object, as Heslin (Note 1) has suggested. Attempts to humanize medical treatment by increased warmth toward and rapport with the patient may have some real therapeutic effect. To the extent that increased involvement is incorporated into the behavioral context for diagnosis and treatment, new service norms may be developing. That is, part of the performance a physician would have to master would be the incidental nonverbal warmth manifested toward the patient. Here too, such prescriptive judgments may well have to be limited not only by the type of treatment required, but also by the gender and age of both the physician and patient.

There are undoubtedly times when the high involvement required by different service occupations can become a source of misattribution. For example, those who are new to a particular culture's service norms might attribute unexpected involvement to a dispositional characteristic, usually an unfavorable one, rather than to the cultural norms. A similar condition may exist for those who use a service the first time. Even if these misattributions can be avoided, it does not mean that patients (or clients or customers) view the service encounter in a positive light. For example, intimate touch, though necessary in some physical exams, often leads to patient embarrassment and a feeling of vulnerability. The consequence of this experience may often negatively affect a later discussion of the health problem. That is, some people may find it very difficult to conduct a conversation about the problem with the physician because of the embarrassment of the exam. Obviously, reluctance to communicate about the problem can detract from the effectiveness of treatment.

Evaluating the Service Component

In modern Western societies, for the most part, we take for granted the professional's necessary tactile involvement with a patient or client. Because comparably high involvement in other settings might well have clear sexual relevance, the circumstances surrounding the service have to be very formalized. Morris (1971, chap. 5), however, notes that such reasonable norms have not always been the case. He describes the extraordinary constraints occasionally placed on gynecologists over 300 years ago. On some occasions, he (presumably there were few female gynecologists) was required to crawl into the pregnant woman's bedroom on his hands and knees so that the woman would not be able to identify the man who would be touching her so intimately. Even at the time of delivery the obstetrician might have to sit at the foot of the bed with the sheet tucked into his collar, covering the the woman and preventing him from seeing what his hands were doing. In addition, Morris (1971, pp. 159-160) claimed that for centuries qualified males were prevented from helping at birth. The result was that unskilled and frequently superstitious women served as midwives, causing unnecessary risks to mother and child.

In most instances of the service function, it appears that both the professional and the patient have clear expectations regarding the role of high involvement in administering the service. When this is the case, attributions regarding the involvement behavior should be directly linked to the requirements of the service. It is also the case, however, that the unscrupulous professional can take advantage of the naive patient or client, and initiate sexual intimacy under the guise of part of the professional treatment. This particular type of problem has been a major ethical issue in clinical psychology. Occasionally the naive, trusting, and troubled client is vulnerable to the therapist who advocates sexual intimacy as part of the treatment.

In most cases, the circumstances that bring a patient or client to see the professional are obvious, that is, the patient or client perceives a need for the service. The related issue, regarding the professional's motivation to enter a specialty requiring a high level of interpersonal involvement, may also affect the typical form of service exchanges. For example, are successful, or at least contented, professionals in various high-involvement specialities different from their colleagues in other comparable but low-involvement specialities? Perhaps those who seek out careers that require high levels of interpersonal involvement are those who enjoy the intense contact with others. Alternatively, some negative selection pressure may be operating; specifically, perhaps those who are stressed by the high level of involvement in some service exchanges either have little initial interest in such careers or decide after some exposure to these careers that high-involvement service exchanges are too stressful. Given the specialized focus and, in some cases, highly selective screening for some of these occupations (e.g., obstetrician, dentist), it seems likely that some general characteristics or motives might be common among many professionals. The identification and analysis of these characteristics may be helpful in trying to understand the management of high-involvement service exchanges.

Task Constraints in Unfocused Interactions

In unfocused interaction, individuals necessarily share a common presence but initiate no explicit communication. In spite of the absence of any direct verbal interaction, the presence of one or more other people in a setting can have a substantial effect on an individual's behavior. To appreciate the potential impact of another person's presence, it may be useful to examine the type and limits of sensory information available from others as a function of distance. Hall (1968, p. 92) has developed a classification system that details sensory input as a function of distance. In Figure 7-1, it can be seen that Hall's system segments interpersonal distance into four zones, each with a close and far phase. Although this classification was developed with an emphasis on focused interactions, its relevance for unfocused interactions is quite direct. The close presence of others with whom direct interaction is not intended still provides important sensory input that may be unwanted. For example, if people are crowded into a theatre lobby, it is likely that individuals

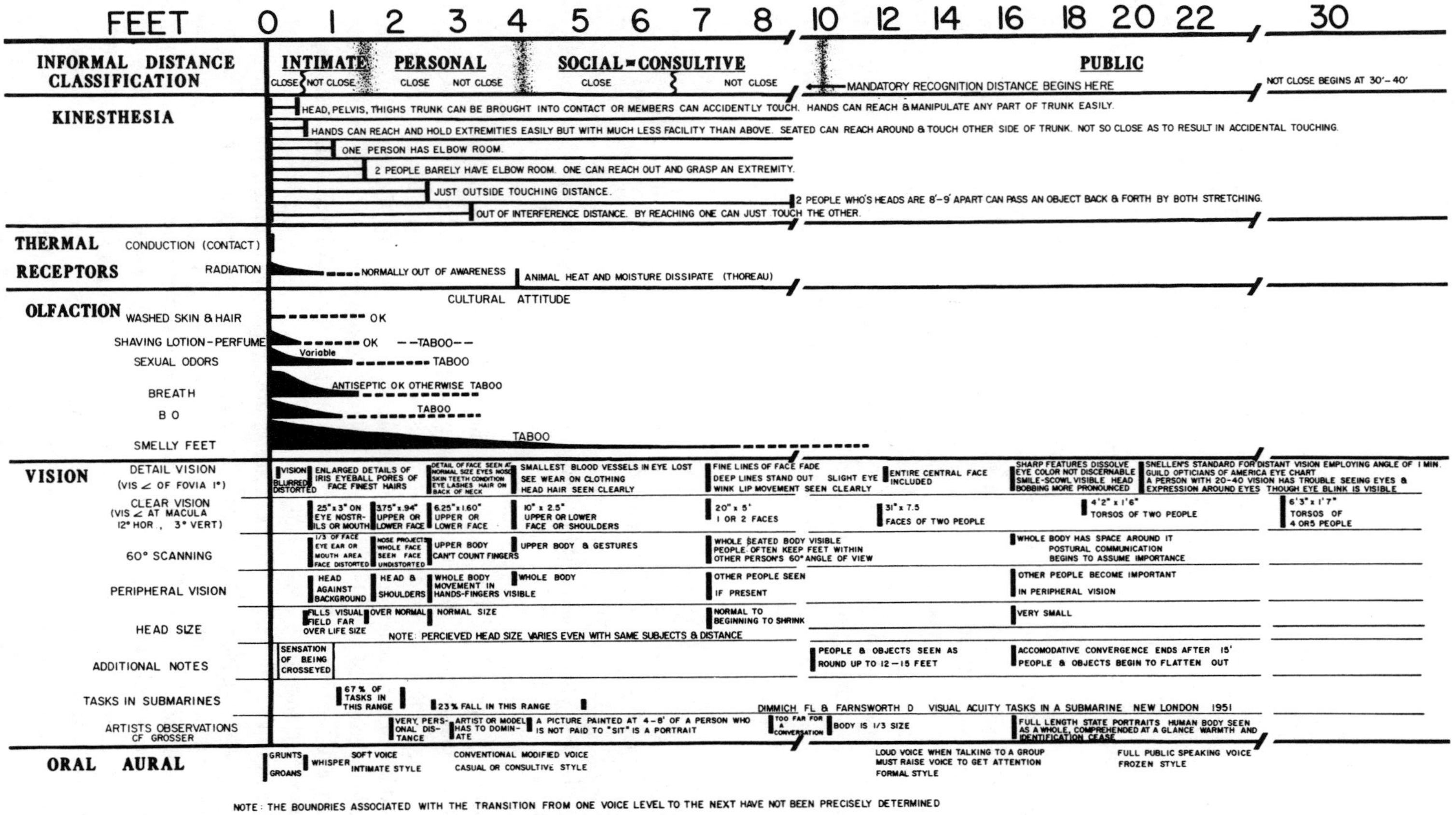

Fig. 7-1. Relationship of distance to sensory input. (Reprinted from *Current Anthropology*, 1968, *9*, 83-108, by E. T. Hall, by permission of The University of Chicago Press. Copyright 1968 by the University of Chicago Press.)

may touch and notice the smell of their neighbors even if they try to avoid them. In addition, accidental glances may occasionally occur between people and produce further discomfort.

It is clear from Hall's scheme that effective sensory input from others generally decreases as the distance from them increases. Typically, individuals must be relatively close to initiate a comfortable focused interaction. A casual, focused interaction might be conducted somewhere in the personal or social-consultive zones described by Hall, for example, 2 to 8 feet. In many situations, however, individuals expecting *no* focused interaction with one another are often brought into arrangements that are as close or closer than those commonly selected for focused interactions.

In this section the discussion will examine three general examples of task-setting categories of unfocused interaction that seem to structure patterns of nonverbal involvement with others: (1) waiting and traveling; (2) studying; and (3) working. In each of these task-setting categories, the individuals may be described as coacting. That is, they are engaged in the same activities or tasks, but each is acting independently. Practically, the task function for these various activities describes how people manage their nonverbal behavior to be more comfortable and more effective at their tasks. Finally, it should be noted that the design and arrangement features of the physical environments exercise considerable influence over the involvement patterns possible in these settings.

Waiting and Traveling

Settings that are designed to accommodate people who are waiting often serve to keep people apart and make interaction more difficult. As an example, Sommer (1974, pp. 73-75) discusses the common design of waiting areas in airports. Seating is usually arranged in a straight line, with all the seats facing the same direction. The chairs are often hard plastic, and they are usually bolted to the floor. If one wanted to promote contact between strangers in these settings, or simply permit family members and friends to talk to one another, such straight line arrangements would make interaction more difficult. That is, people using such settings would have to work against the arrangement of the chairs to orient themselves toward their partners. Although Sommer correctly criticizes this deficiency in the design of these settings, such a criticism also has to be weighed against the individual's concern for privacy and the manner in which these arrangements facilitate that end. Ideally, any given setting should facilitate isolation or interaction as the individual desires. It seems, however, that most public settings are much better suited for promoting isolation than for promoting interaction. Strangers not desiring interaction can be relatively close side by side (e.g., one empty seating separating them), but still be comfortable because the seating does not permit easy visual regard between them. In contrast, an individual might be uncomfortable in a relatively distant arrangement if the chairs were directly facing one another. In this latter instance, the discomfort might be a product of either catching occasionally the unwanted gaze of the other person or perhaps simply feeling that one is under observation by that person.

Obviously, one tactic to avoid catching the unwanted gaze of another is simply not to look in the direction of other people in the setting. The prevalence of gaze avoidance in commuters was the focus of one study conducted in urban and suburban train stations. In that study, the proportion of commuters who initiated gaze toward an experimenter (standing at a doorway or stairway) was approximately twice as high in the suburban station than in the urban station—31% versus 13.5% (McCauley, Coleman, & DeFusco, 1978). The authors judged that the reduced gaze in the urban station reflected a short-term adaptation to interpersonal overload in the city. This interpretation seems reasonable, but it should be noted that the base rate of commuters who passed the experimenter in a 5-minute period was much greater in the urban than in the suburban setting. It is possible that the greater opportunity for looking at other people in the city station simply decreased the probability of looking only at the experimenter.

Whether one is traveling or simply waiting with strangers, similar dynamics probably operate in the management of nonverbal involvement. A basic component in maintaining some privacy in such public settings is to limit tactile involvement with others. But the combination of high density and less than spacious seating in trains, buses, or waiting areas can make it difficult to avoid touching others. Maines (1977) examined one adjustment pattern used by passengers sharing seating on benches in subway trains. Specifically, Maines observed the frequency of elbows forward versus elbows at the side for passengers with a neighbor either less than 6 inches (closed context) or more than 6 inches away from the subject (open context). The elbows forward position usually resulted in an avoidance of touch between neighbors in the closed context, whereas the placing of elbows at the side usually resulted in touch between neighbors in the open context. Overall, approximately 60% of the passengers in the closed context sat with their elbows forward, whereas approximately 40% of the passengers in the open context sat with their elbows forward. The frequency of the elbows forward adjustment in the closed position, however, was very much a product of the race and sex compositions of seated neighbors. The incidence of elbows forward was consistently less in homogeneous race and sex pairs than in heterogeneous race and sex pairs. Thus, an apparent norm of touch avoidance was more strongly held if the neighbor was not of the same race or gender.

Independent of the particular design of seating arrangements, there are some predictable ways in which people arrange themselves when waiting or traveling with one another. In general, strangers will tend to disperse themselves relatively evenly in settings such as an airport, the waiting room of a doctor's office, or the lobby of a theatre. This statement is made with the standard caveat—all other things being equal—which unfortunately is rarely the case. Consequently, people may occasionally be grouped more closely at the area surrounding an entrance or an exit because of the advantage this provides them in simply moving out of the area more quickly. In addition, people may sit relatively close to one another in order to have access to a television or perhaps to avoid warm or cold spots in a room. Because most strangers in these settings do not typically expect to interact with one another, the patterns of spacing, orientation, and visual regard are generally managed so that the degree of potential involvement with others is maximally controlled. For example, if you had to wait in relatively close proximity to a stranger, it would be more comfortable to be seated back to back in separate rows, or even in an adjacent side by side position, than to sit facing the person across a narrow aisle. In fact, it appears that the mere anticipation of others coming into a setting is sufficient to induce an individual to choose a relatively isolated position (Baum & Greenberg, 1975).

Studying

The activity of studying with others present is somewhat similar to that of waiting or traveling with others, but there are some important differences. First, those who share a regular place to study are more likely to be recognized, if not actually known, than are those with whom we may wait or travel. This is particularly the case in high school or college libraries that are frequented by the same populations on a regular basis. In contrast, people who use waiting areas associated with travel, service, or entertainment activities usually represent a larger cross section of the population, which frequents such settings less regularly than a student population might frequent a library.

Not surprisingly, people who use a library (typically to read or study) are more likely to do so alone than are people who frequent other kinds of settings. For example, Bakeman and Beck's (1974) extensive observations of group size in various settings showed that about half of the people they observed in libraries were there alone. In contrast, a much smaller percentage of people (11%-27%) who used settings such as a dining hall, a coffee shop, a shopping mall, or a swimming pool were alone.

Whereas the work setting often necessitates some infrequent, intermittent conversation and involves the individual for an extended period of time, the study setting usually necessitates solitary activity for a shorter period of time. The results of two survey studies of students on college campuses indicated that an average duration of a library study visit was about 2 hours (Schaeffer & Patterson, 1977; Sommer, 1970). In our study almost two thirds of the library users surveyed mentioned avoiding (a) distractions, (b) others, or (c) talkers as the primary reason for their choice of seating locations (Schaeffer & Patterson, 1977). Only 10% mentioned proximity to materials as the primary reason for seating choices. This latter result is consistent with Sommer's (1966, 1968) findings that most students are not concerned with the use of reference materials in a library, but rather with simply finding a quiet location. Although Sommer (1970) found that more studying occurred in the student's own residence (74%) than in the library (23%), concerns about quiet and avoidance of distraction were still important in residential studying. Even though a residence may not be as quiet as a library, it does provide other compensating benefits. In particular, the student could snack, smoke, relax more easily, and still be accessible to friends.

For study settings other than a residence, the more open the setting and the more easily it can be used for other purposes, the less frequently it will be used for studying and the shorter will be the duration of study periods (Rosenbloom, 1977). In particular, Rosenbloom found that students preferred smaller lounges bounded by walls over larger open lounges when they wanted to study. The former were more likely to be used by students arriving alone, and the latter were more often used by groups, frequently for social purposes.

The results of all these studies suggest that minimizing the stimulation from others is a primary concern of those selecting desirable study locations. Such a strategy is also consistent with the arousal-mediated social facilitation effects described by Zajonc (1965). That is, if the presence of others initiates arousal and produces a decrement in learning, then studying may be most effectively managed away from others. Selecting locations of low density where there are few distractions and choosing bounded or partitioned settings can facilitate serious studying. In addition to the type of setting, however, the specific seating position at a table can also affect one's relative involvement with others and the resulting degree of privacy in the setting.

Sommer and Becker (1969) examined the issue of preferred seating location by asking students where they would sit in a library if they wanted to (a) retreat from others or (b) actively defend against others sitting at the table. The retreat condition subjects typically chose seats in the rear of the room, at a wall (rather than aisle) table, in the chair closest to the wall, and facing away from the doorway. These tendencies were maximized when the library room was described as having a high density level. In contrast, the active defense subjects were more likely to face the doorway and select a nonaisle chair. These differences clearly suggested that the retreat subjects were more concerned about reducing their potential involvement with others than the defense subjects were. Although Sommer and Becker were not concerned about the motives that might stimulate either the retreating or defensive strategy of seating location, it might be suggested that the retreat strategy would be more characteristic of an individual who is serious about studying. Such a person could reduce potentially distracting involvement with others by staying far away from the traffic flow and facing away from others so that accidental holding of gaze and evaluative monitoring by others are minimized.

Working

Most working people spend up to half of their waking hours in their job settings—settings over which they often have relatively little control. Most of us can do little to redesign the physical structure of our work settings, with the possible exception of a simple rearrangement of furniture, adding plants or flowers, or hanging a picture or family photo. Many employees do not even have that much flexibility, however. For example, Sommer (1974, p. 104) notes that some architects specify in their contracts that changes, even subtle ones such as the rearrangement of furniture, cannot be undertaken without written permission. Presumably, these architects would require only verbal permission to open the drapes or empty the wastebaskets.

The management of nonverbal involvement in the work setting among those who share only an unfocused interaction seems to be determined primarily by the demands of the job and the physical constraints of the setting. There appears, however, to be relatively little research specifically on nonverbal involvement and work activities. Some direction is provided by the research on related issues, such as privacy. Because the work setting structures primary service and task activities of many people, however, this area merits even a speculative, "soft" analysis.

In many work settings, privacy seems to be a priority concern. For example, in one study of university faculty offices, privacy was the second highest concern, coming only after location of the office (Farrenkopf & Roth, 1980). Privacy is certainly functional for the successful completion of many tasks, but privacy also serves other more personal needs. The extent to which one can control his or her privacy is usually an indicator of status. Often, the high status person has either a larger territory and/or a clearer claim to territory than a low status person does, with the result that privacy is easier to maintain. Practically, the ability to control privacy more easily means that an individual can selectively determine involvement, not only in focused interactions, but also in unfocused interactions. Thus, the boss is likely to have a large office that provides isolation from employees, who, in contrast, probably have little or no opportunity for isolating themselves.

According to Altman (1975), everyone tries to achieve some optimal privacy level specific to himself or herself, the setting, and the particular activity. The way privacy is managed for people of differing status may be quite different. The high status person can usually rely on barriers in the physical environment, for example, the four walls of his or her office, to ensure privacy. In contrast, the low status person may have to rely on less substantial physical barriers or simple behavioral barriers to reduce involvement with others. A good example of this contrast is the private office in Figure 7-2a and the bullpen arrangement of secretaries or clerks in Figure 7-2b. In the open bullpen arrangement the only physical barrier is provided by the arrangement of the desks in a common direction. This arrangement makes it unlikely that one will share accidental gaze with the person in front or behind, but the involvement potential is still considerable with respect to adjacent neighbors. In addition, close neighbors in any direction may be able to overhear phone conversations or discussions with fellow workers.

One physical modification of office areas that has become popular in recent years is office landscaping. The open arrangement of landscaped offices involves a compromise between the usual bullpen arrangement and private offices. In the place of partitions or walls that might separate workers are various plants, cabinets, or bookcases that partially screen neighboring workers from one another. Ideally, the presence of greenery and the openness associated with only partial barriers provides enough privacy but also allows a feeling of spaciousness in the area. An example of the landscaped office can be seen in Figure 7-3. The absence of full partitions and the substitution of plants, shelves, or other partial barriers is characteristic of these landscaped offices. Sommer (1974, pp. 109-110) notes that lower status workers often prefer such an arrangement, apparently because their specific surroundings are usually improved and the landscaped arrangement provides an opportunity for some privacy. The opposing reaction is typical of the middle-range employees who might be forced to move from a partitioned office to a large landscaped room. In this latter case, the employee not only loses some privacy control, but also loses some of the prestige associated with a private office. Of course, the bosses or supervisors are unlikely to join in the landscaped arrangement for the very reasons the middle-level employees do not like it.

(a)

(b)

Fig. 7-2. Illustrations of a private office (a) and an open arrangement of office space (b). (Photos courtesy of Ellen Toler)

Finally, differential involvement should be important in the work setting because of its impact on productivity. Specifically, the presence of others can lead to increased performance on some work tasks (Zajonc, 1965). Apparently, the increased arousal produced by (a) involvement per se, (b) evaluation apprehension, or (c) distraction typically increases performance on relatively simple or overlearned tasks. For more complex and demanding tasks, performance decrements may result from higher levels of arousal.

At this point, a few generalizations can be offered about the relationship of tasks or activities in the work setting to unfocused involvement patterns. To the extent that the task demands clearly require high- or low-involvement patterns, the likeli-

Fig. 7-3. Example of a landscaped office. (Photo courtesy of Ellen Toler)

hood of misattribution from these behaviors should be minimal. Thus, even though coworkers on an assembly line may have to brush against one another in the course of completing their assigned responsibilities, the relevance for interpersonal attributions should be minimal as long as the high involvement is seen as the product of both the task and the available space. This may not be the case for the new worker who has not yet formulated a clear impression of the task constraints on individual behavior. Obviously, simply knowing the source of higher involvement does not mean that the workers are satisfied with the behavioral consequences of their jobs, but it is probably unlikely that they will attribute these consequences to the personal characteristics of their coworkers.

Even though high- or low-involvement levels in the work setting may not be of immediate interpersonal relevance, effects may carry over to influence later focused interaction. For example, a homeostatic principle emphasizing the consequences of understimulation and overstimulation (Milgram, 1970) predicts a kind of compensatory behavioral adjustment in interactions that might follow substantial changes in stimulation. That is, the more important consequences of high involvement on the job may be seen in a delayed fashion in later social behavior. Specifically, an overstimulated person may actively avoid social involvement with others outside of the work setting. In addition, when interactions do occur the residue of stress from overstimulation on the job may have a negative effect on the quality of later exchanges.

Significance of the Service-Task Function

The service-task function describes the direct instrumental use of nonverbal behavior in professional service encounters and in various task-or setting-determined activities. In these various encounters specific levels of nonverbal involvement may be required by the nature of the service or task, or contribute to an effective completion of the service or task.

Presumably, interpersonal affect and motivation have relatively little impact on the specific levels of involvement initiated in service-task exchanges. In a similar fashion, the recipients of differential involvement will usually not attribute this involvement to the dispositional and interpersonal motives of the actors. This latter generalization assumes that the recipients are cognizant of the service or task norms that limit the actor's behavior. Interpersonal dynamics, however, probably become more important if patients, clients, or coactors are not familiar with the relevant norms. This may be the case especially for those who are either new to a particular cultural milieu, or who are uninformed about the nature of the specific service or task. When this occurs, the attributions about the actor's behavior may incorrectly focus on dispositional or interpersonal motives. Such a result may make an exchange more uncomfortable or even jeopardize the completion of a service or a task. It is also important to appreciate that even though individuals may be familiar with behavioral norms for a service or a task, this does not ensure that the service or task exchange is a comfortable one—just ask the patients leaving your local proctologist's office.

The analysis of service patterns of nonverbal involvement is important not as much for interpersonal consequences as for understanding cultural and subcultural norms for behavior in various service activities. For example, the earlier description of obstetrical care typical of the 16th or 17th century (Morris, 1971, chap. 6) clearly suggested that routine medical care of pregnant women was seen as potentially sexually intimate. In effect, the meaning of this professional treatment (and probably others too) was defined by the gender of the professional and the location of the body area examined. Obviously, such an attitude is not likely to promote good medical care. Furthermore, such an orientation clearly contrasts with the functional theme of this book. That is, comparably involving (or noninvolving) behavior patterns can serve very different functions.

Just as service constraints often lead to high levels of nonverbal involvement, task constraints often lead to low levels of involvement. The completion of various tasks and activities frequently requires decreased involvement with those around us. If such decreased involvement is not possible through architectural or design means, then more subtle adjustments in distance, gaze, or orientation can serve to reduce involvement to levels that are less interfering. Most of us can appreciate that involvement with difficult or detailed tasks may require some disengagement from others in order to complete them in a satisfactory or timely manner. In some cases the nature of the task or activity dictates that it be completed in specific settings that require increased isolation from others. For example, developing film is an activity that would be unsuccessful if attempted in the living room. Alternately, taking a bath in one's family room may be possible, but probably inappropriate in our culture (California excepted).

A less extreme example is the task or writing the very words in this chapter. I could attempt this in my office in the Psychology Department, but it is not likely that much would be accomplished. Interruptions and various distractions from colleagues and students make that location undesirable. Consequently, I usually hide away in an infrequently used research room or in a vacant office near my own office. For the duration of any writing period, I prefer isolation, although it is not absolutely required. Of course, individual differences may lead to different ways of managing this kind of task. Some people may be able to recover quickly from interruptions with little or no loss in efficiency. Others may feel a need to be isolated completely before they can even begin to start a project.

A final, interesting issue relates to the use of task involvement as an excuse for either initiating or avoiding involvement with others. For example, personal advice columns occasionally recommend joining various religious or social groups as a means for singles to meet desirable members of the opposite sex. Thus, the group activity becomes the vehicle through which people can get to know one another. In effect, the common task interest provides a license to initiate interaction. More specific short-term tactics might include walking the dog or frequenting the local laundromat (a favorite of television detergent advertisements).

The occasional and deliberate initiation of short-term task involvement might be viewed as a type of interactional strategy. The hurried opening of a technical book or the spreading of important papers on a desk might be staged as one hears an unwanted visitor approaching. If this tactic is not successful in preventing the interaction, it might at least shorten it. When we are at home, callers may be discouraged by the excuse that one is in the shower, giving the baby a bath, or simply sleeping late. There are limits to a legitimate excuse for not seeing others, however. It would not be convincing to say that the lady of the house cannot come to the door because she is watching her favorite toilet paper commercial. In effect, task involvement may be managed so that an individual has some control over his or her access to others and, in turn, controls other people's access to him or her. Task involvement that reflects a long-term job or career interest can also influence general accessibility to others. In this case, however, task involvement is an enduring commitment and not an isolated routine initiated to control interpersonal access.

Summary

The service-task function describes the role that impersonal instrumental goals may have in the management of nonverbal involvement. A number of professional service encounters such as those between a patient and physician, or between a tailor and a customer, require the initiation of high involvement, typically in the form of touch. Generally as the involvement level in these service encounters becomes more extreme, the norms relating to the initiation of touch become more formalized. In this way, the opportunity for misinterpretation of the professional's involvement is reduced and the legitimacy of the professional's service is ensured. Nevertheless, patients or customers who are new to a particular service exchange can misattribute the basis for the high involvement and interpret it in terms of the dispositional or motivational characteristics of the professional. Even if the appropriate service-based attribution is made, the intimate nature of the touch can be stressful.

The task component of the function can serve to either increase or decrease characteristic involvement levels. Many tasks or activities are facilitated by decreased involvement levels. Tasks that are complicated or require considerable concentration typically benefit from the maintenance of minimal levels of involvement with others, for example, studying, writing, or making complex plans. Different antecedent factors proposed in the functional model may predict short-term and long-term task involvement. Specifically, the management of short-term task involvement to control access to others is probably influenced more by experiential and relational-situational factors. In contrast, the selection of long-term commitments to tasks in the form of career choices is undoubtedly affected by individual differences in personal factors. For example, one might expect that the typical forest ranger would differ from the typical sales executive in a variety of traits, perhaps including introversion-extraversion and assertiveness. Such career differences necessarily lead to a difference in the frequency of social contact with others, but these differences may not be reflected in the involvement levels characteristic of their interactions. The whole issue of the selection of social settings and the consequences of these choices seems to be very important in understanding the resulting form of the interactions. The behavior setting approach of Barker (1968) and Wicker (1979) is one perspective that may facilitate such an analysis.

Some tasks may require two or more people to share in a common activity that brings them into greater involvement with one another, for example, some construction tasks, lifting heavy objects, or using common materials at a given workspace. A particularly interesting issue of task involvement is the use of different tasks or activities to control the opportunity for access to others. One might use the tactic of initiating a particular task or activity in order to start an interaction with another person. Thus, the sharing of some attention or effort on a specific activity can become an excuse for initiating involvement with others. More commonly, task involvement may be used to prevent others from initiating contact. Thus, one might manage the appearance of being very busy with a demanding task so that a potential visitor is discouraged from intruding. Finally, it might be noted that the manipulation of task involvement in this fashion can be described as a very basic means of regulating interaction.

Chapter 8

Antecedent Influences

In the last five chapters the discussion has focused on the functions of nonverbal involvement. The salience of a particular function and the manner in which it is expressed nonverbally are often related to the influence of the antecedent factors. The antecedent influences may be grouped into three general categories: (1) personal factors; (2) experiential factors; (3) relational-situational factors. The sequential functional model assumes that the antecedent factors exercise their influence through the preinteraction mediators (see Figure 2-2). Specifically, behavioral predispositions, arousal change, and cognitive-affective expectancies determine both the levels of involvement initiated and the functional bases for the exchange.

An analysis and review of the antecedent factors should promote an understanding of the variety possible in patterns of nonverbal exchange. There are literally hundreds of articles that examine the relationship between one or more of the antecedent factors and some aspects of nonverbal involvement. Consequently, I will not be attempting a comprehensive review of this literature here; a sampling of the research will provide a substantial basis for discussion. The first section will focus on the personal factors of culture, gender, and personality.

Personal Factors

Culture

The impetus for the study of cultural influences on nonverbal behavior can clearly be credited to the work of E. T. Hall (1963, 1966, 1968). Hall's research focused on cultural differences in proxemics, or the study of distance zones, and necessarily stressed the spatial separation between individuals. Unlike many researchers who followed him, however, Hall discussed space in terms of its consequences on other interpersonal behaviors. That is, space was important, not so much in itself, but rather for the way it structured other interactive behaviors such as touch, gaze, body orientation, and even smell. This point is reflected in Figure 7-1.

Cross-cultural comparisons. On the basis of his observations, Hall proposed that societies can be characterized in terms of a contact- or noncontact involvement continuum. For example, Arabs, southern Mediterranean people, and Latin Americans were assumed to be on the contact end of the continuum. People in the contact societies would be likely to stand close to one another, occasionally touch, and use more frequent gestures. In contrast, the English and northern Europeans were assumed to be noncontact people, and consequently to interact at greater distances that made touch unlikely. Presumably, Americans are somewhat between the extremes, but apparently closer to the noncontact end of the continuum.

There is some support for Hall's hypothesized differences in the use of space. For example, Watson and Graves (1966) found that pairs of Arab college students typically sat closer to one another, were more directly oriented, and had higher levels of mutual gaze than did their American counterparts. In another study that compared Latin American and North American students, no differences were found in the selection of distances in a structured interaction (Forston & Larson, 1968). But the experimenters noted that the Latin American pairs seemed to stand closer in casual interactions initiated outside of the experimental session than did the American pairs.

Two studies by Noesjirwan (1977, 1978) suggest that Indonesians, representing a culture not sampled in Hall's early work, may be described as being near the contact end of Hall's continuum. In the first study, conducted in doctors' waiting rooms in Jakarta and in Sydney, Indonesians were more likely than Australians to (a) be accompanied by another adult, (b) sit closer to a stranger, and (c) talk to a stranger. It is interesting that the Indonesians showed such a clear preference for interpersonal closeness, relative to the Australians, even though the Indonesian sample was from an urban, modern, and relatively westernized middle-class setting. Such a sample may be the least likely to show a traditional cultural pattern, yet even this sample was clearly different from the Australians. Consequently, it is possible that the differences observed may underestimate the true differences between the Indonesian and Australian cultures.

In the second study, pairs of Indonesian males in Jakarta and Australian males in Sydney were observed during a brief structured interaction (Noesjirwan, 1978). Consistent with the results of the first study, the Indonesians sat closer together, touched more, and smiled more than did the Australians. The Australians, however, sat in more directly facing orientations and initiated more gaze than did the Indonesians. Noesjirwan proposed that the closer seating and the more frequent touching and smiling reflected a higher level of affiliation in the Indonesian subjects, whereas the increased gaze and more direct body orientation in the Australian subjects reflected a higher level of dominance. Although such an interpretation is plausible, other unknown cultural differences might also contribute to the observed patterns.

For example, another factor affecting cultural differences in the use of nonverbal involvement may be the language used in the interaction. Sussman and Rosenfeld (1982) found that Venezuelan foreign students sat relatively close, and Japanese foreign students sat relatively distant, when they were speaking their own respective languages. When the subjects conducted their discussion in English, however, the Venezuelans sat farther apart from one another and the Japanese sat closer to one another. Thus, when the subjects from these two contrasting cultures conversed in English their differences in seating disappeared. Sussman and Rosenfeld suggested that when the Venezuelan and Japanese students used a foreign language (English), a number of other culturally appropriate cues were activated, including the American distance norms.

The results reported by Sussman and Rosenfeld are also interesting because they have relevance for Hall's proposed explanation for cultural differences in involvement. Specifically, Hall (1966) has suggested that people from different cultures may live in what amounts to different sensory worlds. That is, the Arab and the Englishman may not share common experiences even when they are in the same environment. Hall proposes that the contact cultures emphasize tactile and olfactory input, whereas the noncontact cultures emphasize visual input. These habitual patterns of relating to the world permeate all aspects of everyday life, but their effects on social behavior define the manner in which people relate to one another. In the case of the contact cultures, this general tendency is manifested in closer approaches so that tactile and olfactory information may be gained easily. In contrast, in the noncontact cultures, larger interpersonal distances are maintained so that the interaction partner can be easily focused visually. Thus, according to Hall, culturally specific involvement levels are the by-product of habitual modes of gathering information.

Sussman and Rosenfeld's results seem inconsistent with Hall's emphasis on contrasting cultural styles of relating to the world. It seems unlikely that merely changing the language spoken in an interaction could immediately alter the manner in which one selects and processes sensory information. Those changes, however, are consistent with a Whorfian notion of language serving to structure reality, in this case social behavior.

A final concern in the matter of cross-cultural differences relates to the generalizability of the results. Almost all of the examples cited in Hall's (1966) book involve males interacting with one another. Furthermore, when Hall describes the various encounters that he has observed, the subjects are usually middle- or upperclass members of society, that is, his academic or business acquaintances or college students. The patterns of involvement observed for these individuals are probably characteristic of male middle- or upper-class individuals, but are they representative of those cultures in general? In many cultures outside of western Europe and North America, the majority of the populations are very poor, and their norms for social behavior may be different from that of the middle and upper classes. Furthermore, in at least some of the contact cultures described by Hall, involvement patterns of females are much more constrained than those of males. For example, in traditional Arab and Latin American societies, the contact patterns described of males may be very inappropriate for females, especially when the females are interacting with males. In these instances sex-specific social customs would seem to outweigh any general cultural patterns.

Subcultural comparisons. The research on subcultural differences, at least most of that conducted in North America, does not lead to any clearcut generalizations. Most of this research has examined potential racial differences in involvement. Some of the studies report evidence that blacks prefer closer interaction distances than whites (Aiello & Jones, 1971; Bauer, 1973; Jones & Aiello, 1973), whereas other studies report either the opposite or no differences at all (Baxter, 1970; Jones, 1971; Willis, 1966). One of the better designed studies, which controlled for socioeconomic differences, found no evidence for racial differences (Scherer, 1974). This finding suggests that some of the apparent racial differences are really a function of socioeconomic differences between subjects.

Although the management of distance patterns may not differ as a function of race, there is some evidence for gazing and touching differences between races. Specifically, black listeners may typically look less at a speaker than white listeners (Fugita, Wexley, & Hillery, 1974; LaFrance & Mayo, 1976). In several studies by Willis and his colleagues on race and touch, the dominant pattern is one showing higher levels of touch among blacks than among whites (Smith, Willis, & Gier, 1980; Willis & Hoffman, 1975; Willis, Reeves, & Buchanan, 1976). Research on gaze and touch seems to indicate that whites may be more likely to increase involvement through gaze, whereas blacks are more likely to do so with touch. This conclusion should remain a tentative one until more is known about the potential effects of socioeconomic and situational influences on these racial patterns.

Gender

The relationship of gender to patterns of nonverbal behavior has intrigued researchers for many years. The personal experience of most of us suggests that males and females often do react differently in social situations. It seems likely that, in many cases, such differences are manifested in subtle nonverbal cues. The discussion in this section will focus on two related areas of potential sex differences; those manifested in general interaction patterns, and those reflected in more specific encoding and decoding differences.

Interaction patterns. In same-sex interactions, a substantial amount of research indicates that females typically prefer higher levels of involvement with one another than males do. This preference is reflected by females selecting closer distances than males, both in dyadic interactions (Aiello & Aiello, 1974; Aiello & Jones, 1971; Pellegrini & Empey, 1970) and in larger groups (Giesen & McClaren, 1976; Mehrabian & Diamond, 1971b; Patterson & Schaeffer, 1977). In addition, females engage in more gaze with one another than males do (Dabbs, Evans, Hopper, & Purvis, 1980; Exline, 1963; Exline, Gray, & Schuette, 1965; Libby, 1970). Touch also seems to be more frequent and more positively evaluated among females than among males (Fisher, Rytting, & Heslin, 1976; Jourard, 1966; Whitcher & Fisher, 1979).

It should not be surprising that, in opposite-sex pairs, patterns of involvement as a function of gender are more complicated and conditional. Much of this research was reviewed in Chapter 5 and need only be summarized here. First, as attraction toward an opposite-sex partner increases, the involvement level initiated toward that person tends to increase. Second, in initial encounters in opposite-sex pairs, females seem to react more positively to moderately high levels of involvement initiated by a male partner; however, males' reactions to high involvement by a female partner may be more variable. For example, in one study (Silverthorne, Mickelwright, O'Donnell, & Gibson, 1976), females viewed increased tactile involvement by a male in an initial greeting very favorably, whereas males judged similarly high levels of female tactile involvement less favorably.

In opposite-sex romantic relationships there is clear evidence for the expected high level of involvement, especially for touch (Jourard, 1966; Rosenfeld, Kartus, & Ray, 1976) and mutual gaze (Goldstein, Kilroy, & Van de Voort, 1976; Rubin, 1970). Traditional expectancies regarding heterosexual involvement emphasize the male's typical prerogative in initiating increased involvement, but these expectancies may have changed in recent years. The results of two studies on the meaning of touch in heterosexual pairs suggest that reactions to touch are affected not only by the gender of the person touched, but also by the degree of relationship. In the first study, with unmarried couples, males and females had strongly opposing reactions to sexual touch. Specifically, males viewed sexual touches as pleasant and warm, but females viewed sexual touches as neither pleasant nor warm (Nguyen, Heslin, & Nguyen, 1975). In the second study, with married couples, males perceived sexual touches more negatively than females did. If these results are valid, there is a clear interaction of Gender X Marital Status on perceived pleasantness of sexual touches (Nguyen, Heslin, & Nguyen, 1976).

Analyses of the involvement patterns characteristic of males and females usually emphasize the influence of the sex role socialization that takes place in a child's early years. Although it is not easy to reject completely any biological bases for behavioral differences, the influence of early socialization on traditional sex roles seems to be a more important factor. Traditional norms for young girls typically stress dependence, expressiveness, and warmth in interpersonal relationships, whereas the analogous norms for young boys stress independence, competitiveness, and task accomplishment (Leibman, 1970).

One interpretation of gender differences in interaction has been offered recently by Ickes (1981) in a model of sex role influences. Ickes used the common sex role orientation categories of masculine, feminine, androgynous, and undifferentiated in constructing his model. The masculine orientation can be described as essentially instrumental in nature (active and controlling), whereas the feminine orientation is essentially expressive (reactive and emotionally responsive). Androgynous individuals possess both instrumental and affiliative capabilities, whereas undifferentiated individuals possess neither capability. Ickes discussed a number of hypotheses from his model for which there are some supporting results. A few of these hypotheses will be discussed here and their relevance to the overall pattern of gender differences considered.

Ickes' analysis of sex role orientation influences emphasizes two separate concerns, actual behavioral involvement initiated in an interaction and satisfaction with this level of involvement. For example, two stereotypic (ST), or masculine, males should typically prefer and actually initiate low levels of involvement in an interaction. Two ST, or feminine, females should typically prefer high involvement, but because both lack the instrumental capacity necessary the actual level of involvement will be low. Consequently, the ST-ST female pair would be dissatisfied with low involvement. Ickes rejects the notion that the contrasting orientations within

ST-ST mixed sex pairs result in a kind of interdependence that produces a mutually satisfying interaction. Instead, the ST male who has the instrumental skills to manage increased involvement is not motivated to initiate high involvement because his expressive interests are too low. The ST female, in contrast, has the expressive interest, but does not have the instrumental capacity. The result is a low level of interaction involvement, one that is comfortable for the ST male but not for the ST female. Data from the Ickes and Barnes (1978) study provide support for this last hypothesis. Thus, it can be suggested that some of the incompatibility in interactions between males and females may be a result of adhering to, not violating, traditional sex role orientations.

According to this model, the potential for higher levels of involvement that are mutually satisfying is present when both members of a pair are androgynous. Results from three different studies indicate support for this last prediction. Specifically, androgynous same- and opposite-sex pairs consistently showed both higher levels of involvement and greater satisfaction with that involvement (Ickes & Barnes, 1978; Ickes, Shermer, & Steeno, 1979; Lamke, 1979). Furthermore, involvement levels were also high in mixed-sex dyads in which one person was androgynous.

In summary, Ickes' model and the related data suggest the androgyny, not stereotypic femininity, facilitates increased involvement. Consequently, the apparent complementarity in stereotypic mixed-sex interactions and the similarity in stereotypic female-female interactions may not serve to increase involvement. Rather, at least one member of a pair has to have instrumental skills and expressive interest, in order to maximize interactional involvement.

Ickes' model and the related results seem consistent with the trends described earlier that showed relatively low involvement in male-male interactions. But the relatively higher levels of involvement characteristic of the research of male-female and female-female pairs seems inconsistent with Ickes' model (i.e., assuming that most subjects in those studies have stereotypic sex role orientations). Ickes commented on this issue of generalizability and noted that to the extent natural settings (or for that matter, other research settings) are more structured than the setting in which he conducted his research, situational cues and norms may override the dispositional sex role orientations. Thus, there may be increased situational pressure for higher involvement in male-female and female-female pairs. In addition, it is clear that many of the field settings used for research on gender differences necessarily result in a selection of subjects who know one another. This circumstance can also contribute to females generally (i.e., independent of sex role orientation) being more involved with their interaction partner than is typical of the encounters between strangers in the Ickes and Barnes (1978) and Ickes et al. (1979) studies. The merit of these ad hoc explanations for inconsistencies between Ickes' model and general trends in research on gender differences is uncertain; however, Ickes' model provides some intriguing insights and hypotheses regarding gender differences that deserve close attention.

Encoding and decoding differences. The discussion of gender differences in nonverbal involvement focused on rather broad differences in characteristic interaction patterns. In contrast, potential gender differences in encoding and decoding identify more limited, yet basic, contrasts in the way that feelings are interpreted and expressed. In fact, it might be suggested that gender differences in encoding and decoding may contribute to the differences described in interactive behavior.

Although the pattern of differences is not completely consistent, the majority of the research on decoding suggests that females are better (i.e., more accurate) decoders of nonverbal affect (Hall, 1978). In her review, Hall considered two contrasting explanations for the advantage of females over males in decoding accuracy. First, because women have traditionally had less status and power than men in our society, increased nonverbal sensitivity may be socially adaptive. That is, the ability to decode accurately the nonverbal behavior of powerful others may provide some leverage in relating to such people. Hall (1978) notes that because the advantage of females in decoding sensitivity is not absent at earlier ages, this explanation may be questioned. That is, if increased nonverbal sensitivity is learned, then the advantage of females should develop slowly over a period of years, but this does not seem to be the case.

An alternate explanation is simply that females may be innately more sensitive to nonverbal cues, or at least predisposed to learning such cues quickly. From an evolutionary standpoint, there would be selective value in such sensitivity for the survival of offspring. In addition to these two contrasting speculations, gender differences in decoding might also be linked to any one of a number of factors that are correlated with gender, such as personality or various socialization practices.

The results on encoding differences may be less clear, but they also suggest some advantage for females in encoding accuracy, at least in some dimensions of expression. Specifically, females may be better encoders of spontaneous facial expressions of affect than males (Buck, 1975; Buck, Savin, Miller, & Caul, 1972; Fugita, Harper, & Wiens, 1980; Woolfolk, Abrams, Abrams, & Wilson, 1979). To the extent that these results are reliable, two contributing factors may determine the advantage of females in encoding accuracy. First, some research suggests that more accurate encoders show less physiological reactivity to emotional stimuli than less accurate encoders do (Buck et al., 1972; Notarius & Levenson, 1979). Although this seems counterintuitive at first glance, Buck (1980) suggests that the active *inhibition* of outward expression may contribute to greater physiological reactivity. Presumably feelings of guilt and anxiety about the inappropriate expression of emotions trigger increased arousal. Because males in our culture are usually taught to be internalizers of affect, by hiding or masking their emotion, they are more likely to be less expressive outwardly, and at the same time, more reactive physiologically than females are. Results from one study by Buck (1977) on children 4 to 6 years of age support this kind of social learning basis for sex differences in encoding. Specifically, Buck found a negative correlation between age and encoder accuracy for the boys but not for the girls. This pattern is what one would expect if boys in the 4 to 6 age range are gradually being taught to inhibit their expressiveness.

A final qualification of the apparent sex differences in encoding is warranted. Most of the data on encoding differences seem to be limited to those feelings that females may appropriately express, for example, happiness, sadness, fear. Males, however, may be more accurate encoders of hostile and aggressive feelings than females are (Buck, 1977). Again, in our culture, expression of the latter feelings is probably more appropriate for males than for females. Thus, just as learned sex role orientations apparently contribute to contrasting styles of interaction, the same may be true for patterns of encoding accuracy. Finally, support for this social learning explanation of sex differences in encoding can be found in a recent study of sex role orientation and encoding accuracy. In that study, for both male and female groups, increased encoding accuracy was generally related to increased feminine scores on a test measure of masculinity-femininity (Zuckerman, DeFrank, Spiegel, & Larrance, 1982).

Personality

The pursuit of personality correlates of nonverbal involvement would seem to be a logical result of the differences each of us notices in the behavior of others. (This discussion of personality correlates of nonverbal involvement is adapted from Patterson, 1982b.) Even the layman's description of the "pushy" acquaintance or the "reserved" coworker clearly suggests relevant behavioral manifestations of these characteristics. Our personal experiences with others certainly suggest that people tend to behave consistently over time, but is this also the case with specific forms of nonverbal involvement? A few studies have demonstrated clear evidence for the stability of selected behaviors over time. For example, in two separate studies examining the stability of approach distances in interview settings, the correlations between the first and second approaches were approximately $r = .90$ (Daniell & Lewis, 1972; Patterson, 1973a). This very high degree of stability for approach distances to the same interviewer was manifested for intervals from 20 minutes to 2 weeks. When different interviewers were used for the two sessions, the stability coefficients still averaged $r = .80$ (Daniell & Lewis, 1972). Data on gazing behaviors also indicate high levels of stability, both within a given interaction (Kendon & Cook, 1969; Libby, 1970) and across interactions (Daniell & Lewis, 1972; Patterson, 1973a). Finally, there is evidence that the degree of forward lean and body orientation in seated interactions are relatively stable over time, though perhaps less stable than approach distance and gaze (Patterson, 1973a).

These findings on intraindividual stability over time indicate that people apparently do use at least some of their involvement behaviors in a consistent manner over time. This, however, does not mean that situational influences such as the type of setting or activity or varying role relationships cannot modify a stable pattern of nonverbal involvement. These influences will be discussed later in this chapter.

Because of the considerable volume of research on personality correlates of nonverbal behavior, this discussion will be somewhat selective in the studies examined. A broad dichotomy can be suggested regarding the focus of the research on personality and nonverbal involvement; namely, (1) comparisons between normal and abnormal populations, and (2) comparisons between personality types within normal populations.

Normal-abnormal differences. There is considerable evidence that psychiatric patients, particularly those diagnosed as schizophrenic or depressive, generally show less social involvement with others than do normal subjects. In fact, such patterns may be at the very basis of these psychiatric diagnoses. Noninvolvement or even avoidance among psychiatric patients may be manifested by larger interpersonal distances (Horowitz, Duff, & Stratton, 1964; Sommer, 1959), nonconfronting body orientations (Sommer, 1959), and distinctly lower levels of gaze directed at others (Rutter & Stephenson, 1972; Waxer, 1974).

The dynamics underlying the differences in gaze were examined in an interesting study by Williams (1974) on normal and schizophrenic patients. Williams sought to determine if the lower level of gaze initiated by schizophrenic patients was part of a general pattern of avoidance of a wide range of environmental stimuli, or was specific to the avoidance of people only. The former alternative is consistent with the view that schizophrenics are habitually overstimulated by input from the environment, whereas the latter alternative focuses the problem more narrowly in the interpersonal domain. The study involved observing gaze patterns in schizophrenic and control subjects in a waiting room. The control subjects were a mix of nonschizophrenic patients and a small number of hospital employees. The salient gaze targets were either a television program or the confederate. In the first part of the waiting period, when the confederate was silent, the proportions of television watching and occasional confederate-directed glances were comparable in the two groups of subjects. When the confederate tried to initiate a casual, impersonal conversation, however, substantial differences appeared in the gaze patterns of the schizophrenic and control subjects. Although confederate-directed gaze increased in both groups, the increase in the control group was noticeably greater. At the same time, the decrease in television watching in response to the confederate's comments was much less for the schizophrenic subjects. These findings are consistent with the suggestion that the schizophrenic's gaze aversion is specific to other people and not indicative of a broader stimulus avoidance pattern.

More recent work by Rutter (1977, 1978), however, suggests that the duration and timing of gaze by schizophrenics is really comparable to that of normals. Specifically, Rutter suggests that gaze avoidance may be more a product of focusing conversations on their problems, which are personally embarrassing, than a product of stable individual styles. Thus, the schizophrenics may be responding just as normals would if the normals had to discuss personally embarrassing issues. This interpretation cannot account for the differences found in the Williams (1974) study, but it may identify a potential confound occasionally present in comparing the behavior of normal and schizophrenic subjects, namely, the degree of potential embarrassment in typical conversations involving the two groups.

Extreme levels of interpersonal avoidance may be typical of a very different kind of abnormal group—violent individuals. In separate studies, two with adult male prisoners (Kinzel, 1970; Roger & Schalekamp, 1976) and another with underachieving male adolescents (Newman & Pollack, 1973), aggressive subjects reacted much more strongly to an approaching experimenter than did the nonaggressive subjects. The differences were particularly striking in Kinzel's study with prisoners. In this study, the male experimenter sequentially approached each prisoner from eight different directions until the subject told him to stop. The average area required by the aggressive prisoner was over 4 times that required by the nonaggressive prisoner. This contrast was clearly not just the product of some casual cognitive assessment.

Kinzel reported that several of the violent prisoners reported perceiving the experimenter "rushing" or "looming" at them as he walked closer. Others clenched their fists, experienced goose pimples, or had to turn around to view the experimenter when he approached them from behind. The difference between the violent and nonviolent groups was greater for approaches from the rear. Kinzel proposed that the larger approach distance required from behind reflected concern about homosexual attack, a realistic fear in the prison environment. But if it is assumed that an individual is generally more vulnerable to an attack from behind, simple concern for personal safety may sensitize one to approaches from behind.

Differences within normal populations. Research on personality correlates of nonverbal involvement has been voluminous. Instead of merely sampling some representative number of studies from this research, I will concentrate on a few dimensions that offer some promise for theoretical development. A first dimension is one that may be described as *social approach-avoidance.* Social approach-avoidance is a convenient descriptive label for a dimension that includes affiliation, introversion-extraversion, and social anxiety. Although these three characteristics are nominally distinct, empirical evidence suggests they are highly related. Specifically, a factor-analytic study of these dimensions showed that a majority of items from scales of affiliation, introversion-extraversion, and social anxiety loaded on a common social approach-avoidance factor (Patterson & Strauss, 1972). Consequently, the discrete findings on these three characteristics may reflect a pattern relating a more general social approach-avoidance dimension to nonverbal involvement. This pattern is manifested in a variety of different results.

For example, individuals scoring higher on affiliation scales apparently prefer closer seating arrangements than do low scorers (Mehrabian & Diamond, 1971a; Clore, Note 6). There is also some evidence that high affiliative females look more at others (Exline, 1963). Ellsworth and Ludwig (1972), however, suggest that such an effect may depend on the subject's expectations of approval. Specifically, those anticipating approval may look more than those who do not. The relationship between nonverbal involvement and extraversion parallels that described for affiliation. Extraverts choose closer seating distances than introverts (Cook, 1970; Pedersen, 1973a; Patterson & Holmes, Note 7) and engage in higher levels of eye contact (Kendon & Cook, 1969; Mobbs, 1968). In summarizing the research on vocal cues and personality, Siegman (1978) reported that extraversion has been consistently related to a louder speaking voice and a faster tempo of speech. Also, extraversion is correlated with a high amount of speaking (Campbell & Rushton, 1978). Research on social anxiety indicates that those who score highly on social anxiety behave as the low-affiliation and introverted subjects do. Specifically, increased levels of social anxiety have been marginally related to more distant approaches (Patterson, 1973b, 1977a) and to decreased talking and gaze (Daly, 1978) in interview settings. Although much of the evidence relating each of these three personality dimensions to nonverbal involvement indicates only weak to moderate relationships, the convergence among these dimensions provides more general support for the predictive validity of a common social approach-avoidance dimension.

A second important personality dimension is that of *internal-external locus of control*. This dimension was introduced by Rotter (1966) who drew a contrast between internals, individuals who perceive themselves as generally being in control of their own fate, and externals, individuals who perceive themselves as generally being subject to forces outside of themselves. Duke and Nowicki (1972) examined the relationship between locus of control and the regulation of interpersonal distance. They proposed that the combined effect of internal-external control and situational expectancies influences the degree of preferred closeness to others. Specifically, internals and externals are predicted to act similarly in situations in which clear expectancies are present for the reactions of others, for example, interacting with friends or relatives. In settings for which specific expectancies are not available (e.g., interacting with strangers), however, externals will be more reserved and distant than internals. If Duke and Nowicki's model is extended to other behaviors, a general prediction can be offered that externals, compared to internals, will prefer lower levels of involvement because of the lack of control they feel when interacting with strangers.

Although results from two studies reported by Duke and Nowicki (1972) supported these predicted differences in distancing by internals and externals, results from another recent study are in apparent conflict with Duke and Nowicki's predictions. In the latter study, externals talked more and looked at one another more than internals (Rajecki, Ickes, & Tanford, 1981). In this case, however, increased talking and looking by externals may result from an increased need for social comparison. If externals are less confident and feel less in control, then talking with and looking at others may permit them to benefit from the experience of others. Finally, there is evidence that internal-locus-of-control subjects are more assertive in the manner (paralinguistic level) than in the content (verbal level) of their conversations, whereas the opposite pattern holds for external-locus-of-control subjects (Bugenthal, Henker, & Whalen, 1976). Because the paralinguistic channel may be more influential in transmitting one's intention or motivation than the verbal channel, internals may be more effective in managing assertiveness or power.

As the situational or role expectancies become more structured, a generalized locus of control expectancy should have less impact on the initiation of nonverbal involvement. In other words, the interaction of locus of control and role expectancies may better predict nonverbal involvement than either dimension in isolation.

The dimension of *field dependence-independence* is one that has substantial relevance for a wide variety of social behaviors. The field dependence-independence dimension contrasts individuals whose cognitive styles reflect reliance either on external referents (field dependent) or on internal referents (field independent). Thus, the independent person has a clearer differentiation of his or her own self from others than the field-dependent person has. In terms of social behavior, this dimension implies greater autonomy in social relations for the field-independent person, and a greater reliance on others for the field-dependent person (Witkin & Goodenough, 1977).

Given these general differences we might expect that field-dependent persons would prefer greater involvement with others than field-independent persons. In fact, three different unpublished dissertations cited by Witkin and Goodenough (1977) showed such a contrast in subjects' use of interpersonal distance. In two studies, field-dependent subjects stood closer to the person with whom they interacted than did field-independent subjects (Holley, 1972; Justice, 1969). In the third study, field-dependent subjects emitted more dependency behaviors, such as palms-up gesturing, lip and tongue activity, and mouth touching, when seated at 5 feet than at 2 feet (Greene, 1973). In contrast, field-independent subjects did not increase their use of the dependency behaviors at the greater distance. Field-dependent people may also gaze at others more than field-independent people (Konstadt & & Forman, 1965; Nevill, 1974).

If field-dependent individuals do prefer higher levels of involvement with others than field independents, this pattern may be the result of either or both of two related motives. First, field-dependent individuals may simply prefer greater involvement with others because their perceptions of themselves are more likely to be linked to their relationships with others. Consequently, they may be more comfortable with high-involvement exchanges than are field-independent individuals. Alternately, because field-dependent people seem to rely more on others for information, higher levels of involvement may facilitate the social comparison necessary to obtain information.

The dimension of *self-monitoring* (Snyder, 1974) is another personality characteristic that may be especially relevant for the management of nonverbal involvement. Snyder describes those who score highly on self-monitoring as concerned about both effective self-presentation and adjustment to others in social settings. More specifically, high self-monitors endorse items reflecting concern with the social appropriateness of their self-presentation, sensitivity to changing situational cues, and an ability to modify self-presentation to fit differing purposes. Such a dimension should have considerable relevance for managing one's level of nonverbal involvement. In fact, Lippa (1976) found that high self-monitoring subjects were generally better able to control their expressive behavior by facilitating the expression of more desirable characteristics, while inhibiting the expression of less desirable characteristics (e.g., anxiety). Self-monitoring may also affect other aspects of interaction behavior. In one study, high self-monitoring subjects were more likely to talk first, initiate later conversational sequences, feel more self-conscious about their behavior, and use their partner's behavior as a guide for their own actions (Ickes & Barnes, 1977).

The description of the self-monitoring dimension and the results just cited do not suggest a simple relationship between self-monitoring and nonverbal involvement. Rather, an increased level of self-monitoring should be related to both an increased awareness to social cues and an ability to manage one's nonverbal involvement. Thus, the high self-monitoring individual's concern with social appropriateness may result in high levels of nonverbal involvement in one setting and low levels in another. Finally, although self-monitoring may offer considerable promise for identifying individual style differences in social interaction, a recent factor-analytic study of the self-monitoring scale suggests that the scale is not a unidimensional one (Gabrenya & Arkin, 1980). It is interesting to note that one, and possibly two, of the factors identified by Gabrenya and Arkin appear to be comparable to the social approach-avoidance dimension discussed earlier.

Other Personal Factors

There are, of course, a number of other personal factors that may contribute to distinct patterns of involvement in social interactions. One that has been researched in some detail is that of age. For example, Aiello and Aiello (1974) note that as children grow older they use larger distances in relating to others in interactions. Decreased involvement is also reflected in a decline in the use of touch by children as they grow older (Willis & Hoffman, 1975; Willis & Reeves, 1976). In general, it appears that by the adolescent years children are closely approximating adult norms of interpersonal involvement.

Various other factors, such as socioeconomic class, occupation, or religion, may also affect habitual patterns of nonverbal involvement. Although there may be little systematic research on these factors, personal experience certainly suggests that differences on some of these characteristics contribute to differences in expressing nonverbal involvement. In some cases the resulting patterns appear to be very affected presentations. A good example might be the casual intimacy suggested by the greetings common among show business people. In the fall of 1982, these stereotyped exchanges were satirically portrayed by Garry Trudeau in the *Doonesbury* comic strip. In one scene, Duke, the slightly crazy, greedy, but definitely not "in" character, meets his old boyhood acquaintance Sid who made good in Hollywood. Duke's outstretched hand is ignored by Sid who gives him a hug and a kiss. Sid responds to Duke's bewilderment by reminding him that he's in California now. In this instance such casual use of tactile involvement is probably a product of both occupation and geographical location. In any case, it is a greeting between acquaintances that would not be typical of people in most other occupations and locations.

Experiential Factors

Experiential factors identify the residual influence of recent and/or similar experiences on later interactions. The mechanisms mediating these experiential influences seem to emphasize either learning-reinforcement or stimulation regulation explanations. The experiential influence of learning or reinforcement may be either vicarious (social learning) or direct (operant or classical conditioning). In the former instance, one might observe the interpersonal behavior of another individual and weigh the consequences of this pattern. For example, a recently recruited salesperson may watch the skillful and highly involving behavioral routine of a seasoned salesperson. Obviously, if this routine is successful, the probability increases that the newcomer will adopt it. The opposite should be true for a behavioral routine that is unsuccessful. The influence of direct reinforcement on one's own behavior is obvious. Successful patterns of involvement will tend to be repeated, whereas unsuccessful ones will not. Such very general comments have to be qualified by the relationships between people and the setting constraints. A pattern of high involvement with a good friend may produce a favorable response, but if the same pattern were initiated toward one's boss, it would probably be seen as inappropriate, especially in the work setting.

Recent social experiences may also be important because of their residual effects of overstimulation (Milgram, 1970) or understimulation. That is, from a stimulation-regulation perspective, one can assume that deviations from some optimum level of involvement over time produce compensatory adjustments in the future. This kind of homeostatic mechanism is similar to that proposed in equilibrium theory (Argyle & Dean, 1965). In the case of equilibrium theory, the predicted adjustments immediately follow the partner's behavior, whereas the experiential focus extends these effects and their adjustments over time. Thus, several intense, highly involving interactions (particularly if they are also negatively toned) should produce overstimulation that, in turn, leads to a temporary avoidance of additional stimulating interactions. In contrast, the lack of adequately stimulating interactions should result in an individual exerting greater effort to initiate such exchanges.

To the extent that interactants do not share common recent experiences, experiences may contribute to present interaction in a fashion that the interaction partner finds difficult to anticipate or understand. Chapple (1970, pp. 115-121) discusses some of the complex dynamics associated with mutual adjustments in interaction rhythms over time. Chapple notes that our interactional experiences and adjustments develop on a foundation of personal stimulation preferences that may be determined by personality or other individual difference factors. Thus, what is overstimulating for one individual is understimulating for another. Daily patterns of interaction may be superimposed on these individual stimulation preferences to determine each person's approximation of the optimal level of interaction. As we move from the individual as a unit to the pair as a social system, however, the potential difficulties for developing a comfortable meshing of preferences are obvious. As daily experiences run counter to preferred levels of interactional involvement, the adjustments of both members of a pair may be directly opposing.

A variation on an example Chapple cites is the harried wife who comes home to her househusband after a hard day at the office. The husband, however, has had only limited interaction with the baby and the cat and feels a need to have some meaningful conversation with his wife. Developing a mutually satisfying exchange will probably be difficult under such circumstances because each person's dominant adjustment runs counter to the other person's dominant adjustment.

Another homeostatic perspective that might be used to describe the effects of recent experience on patterns of involvement is Altman's (1975) privacy-regulation model. Altman proposed that each individual is motivated to achieve his or her own desired level of privacy as closely as possible. In attempting to achieve this desired level of privacy, a person may adjust his or her own verbal and nonverbal behavior to approximate the desired privacy. Thus, if one is unable to achieve sufficient privacy, the experience should lead to decreased involvement with others. The successful completion of a complex, solitary task in a setting with many others present may require deliberate avoidance of others. In contrast, if one were trying to get social comparison information from others, the desired privacy level might be very low. In such a case increased involvement with others would be sought. In effect, when the discrepancy between ideal and objective privacy levels is sufficiently large, behavioral adjustments in involvement may be initiated to reduce such a discrepancy. Thus, a negative feedback mechanism provides the means for evaluating recent experience.

Finally, it may be noted that a different perspective in experiential influences, namely, Helson's (1964) adaptation level (AL) approach, seems to make predictions that are in direct opposition to those of a stimulation-based homeostatic model. In particular, AL theory predicts that successive deviations from the AL (weighted average) of past involvement become incorporated into a new AL. The result is that additional experiences at the same "objective" level of involvement are perceived as less extreme. If this were the case, then continued overstimulation should result in the gradual formation of a new higher AL for involvement. Repeated instances of the same level of involvement should produce milder adjustments because this involvement level is not perceived to be as extreme.

Although there has been little systematic research on the influence of past experience on later involvement patterns, there is no doubt that past experience does influence subsequent behavior. Stimulation-regulation and AL explanations of past experience predict distinctly different processes and outcomes affecting nonverbal behavior. Obviously, an examination of such issues requires measurement of nonverbal involvement over time and across different circumstances. It seems likely that the demands posed by this kind of research have discouraged such studies. Nevertheless, the experiential changes represent an important influence on developing patterns of nonverbal behavior, influences that deserve closer attention.

Relational-Situational Factors

Although relational and situational factors independently affect nonverbal involvement, it is appropriate to consider them jointly because each interacts with the other. Thus, the effect of relationship on nonverbal involvement is often moderated by the nature of the setting. The discussion of the intimacy function in Chapter 5 included a substantial amount of research on relationship and nonverbal involvement. The general pattern of increased involvement with increasingly intimate relationships is not characteristic of all exchanges. For example, interactions between males are less affected by relationship intimacy than are those involving females. The role of situational influences further qualifies generalizations about relationships. Although there is little research directly on the interactive effects of Relationship X Situation, a discussion of situational influences on nonverbal involvement should facilitate an appreciation of potential Relationship X Situation effects.

The behavior setting approach of ecological psychology (Barker, 1968; Wicker, 1979) provides one perspective for analyzing situational variables. The ecological approach stresses the role of physical, social, and selection characteristics of a setting in contributing to the homogeneity of behavior across individuals. At a very general level, different kinds of people are attracted to different kinds of settings. That is, individuals can take the initiative in entering one or another setting. At the same time, the setting (or more accurately, the people who control the setting) can selectively admit individuals to its activities. Thus, entrance to and participation in the behavioral program of a neighborhood bar, a local political group, or a church's annual picnic is a joint product of one's interest and the setting's approval of one's admission. In many cases, the selection criteria for the setting may be minimal, for example, meeting a minimum age requirement or simply having the price of admission. In other cases, the minimal standards may be very demanding and permit entrance to only a small number of people. An example of such criteria might be the superior IQ required of MENSA members or the $25,000 initiation fee at a posh country club. Obviously, the more exclusive the membership in a particular setting, the more the members will have in common. This increased communality should, in turn, be reflected in greater behavioral homogeneity among its members. When the mutual self-selection and setting-selection processes are complemented by both the design constraints and the normative or social constraints in a structured situation, the contribution of individual difference factors to nonverbal involvement may be minimized.

Another situational mechanism that interacts with relationship variables is that of territoriality. Altman (1975, chaps. 7 & 8) discusses the role of territory in a variety of circumstances and notes that territory frequently serves as a social-regulation mechanism. In contrast to the naive assumption that territoriality may contribute to conflict and disruption, Altman provides evidence that conflict is actually reduced when territorial claims are stabilized.

More interesting in terms of the interaction of Situation X Relationship is the effect of territory on the dominance and control of an exchange. We are all sensitive to the location of the interactions we have with family, friends, acquaintances, or coworkers. In our own territories (e.g., at one's home or office), we are typically more comfortable, relaxed, and in control than we are in the territory of others. It is also likely that the territory holder can more easily manage his or her own preferred involvement level, the pace of the exchange, and the termination of the exchange. In fact, being in one's own territory may help to equalize an exchange that might otherwise favor the partner in a more neutral setting. For example, when an employee hosts a cocktail party in his or her own home, it is comfortable and appropriate to initiate higher levels of involvement with the boss than those that might be common at the office. In effect, the territory holder has greater flexibility in behavior at home than at other locations.

The fact that almost all empirical research has been limited to a single situation at a time makes an assessment of the interactive effects of Relationship X Situation obviously difficult. Nevertheless, we can expect that the patterns of nonverbal involvement that are characteristic of various relationships in one setting may be different in another setting. Finally, it might be noted that, as empirical research begins to sample behavior patterns across different kinds of settings, the potential generalizability of results will simultaneously increase. This increased generalizability or external validity is a goal of research that critics of social psychology have strongly urged in recent years.

The Mediation of Antecedent Influences

Thus far, the discussion in this chapter has emphasized the behavioral correlates of personal, experiential, and relational-situational factors. The mediators that more directly determine the course of nonverbal involvement—behavioral predispositions, potential arousal change, and cognitive-affective assessment—were discussed briefly in the second chapter's presentation of the functional model. An appreciation of the role of the antecedent factors in interaction requires a closer look at these mediators.

First, behavioral predispositions represent habitual, relatively stable tendencies for enacting behavioral involvement. These predispositions set some broad limits on the potential range of involvement initiated by each person. In general, it is presumed that individual or group differences such as those included in the personal factors (culture, gender, personality) determine such habitual tendencies for nonverbal involvement. For example, individuals from contact cultures, females, and extraverts typically prefer higher levels of involvement than opposing types of individuals. Generally, it might be expected that contrasting predispositions are more likely to result in greater instability of exchange over time than are similar predispositions. In such a circumstance, each person's preferred level of involvement might be outside the other person's comfortable range. The result is likely to be a series of compensatory adjustments that leave one or the other partner uncomfortable. Such a prediction is also consistent with Cappella and Greene's (1982) discrepancy-arousal model. Of course there may be exceptions to such a series of ineffective adjustments that leave each person uncomfortable. That may not be the case when the partners assume complementary roles that are consistent with contrasting patterns of involvement, for example, the superior who initiates high involvement and the subordinate who remains aloof and passive.

Generally, it is presumed that behavioral predispositions are not explicitly represented in cognitive awareness. In effect, such habitual tendencies are a given, about which there is little need to reflect. Even when an individual may be sensitized to a condition of instability in an exchange, it is unlikely that the instability will be attributed to one's own behavioral patterns. Rather, the actor is likely to attribute the problem to the situation or to the partner. Thus, a person's behavioral predispositions for nonverbal involvement will most commonly be classified as indicative, that is, spontaneous and nonreflective.

The initiation of arousal change, the second preinteraction mediator, usually occurs in tandem with the cognitive-affective assessment. Undifferentiated arousal change may precipitate the cognitive-affective assessment, or the opposite occurs—the cognitive-affective assessment leads to arousal change. The former sequence describes the pattern proposed by Schachter and Singer (1962) in their theory of emotions. Although such a sequence is obviously possible, it seems more likely that the opposite pattern is more common. That is, typically, changes in an interactive pattern by one individual are recognized and have a meaning at some level by the other individual. This meaning, in turn, can precipitate an arousal change that may require some further cognitive work. Thus, the proposed dominance of the latter sequence suggests that arousal change is more likely an effect than a cause of some cognitive work.

Finally, it should be mentioned that arousal change is important not only for its link to cognitive-affective assessment, but also for its role in facilitating a dominant response. An example of this last circumstance is a situation in which the high involvement of another is threatening. A dominant response under threatening circumstances might be flight from the situation or, at least, compensatory avoidance. Without the accompanying arousal such avoidance responses would be less intense and probably occur with a longer latency.

The influence of the last mediator, cognitive-affective assessment, on subsequent interactions has long been a concern for researchers in social psychology. Frequently, preinteraction expectancies or attributions have a substantial effect on the development of an interaction. For example, Kelley's (1950) classic study showed that students who were led to believe that their guest instructor was a cold person not only rated him as a colder and more distant person, but initiated less discussion with him than students who had been led to believe that he was a warm person. One form that this preinteraction expectancy may take is the self-fulfilling prophecy (e.g., Merton, 1948, 1957; Rosenthal, 1966; Rosenthal & Jacobson, 1968) or behavioral confirmation process (Snyder, Tanke, & Berscheid, 1977). Such a process would involve the perceiver's acquisition of an expectancy that affects his or her behavior toward the target in such a way as to elicit a pattern of reciprocated behavior. In turn, this reciprocated behavior appears to confirm the validity of the original expectancy. Further, the perceiver is typically unaware that his or her expectancy may be inaccurate, and unaware that his or her own behavior plays a role in influencing the target's confirmatory behavior (Snyder, Tanke, & Berscheid, 1977).

The opposing pattern, reflecting a behavioral compensation strategy, was discussed in some detail in Chapter 6. The likelihood of one or the other strategy predominating is probably a product both of the anticipated outcome (positive or negative) and the potential for affecting that outcome. Specifically, when the anticipated outcome of the interaction is positive, there is no need to expend compensatory efforts to ensure such an outcome. Similarly, if the anticipated outcome is negative, but one cannot change that outcome, no compensatory effort will be initiated. A behavioral compensation strategy may be expected only when the anticipated outcome is negative, but modifiable. For example, in the Ickes, Patterson, Rajecki, and Tanford (1982) and Bond (1972) studies, subjects apparently initiated greater involvement in an attempt to improve an anticipated uncomfortable interaction with an unfriendly partner.

Of course, our cognitions about an anticipated interaction are not limited solely to the person with whom we may be interacting. Occasionally, information about the situation may be particularly influential in affecting our behavior. For example, Baum and Greenberg (1975) found that subjects expecting to be in a crowded group chose more remote (low-involvement) seating arrangements than those without such expectations. Similarly, the anticipation of entering a specifically defined behavior setting like a party, a funeral, or a meeting with superiors probably leads to the initiation of differing involvement strategies appropriate to the setting. Whether one attributes such behavioral patterns to the enactment of scripted behavior (Schank & Abelson, 1977) or self-presentation strategies (Goffman, 1967, 1972), the effect is the same—knowledge about the setting affects the pattern of behavioral involvement. More important, knowledge about the setting allows the individual to *initiate* behavioral strategies, not merely react to others in the setting.

An Overview of Antecedent Influences

Although it is convenient to describe and analyze the antecedent influences in isolation, they obviously do not naturally occur this way. Different factors interact with one another to produce unique effects on the involvement patterns observed. At this point, it may be helpful to describe some ways in which the various antecedent factors combine to produce their effects. At the most elementary level, the antecedent influences, especially the personal factors, structure interaction through a variety of self-, other-, and setting-selection processes.

Culture, gender, personality, age, and socioeconomic class are characteristics that predictably determine a variety of selection mechanisms. For example, the fact that one lives in a Western, industrialized country typically provides individuals with a greater potential variety of social experiences than those who live in a primitive society. That is not a judgment of the value of the contrasting societies, but merely a description of the variety of settings available in those cultures. Pervasive cultural differences lead both to the differential availability of activities and settings and to different norms for similar settings and activities.

These cultural constraints are, in turn, further specified by gender, personality, age, and socioeconomic class influences. Complementary selection pressures from the setting and the individual result in different kinds of people inhabiting practically different worlds within the same culture. For example, in spite of changing sex role norms, females are still more likely to be secretaries or nurses than are males. In contrast, males are more likely to be lumberjacks or stock car racers than are females. Introverted, nonassertive individuals are probably less likely to choose careers, and be chosen for positions, in sales than are extraverted, assertive individuals. Few senior citizens will be found scrambling up and down the slides at playgrounds, just as there are few children at Gray Panther meetings. In a similar fashion blue-collar workers are distinctly underrepresented in yachting clubs as are the very wealthy in bus stations.

Although these examples are extreme ones, they are characteristic of the kinds of contrasts that may be found in different settings as a function of a complex of individual difference variables. In general, the more unique one's personal characteristics, the more likely it is that one will have a more limited range of social contacts, and these typically with similar others. Such selectivity operates even on those who are wealthy or powerful, not simply on the poor or weak. There is, however, an important difference in the source of the selection pressure. Those who are wealthy or powerful actively *choose not* to enter the settings of the poor or powerless. In contrast, the settings of the wealthy and powerful *exclude* the poor or powerless. Thus, for the upper class, the initiative for selection rests with them, whereas this is not the case for the lower class.

Once entry into a setting is secured, antecedent factors exert a more direct influence on specific involvement patterns with others in that setting. The earlier review in this chapter described the particular isolated effects of personal, experiential, and relational-situational factors on nonverbal exchange. But just as the antecedent factors combine to produce unique effects on selection pressures for entering various settings, the same factors combine to produce unique effects on patterns of nonverbal involvement once individuals are in the setting. For example, the personality dimension of introversion-extraversion may interact with the experiential factor to reinforce contrasting patterns of involvement. That is, chronic arousal level differences between introverts and extraverts may mediate the initiation of contrasting involvement patterns. If, as Eysenck (1967) suggests, introverts are more easily aroused by a variety of stimulus situations than are extraverts, then comparable patterns of involvement (high or low) will produce contrasting experiences for the two groups. A pattern of high involvement initiated by a partner may produce over-arousal and avoidance in the introvert, but optimal arousal and approach in the extravert. Future similar interactions will probably precipitate anticipatory strategies consistent with the earlier outcomes. That is, introverts will attempt to minimize involvement and extraverts will attempt to maximize it.

In a similar fashion, other antecedent factors will interact to determine specific effects on involvement patterns. The potential combinations of these factors are too diverse to cover here. It is clear, however, that a simplistic consideration of each of the antecedent factors in isolation will not provide a satisfactory appreciation of the practical influence of these factors.

A comparison of the focused effects of the antecedent factors on the interaction stage itself provides some interesting contrasts. The behavioral predispositions, structured by the personal factors, reflect an individual's characteristic patterns of nonverbal involvement. Such habitual patterns typically operate outside awareness and, in the absence of any behavioral management, determine the initiation of an exchange. These behavioral predispositions not only limit an individual's typical involvement level, but also help to structure the person's expectancies about the involvement of others. That is, each individual's own preferred level of involvement contributes to the development of a norm for the anticipated involvement of others. Thus, the extravert not only prefers greater involvement with others, but may also view higher involvement from others as appropriate. In effect, behavioral predispositions influence both the characteristic patterns of involvement and the expectancies about appropriate involvement from others. Furthermore, as Cappella and Greene (1982) note, the greater the discrepancy between the anticipated involvement of each party, the greater the probability that compensatory adjustments will result.

The experiential and relational-situational factors are more likely to precipitate some cognitive activity that may trigger functional attributions about the interaction. In such a circumstance, the functional assessment may override the influence of the behavioral predispositions. For example, even though I may be introverted, I know that my potential success in a job interview depends on my being friendly, outgoing, and assertive. Thus, the social control assessment of the job interview is sufficient to stimulate an extraverted performance. Obviously, *if* I do not have the skill to initiate such a performance, knowing that I *should* act extraverted will do little for me. In practice, the joint influence of one's habitual level of involvement and one's functional cognitions determines the development of an exchange. To the extent that cognitive expectancies are explicit and important, it might generally be predicted that the functional attributions will be more critical in the exchange than behavioral predispositions.

Summary

In this chapter the role of the antecedent factors in developing interaction patterns was reviewed and analyzed. Most of the discussion focused on the personal factors —culture, gender, and personality—because of the voluminous research on these variables. It was proposed that the substantial influence of personal factors was manifested primarily in behavioral predispositions, and as such, this influence did not typically register in cognitive awareness. In contrast, it was proposed that the experiential factors and, more importantly, the relational-situational factors have a directing cognitive component. That is, evaluative cognitions about past experience, particular relationships, or the situation may help to determine patterns of nonverbal involvement. Specifically, these evaluative cognitions are basic to the development of functional attributions concerning an interaction. An understanding of the functional bases for nonverbal exchange would seem to be more dependent on analyzing the influence of the experiential and relational-situational factors than on analyzing the influence of the personal factors. Unfortunately, research up to the present has not focused enough on the experiential and relational-situational factors. It may be hoped that an emphasis on a functional perspective will change this condition.

Chapter 9

An Overview: Problems and Prospects

The functional perspective outlined in this book attempts to provide a relatively comprehensive and integrative approach to understanding nonverbal behavior. The circumstance that precipitated this effort included a vast inventory of empirical research linked only occasionally to limited theoretical models. Of course, I am responsible for some of the previous theoretical deficiencies in this area. The intimacy-arousal model (Patterson, 1976) may have been an improvement on equilibrium theory (Argyle & Dean, 1965), but it now seems too simplistic and mechanical in light of the complexity of nonverbal exchange. In addition, the results of more recent research, some of it from our own laboratory (Ickes, Patterson, Rajecki, & Tanford, 1982; Patterson, Roth, & Schenk, 1979; Patterson, Jordan, Hogan, & Frerker, 1981), highlighted some of the weaknesses of the earlier models and provided direction for developing this functional approach. An overview of the present model might proceed best by first attending to a general evaluation of the functional perspective.

Evaluating the Functional Perspective

Before specific issues relating to the present model are addressed, it may be helpful to evaluate the utility of the functional perspective in general. At least three major advantages of a functional perspective may be proposed. First, a functional perspective pursues the issue of the purpose behind specific behavioral patterns. Such an approach coincides with the recent emphasis in psychology on the directing effects of cognitions on behavior. It should be noted that a functional perspective, in analyzing purpose, emphasizes primarily the *reasons* underlying behavior. In the present model, the reasons may be generally classified into the intimacy, social control, and service-task categories. This is not the place to review the controversy regarding the distinction between reasons and causes (see Buss, 1978, 1979; Harvey & Tucker, 1979; Kruglanski, 1979). But attention to the purpose or reason behind behavior provides an opportunity to recognize the individual's initiative in behavioral sequences. That is, one's involvement patterns may be seen as more than mere mechnical reactions to the behavioral input of another person. Instead, these patterns are often part of a larger context of meaningful, coordinated behavioral sequences.

A second general advantage of the functional perspective is its compatibility with a multivariate description of nonverbal behavior. Much of the research on nonverbal behavior has been developed and analyzed from a channel approach. Empirical studies often focus on only one behavior at a time and, in doing so, ignore the underlying processes common across different behaviors. Consequently, it is easy to isolate research on distance from that on gaze, and each, in turn, from the research on touch. It should be obvious, however, that the significance of any channel is necessarily dependent on the behavioral context provided by the other channels. Although there are exceptions, in general, the behavior of others is meaningful to the extent that it is reflected in an organized pattern, not simply in an isolated cue.

A third advantage of the functional perspective is that it can provide a framework for applying our considerable knowledge about interpersonal processes to the analysis of nonverbal behavior. That is, research on a variety of social psychological processes can suggest specific dynamics that are characteristic of different functions. For example, research on attraction, impression formation, or helping behavior may provide insights into motivation related to the intimacy function. Research on persuasion, conflict, aggression, leadership, and impression management may be especially relevant for understanding social control motives. A beneficial consequence of developing this link between the nonverbal literature and the general social psychology literature is the opportunity for promoting a more comprehensive view of social behavior. Specifically, the nonverbal researcher may be sensitized to the broader social processes that mediate nonverbal exchange. In addition, the social psychology researchers may be sensitized to some of the more subtle behavioral manifestations of the processes they study.

This functional perspective is not without its limitations, and these, too, must be considered. First, it is important to realize that inferences about functions are often very tentative and based on minimal evidence. A basic issue here is simply whether or not such intentions are available in one's awareness. Nisbett and Wilson (1977), in their critique of research on the verbal reporting of mental processes, conclude that in many situations people cannot accurately verbalize the cognitive processes that apparently guided their behavior. The issue of accessibility to one's cognitive processes or the accuracy of verbal reports about them is clearly separate from positing that such cognitive processes occur. But practical testing of hypotheses about the influence of various cognitive processes would indeed be difficult if such verbal reports were not valid. The contrasting view, however, that is, that verbal reports of cognitive processes can be valid, at least under the right conditions, has been gathering support (Cotton, 1980; Ericsson & Simon, 1980; Smith & Miller, 1978; White, 1980). A less direct, and also less reactive, way of inferring functional bases for interaction is simply to observe consistencies in behavior over time and across different actors. This is basically what Goffman (1959, 1963, 1967) has done in analyses of social behavior from a dramaturgical perspective. In Chapter 3, it was suggested that a communicative pattern (in this case typically one characteristic of a social control function) might be expected in situations in which there are one or more of the following: (a) evaluational pressures; (b) a need to relay sensitive judgments; and (c) attempts to amplify verbal reactions. Such circumstances may increase the likelihood of social control, but specific inferences about functions can obviously be unreliable.

A second concern about the functional perspective is that many behavioral sequences apparently serve more than one function. Some allowance was made for this circumstance in differentiating between the molecular functions—providing information and regulating interaction—and the molar functions—intimacy, social control, and the service-task function. Thus, it is appropriate to identify specific isolated behavioral cues as either informative or regulatory, while, at the same time, describing overall exchange in terms of one of the molar functions. Even at the molar level of describing the function of an exchange, however, it may often be the case that multiple functions are operating. Characteristic of such exchanges may be interactions between family members, loved ones, or good friends, in which the intimacy of the relationship is reflected in a generally high level of nonverbal involvement, but attempts to influence the partner are also reflected in a timely touch, gaze, and an exaggerated smile, or in a cessation of gaze and a feigned expression of dismay. The fact that some interactions are characterized by the initiation of multiple functions may say more about the complex nature of social behavior than it does about the inadequacies of this model. It must be admitted, however, that such a circumstance is a complicating one that makes the task of description and prediction more difficult.

A final consideration, related to the second issue, is the testability of the functional model. The issue of testability arose when the manuscript on the functional model was originally submitted to *Psychological Review* (Patterson, 1982a). One anonymous reviewer suggested that more focused and specific theories, like equilibrium theory, were preferable to the functional model from the standpoint of disconfirmability. Such a judgment is a fair one. Equilibrium theory is a more testable theory than the functional model. Furthermore, the dimension of testability clearly represents an important criterion for evaluating the merit of a theory. One counter to this criticism is that deficiencies in testability might be balanced by the functional model's relative comprehensiveness. A more direct reply to that criticism is my belief that the functional model does provide a fertile basis for a variety of important and testable hypotheses, even though the functional model as a whole may not be as disconfirmable as equilibrum theory. At this point, I would like to consider some of the issues that will be very important in research on the functional model. These issues relate to both methodological and substantive problems in research.

Directions for Research

Methodological Issues

Specific measures. An examination of the functional model requires that the proposed influence of the mediating factors, especially cognitive-affective assessment and arousal change, be critically evaluated. In order to accomplish this evaluation, some reliable means of measuring cognitive and arousal responses must be available. With the proper equipment, assessing arousal change in the laboratory or in a controlled environment, such as a hospital (see Whitcher & Fisher, 1979), is clearly possible. In our own research program, we have been able to monitor electrodermal responses or heart rate changes in the vast majority of subjects without undue loss from measurement problems. A small percentage of subjects may be unresponsive on a particular index (e.g., 5%-10%), and occasionally a subject will produce some movement artifacts (e.g., moving or tapping the finger on which the electrode is attached). In the former circumstance, the unresponsive subjects are dropped from an analysis. In the latter circumstance, movement artifacts can usually be identified, and if they occur infrequently they will result in a loss of only a small part of a subject's data.

The issue of the reactivity of such measures is a different, more difficult problem. Obviously, one cannot unobtrusively monitor the physiological reactions of subjects, at least not by traditional methods. But appropriate use of engaging tasks, distracting cover stories, or focusing on the waiting period before the "experiment" starts can reduce the problem of reactivity. Alternately, capitalizing on measurement in a natural setting such as a physician's office or a hospital (Whitcher & Fisher, 1979) should limit reactivity.

Assessing the mediating cognitions presents some obvious procedural difficulties. In the past, our research and that of others relied primarily on relatively structured ratings of different elements of an interaction. For example, subjects might be asked to rate how they felt, what they thought of the other subject, or how they perceived the interaction itself. These ratings were assumed to reflect thoughts and feelings present during the interaction. Although such ratings may be informative, they cannot provide much insight into *sequential* changes in thoughts and feelings, especially as they relate to specific critical changes in the patterns of nonverbal behavior. But there are means by which the assessment of sequential changes in thoughts can be accomplished.

First, it should be noted that the simple listing of thoughts for a specific interval can be managed quite easily. For example, Cacioppo and Petty's (1981b) thought-listing procedure requires subjects to record the separate thoughts they recalled from a specified period in the experiment. Cacioppo and Petty report that this measure can be reliably scored, is sensitive to experimental manipulations, and can reflect motivational changes. In work in our own laboratory, we are employing a variant of the thought-listing procedure with the help of a videotape replay of the interaction. The purpose of this technique is simply to assess changing cognitions over the period of the interaction. The subject views the replay of the interaction until a specific thought or feeling from the interaction is recalled. Then the subject simply stops the videotape and writes the thought or feeling on a response sheet. The experimenter times the replay of the videotape so that the exact time of each recalled thought may be recorded. Thus, a sequential, time-tagged log of the thoughts and feelings is possible. Subjects appear to be able to manage the recall task quite well. In addition, the variety and occasional extremity of thoughts listed suggest that some of the subjects are being very candid. For example, in our first study employing the thought assessment procedure, some male subjects listed inferences about the potential drug use of the other subject and sexual comments about the female experimenter (Patterson & Prevallet, Note 8). We have been able to score reliably the listed thoughts in terms of the target of the thought and its polarity.

There are two other indicators of general thought content or style that are worthy of mention. Although these measures do not identify specific thought content, as the thought-listing technique does, they can provide a sequential record of changes in the focus of attention. The first is a measure that classifies the form of personal pronoun usage by subjects. For example, in research by Wegner and Giuliano (1980), personal pronoun usage of subjects was examined in a sentence completion task. They found that among subjects whose arousal was increased by running in place, there was a greater frequency of first person pronouns than among control subjects. In our research, we were interested in determining if patterns of personal pronoun use in conversations were correlated with particular personality dimensions. Our results indicated that self-monitoring was negatively correlated with the frequency of first person singular pronoun use and inner directedness was negatively correlated with the frequency of third person pronoun use (Reidhead, Ickes, & Patterson, Note 9). Thus, the high self-monitor avoids too much self-reference, whereas the inner-directed person avoids third person references. This pronoun classification might also reflect changing situational or interpersonal constraints and the targets of thought associated with them. For example, will first person singular usage increase in highly evaluative circumstances (e.g., a job interview or meeting your new mother-in-law) that stimulate cognitions about self-presentation? Changes of this type might generally characterize the initiation of the social control function. In contrast, in an intimacy-focused exchange, will the first person singular pronouns decrease while first person plural and second person pronouns increase? Such a pattern might reflect a concern about either the relationship or the other person.

The second potential behavioral indicator of thought content is the electromyogram (EMG). The EMG measures the degree of muscle activity monitored through electrodes placed at specific locations on the body. In a recent article, Cacioppo and Petty (1981a) reviewed the research on EMG records of muscles controlling expressive movements in the face. Of particular interest are results related to changes in facial muscle activity over intervals in which cognitive activity should be maximized, for example, following persuasive messages. In general, Cacioppo and Petty found increased speech muscle activity both during and immediately following the presentation of persuasive messages. Presumably, cognitive responses to the persuasive message trigger the facial muscle activity. In addition, the anticipation of positive versus negative events may activate different patterns of facial muscles. Thus, EMG measures of facial muscle activity may signal not only the amount of cognitive activity, but also the valence of this activity. Such a measure might be employed in a waiting period before an interaction when the subject is isolated. In this interval the subject might be given an expectancy manipulation about the other "subject" and the EMG record could provide some information about how the expectancies are processed.

In summary, the more subtle and elusive arousal and cognitive responses that constitute the critical mediators in this theory can be measured in different ways. The more recently developed techniques of cognitive assessment provide the potential for relatively continuous measurement of some aspects of thought patterns in interactions. With the exception of the unobtrusive classification of pronoun usage, the other measures described here can be quite reactive. Nevertheless, sensitivity to this concern and creativity in structuring the interaction setting can make the problem of reactivity a manageable one.

Research paradigms. A final methodological issue that might be discussed here is the general concern for a paradigm in which the measures just described may be assessed. In the recent studies in which we have monitored arousal change (Ickes, Patterson, Rajecki, & Tanford, 1982, study 2; Patterson, Jordan, Hogan, & Frerker, 1981), the experiment is portrayed as a study of the relationship between physiological activity and a decision-making task. In this setting a subject is paired with a confederate who is typically programmed to maintain a specific level of involvement for a critical interval. The subject and confederate are seated in the middle of a 3.2 X 6.1 meter room. A camera is focused on each of them from a diagonal position. In fact, only the camera focused on the subject is actually recording. The position of the camera permits the inclusion of the back and side of the confederate in the picture so that the subject's gaze and orientation toward the confederate can be reliably judged. Figure 9-1 is a representation of the experimental setting.

A few other characteristics of the setting should be noted. First, the physiograph is located in a hallway behind the experimental room. The operator of the physiograph is able to synchronize the videotape to the physiological record by means of a switch that simultaneously registers a mark on the physiograph paper and briefly turns on a light in the experimental room. The light is above and behind the subject on a side wall. It is positioned so that the confederate, but not the subject, can see it. The light is also visible on the videotape. The light is important not only in signaling the start and the end of the session, but it can also be used to signal a specific manipulation change to the confederate, for example, for the confederate to move from a control period of baseline involvement to one of increased or decreased involvement.

The critical subject-confederate exchange might be either the focused issue described in the instructions, for example, a decision-making task, or a "waiting period" during which the physiological measures are supposedly stabilizing. In the former case there is no deception about the exchange that is videotaped. In the latter case, the subject is led to believe that the decision-making task will follow the interval needed for stabilizing the physiological measures. In fact, the interaction phase of the study is limited to the waiting period. With this latter procedure, we have also tried to make the subject less self-conscious by rigging a phony switch on the camera that apparently turns off the camera. An added red light on the front of the camera is turned off when the switch is flipped. When the waiting period is completed, the subject is informed that the interaction phase of the study is over and that the camera had recorded the exchange.

The last stage in the procedure begins by obtaining ratings from the subject on himself or herself, the other "subject," and their interaction. Finally, the videotape thought-listing measure is taken. When this is completed, the subject is debriefed and consent is requested for using the videotape record in the analysis. It is impor-

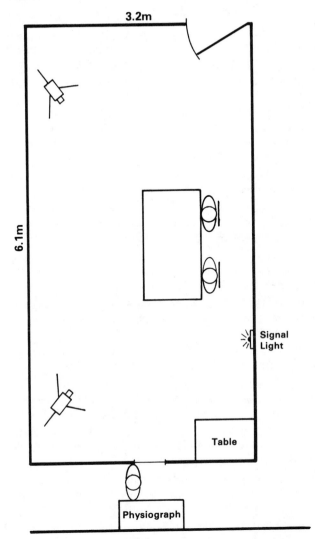

Fig. 9-1. Overhead view of the physical setting in the Patterson paradigm.

tant to appreciate that because the experimenter records the point in the interaction at which each thought was listed, the behavioral measures from the videotape, the physiological changes, and the specific thoughts can all be precisely time-tagged. Although the thoughts are necessarily listed after the fact, this procedure provides a means for the relatively continuous measurement of behavior, arousal, and thought changes.

This first paradigm permits relatively comprehensive monitoring of a subject's responses over time. It is obviously a very structured and reactive setting for an interaction, however. In contrast, Ickes and Barnes (1977) have developed a much less structured and less reactive paradigm for studying interaction. In their case, there is no attempt to record physiological change because it would necessarily be incompatible with an unstructured and nonreactive setting. Ickes (1982) has discussed this paradigm in detail elsewhere, so only its general characteristics will be described here. Basically, two naive subjects, apparently recruited for different experiments, are met by the experimenter and led to the observation room. At this point, the experimenter informs the subjects that he or she has just run out of the questionnaires needed for the first part of the study. The experimenter explains that while he or she is getting copies made, the subjects can wait for a minute or two in this psychology storage room. In the room are a large table on which the subjects can place their books and coats and a long couch against the wall. The experimenter suggests that the subjects might take a seat on the couch and then leaves them alone for exactly 5 minutes.

In this "storage room," opposite the couch, is a large stack of boxes behind which is a concealed videocamera. The top and side views of this arrangement can be seen in Figure 9-2. Prior to meeting the subjects, the experimenter turns on the videocamera and turns off the lights in the room so that everything is prepared for the pair of subjects. After the 5-minute period is completed, the experimenter returns to the room and informs the subjects that part of the experiment is already completed. The subjects are debriefed and consent is sought to use the videotapes for data analysis. The last stage involves the completion of a questionnaire about the waiting period, personal reactions, and judgments of the other subject.

Ickes (1982) reported that this unstructured interaction setting seems to be a particularly useful means for examining the role of individual difference variables in social interaction. Presumably, the minimal structure of the setting makes it easier to determine the influence of personality and other individual difference variables. In our laboratory, we have modified this paradigm to include the videotape thought-listing procedure after the waiting period is completed. Although Ickes and Barnes (1977) designed this paradigm for use with pairs of naive subjects, it obviously could be modified to include a confederate in the pair who might be instructed to enact a particular pattern of involvement.

This section on methodological issues highlighted some basic issues involved in researching questions about the functional model. The tactics and procedures discussed here reflect recent developments in both my own research and that collaboratively undertaken with Bill Ickes and his students. My graduate school exposure to Don Campbell's emphasis on the virtues of the heterogeneity of methods leaves me confident in believing there is no single right way to do research. The obvious contrasts in the two paradigms discussed here are a good example of different procedures that have unique strengths and weaknesses. It might be hoped that creative approaches to conducting research will keep pace with the technology of recording behavior.

Substantive Issues

After the general evaluation of the functional perspective and a consideration of methodological issues, it seems desirable now to narrow the focus to more specific substantive issues that flow from the dynamics proposed in the functional model. I hope in this discussion to identify some problems that are worthy of further

a. TOP VIEW

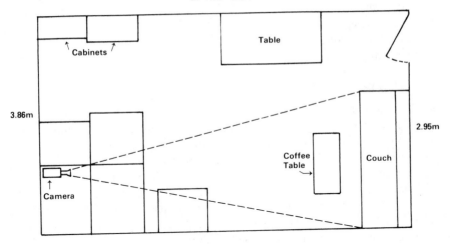

b. SIDE VIEW

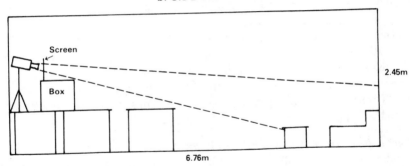

Fig. 9-2. Schematic views of the physical setting in the Ickes paradigm. (From Ickes, 1982)

research. Although these issues are obviously relevant to an evaluation of the functional model, in a larger sense that is secondary. Independent of that evaluation outcome, the pursuit of these problems should facilitate a better understanding of nonverbal exchange.

Defining nonverbal involvement. In the first chapter it was proposed that nonverbal involvement might be operationalized in terms of the following behaviors:

1. Interpersonal distance.
2. Gaze.
3. Touch.
4. Body orientation.
5. Lean.

6. Facial expressiveness.
7. Talking duration.
8. Interruptions.
9. Postural openness.
10. Relational gestures.
11. Head nods.
12. Paralinguistic cues.

That list was admittedly tentative and ripe for additions or deletions. The fact that nonverbal involvement is not operationalized with any precision, however, frequently makes it difficult to describe confidently the effective changes in behavioral involvement. Basic to the difficulty is the lack of an adequate system for weighting the component behaviors that contribute to overall involvement.

Weighting schemes for other specific criterion measures have been proposed in the past. One example is Mehrabian's (1969b) system of weights for predicting liking. From his empirical data, Mehrabian computed the following weights in contributing to interpersonal liking: (a) –.6 for distance; (b) .3 for eye contact; (c) .3 for forward lean; and (d) –.1 for orientation. Of course, the prediction of interpersonal liking is not the same as the prediction of the total involvement level. Consequently, Mehrabian's system does not have direct relevance for an assessment of total involvement. As far as I know, there is no published attempt at developing this kind of general system of weights.

One might speculate that touch, gaze, distance, facial expressiveness, and paralinguistic cues would be more important in determining overall involvement than the remaining involvement cues. But that is an empirical question that might be answered with careful research. On the other hand, it is also possible that a single set of weights that might generalize across situations and relationships will not be found.

Verbal behavior and nonverbal involvement. The present analysis of nonverbal involvement has generally avoided (for the sake of relative simplicity) the verbal behavior of interactants. Such an approach necessarily gives an incomplete picture of the interactive exchange. Eventually, some integration of the verbal and non-verbal dimensions will be required for a comprehensive description of interactive exchange.

There are some options already available for classifying verbal behavior in a manner analogous to the nonverbal involvement dimension. For example, Wiener and Mehrabian (1968) analyze verbal behavior along an immediacy dimension that is comparable to Mehrabian's (1969b) nonverbal immediacy dimension. According to Wiener and Mehrabian, the verbal immediacy dimension refers to the degree of intensity and directness between a speaker and the object or person about which (whom) the individual speaks. Judgments of activity-passivity, order of occurrence, duration, and probability of occurrence, among others, are basic to an assessment of verbal immediacy. A second alternative is Stiles' (1978) taxonomy of verbal response modes. In this taxonomy each utterance is classified in terms of its grammatical form and communicative intent. Communicative intent identifies utterances in terms of the following categories: (a) advisement; (b) interpretation; (c) confirmation; (d) reflection; (e) disclosure; (f) question; (g) edification; and (h) acknowledgment. A third approach is the one most commonly used in analyzing verbal exchanges, namely, verbal intimacy or self-disclosure. The research on self-disclosure is almost as extensive as that on nonverbal involvement.

An examination of the link between self-disclosure and nonverbal involvement may suggest some interesting hypotheses about the dynamic relationship between verbal and nonverbal behavior. First, it should be emphasized that other theoretical analyses, including those on intimacy (Argyle & Dean, 1965; Patterson, 1976) and expressiveness (Cappella, 1981; Cappella & Greene, 1982), have attempted to integrate verbal and nonverbal behavior into a common dynamic process. This is not a new development. What I would like to stress here, however, is the potential of the functional model for explaining the contrasting patterns of empirical results characteristic of verbal and nonverbal research. The clearly dominant pattern found in self-disclosure research is one of reciprocity, a pattern that is even stronger than the pattern of compensation characteristic of research on nonverbal exchange. Firestone (1977), in reviewing this puzzling contrast between verbal and nonverbal research, noted that attraction does not seem to be an adequate mediating explanation for reciprocity in self-disclosure. In support of this judgment, he cites results from a study by Derlega, Harris, and Chaikin (1973) showing that high disclosure from an unlikable other is reciprocated as much as high disclosure from a liked other. My own judgment is that to the extent that attraction or liking per se cannot explain the reciprocity of self-disclosure, such reciprocity is not likely to be in the service of the intimacy function.

An alternate explanation is that some, and perhaps much, of the reciprocity shown in self-disclosure is a manifestation of the social control function. Thus, the reciprocation of self-disclosure, particularly higher levels of self-disclosure, may be a purposeful, managed interaction strategy. Consistent with this view is Cappella's (1981) suggestion that pressure for topic continuation in a verbal exchange is a potentially important factor in reciprocated self-disclosure. That is, a relatively comfortable and orderly conversation requires related responses from the interactants. Although such matching may occur spontaneously at lower levels of self-disclosure, it seems likely that high disclosure from another is distinct enough to bring the consideration of an appropriate response into awareness. When this happens, a deliberate strategy of matching may structure the response. The existence of deception clearly shows that such deliberate response strategies for verbal behavior are common. Reciprocated self-disclosure may simply be another instance of such deliberate strategies, one that might serve to make the interaction more pleasant, impress the other person, or simply enhance one's own self-image.

Intimacy and social control. The contrast between the intimacy and social control functions is basic to understanding the role of different motive systems in nonverbal exchange. At the heart of this contrast is the description of intimacy behavior as spontaneous and *indicative* versus social control behavior as managed, purposeful, and *communicative.* One approach to studying the contrast between the intimacy and social control functions is to examine the situational factors that contribute to evaluative and self-presentation pressures. These pressures presumably trigger the cognitive activity that leads to the managed, social control patterns.

A related tactic for identifying intimacy versus social control patterns is an assessment of the apparent consistency between interpersonal affect and nonverbal involvement. It is presumed that an intimacy pattern is necessarily characterized by consistency between interpersonal affect and nonverbal involvement. Thus, within the situational constraints, the level of nonverbal involvement with another person is proportionate to the underlying degree of positive intimacy felt toward that person. In other words, disliking leads to decreased involvement and liking leads to increased involvement. Social control patterns *may* be characterized by inconsistency between interpersonal affect and nonverbal involvement. Thus, one might very well stand close to, gaze, and smile at a disliked superior because that is a diplomatic way to relate to a person who determines the longevity of your employment. On the other hand, one might feign indifference toward a liked other in order to manipulate that person into initiating some expression of interest. Flirting is an interesting phenomenon that includes a balance between indifference and interest in another person, which is designed to signal interest without risking too much in being rejected. That is, the routine is subtle enough that it cannot be judged a direct approach. In these examples, the behavioral patterns are characterized by an inconsistency between behavior and affect.

Another issue that deserves consideration in analyzing the intimacy-social control distinction is the role of the social control function in intimate relationships. At first glance, one might naively assume that close relationships, such as parent-child, husband-wife, or best friend pairs, would be exclusively guided by the intimacy function. A little reflection on this judgment should make it apparent that in close relationships, manipulation (social control) strategies may be common. This should not be surprising, because so much of personal importance is determined by the joint decisions we make in our intimate relataionships. Because individuals differ in their preferences, even when they are in an intimate relationship, they will often try to influence a spouse, family member, or good friend. By encoding these influence attempts nonverbally, there may be less opportunity for direct conflict than if they were addressed verbally. Again, there may be safety in the ambiguity of such manipulative strategies. No matter how "open" intimate relationships are, there are always opportunities for manipulative, social control patterns. One might predict, however, that as an excessive amount of behavior by one party in a relationship is viewed as manipulative by the other party, the stability of that relationship may be jeopardized. In fact, an assessment of the frequency and/or intensity of social control patterns in marital relationships may provide an index of marital harmony.

A final, more specific concern that might be mentioned in this analysis of intimacy and social control is the possibility of predicting specific behavioral contrasts in the initiation of the two functions. One suggestion may be developed from the research on deception that indicates that deceivers are apparently more sensitive to managing facial behaviors than lower body behaviors. For example, individuals may smile more when they are being deceptive than when they are being truthful (Ekman & Friesen, 1974; Mehrabian, 1971). At the same time, body cues (such as tapping one's foot or general lower body movement) may leak out signs of stress that are indicative of lying. To the extent that one can monitor and manage specific behaviors, including verbal behavior, smiling, and gaze, these behaviors should be most affected in initiating a social control pattern. To the extent that other involvement behaviors, including lean, paralinguistic cues, or postural openness, are not so well monitored or managed, they should change less during the initiation of a social control pattern. The latter behaviors should be more affected by the initiation of an intimacy pattern. That is, they would spontaneously indicate a changing level of perceived intimacy.

The proposed contrast between the intimacy and social control functions should sensitize researchers to conditions under which nonverbal behavior can be clearly deliberate and managed. There is considerable potential for developing important hypotheses about behavior through extended analyses of these two basic motive systems. The few issues mentioned here deserve consideration, but more detailed comparisons between the intimacy and social control functions should stimulate many other interesting questions.

Role of cognitions. Earlier in this chapter, I described the use of the videotape replay as a new technique that seems promising in approximating a continuous assessment of cognitions during interactions. In this section I will describe some of our early results in using the videotape replay meaures and speculate about the cognitive mediation of nonverbal involvement.

In one of our recent studies, subjects were videotaped and skin conductance measures were taken when they heard either a friendly or an unfriendly expectancy about the other subject (confederate) and when they later shared a waiting period with this person (Patterson & Prevallet, Note 8). The expectancy manipulation was casually mentioned before the confederate appeared at the experimental room, permitting the confederate to remain blind to the manipulation. When the waiting period was finished, the subject first completed a rating inventory on his or her impressions and then completed the listing of cognitions from the videotape replay. Some of the analyses of the thought listing have been completed and a few significant patterns are particularly interesting. First, as the number of self-thoughts increased, the tonic skin conductance level (SCL) measure of arousal also increased. Second, as the number of self-thoughts increased, the waiting period was judged to be more uncomfortable. Finally, as thoughts about the environment (e.g., the room is cold, today is very humid) increased, there were fewer skin conductance responses (SCRs). Thus, the number of environmental thoughts was negatively related to an SCR measure of arousal. These results provide some validating support for the thought-listing procedure. They also suggest, however, that different types of thoughts (following the expectancy manipulations) have contrasting effects on arousal and comfort. Such a pattern would hardly be surprising in a therapy or biofeedback context, but, as far as I know, results like these are new in interaction research.

Up to this point we have not had enough variability in the valence of reported thoughts (i.e., positive, neutral, or negative) to make any use of this dimension in predicting other behaviors. It is possible that our system for scoring thought valence is not yet discriminating enough to permit reliable distinctions in valence. Nevertheless, eventually, we may find that the valence of thoughts can qualify the patterns indicated in some of these early results.

Our procedure in videotaping the interactions so far has involved focusing the camera directly on the subject. Although such a vantage point is necessary in measuring the subject's nonverbal behavior, it may introduce a substantial bias in the reporting of thoughts. That is, directing the subject's attention to himself or herself probably accentuates objective self-awareness and increases the likelihood that self-thoughts will be reported (Duval & Wicklund, 1972). A divergent perspective analysis (Jones & Nisbett, 1971) stresses that the subject's actual perspective in the interaction is not matched by the videotaped record. Consequently, the cognitions listed after viewing the videotape may not match those that actually occurred earlier in the interaction. We are now planning research that will vary the camera perspective in an attempt to determine just what those differences may be. It is quite possible that a camera perspective from behind the subject (i.e., the subject's perspective) that focuses on the room and the confederate will stimulate the recall of more other- and environment-related thoughts. In turn, these thoughts might better predict the behavior we are trying to understand.

Personality influences. The role of personality in determining specific functional sequences in nonverbal exchange is another interesting line of research, and a potentially fertile one for studying characteristic interaction styles. Perhaps the most promising dimensions for additional research are those of self-monitoring, internal-external locus of control, and Machiavellianism. The self-monitoring and locus of control dimensions emphasize one's real or perceived mastery in relating to others or to the environment. One might generally assume that those who are high self-monitors or internal control types may be more sensitive to interpersonal and environmental changes that require deliberation and management in interpersonal behavior. Thus, the cognitions and behavior patterns of high self-monitoring and internal control individuals might more frequently reflect the social control function than those of the low self-monitoring and external control individuals.

The dimension of Machiavellianism is one that should have very direct relevance for the social control function. Results from work by Exline and his colleagues (Exline, Thibaut, Hickey, & Gumpert, 1970) showed that high Machiavellian subjects who were induced to cheat on an experimental task gazed more at the experimenter following the accusation of cheating than did low Machiavellian subjects who were induced to cheat. The manipulative tendencies of Machiavellian individuals may well precipitate more frequent and more polished (i.e., more convincing) social control patterns than those who are not Machiavellian. These three dimensions are only a sample of those that may predispose individuals toward different kinds of functional exchanges. More generally, other personal factors may similarly suggest dynamics that may relate individual differences to specific functions and/or behavioral strategies.

Personal Observations

I want to finish this overview with a few personal observations about the issues discussed in this book. In doing so it is important to distinguish between *a* general functional perspective and *the* specific sequential functional model discussed here. I am relatively confident of the utility of a functional perspective in contributing to a further understanding of nonverbal behavior and exchange. Research should be addressing questions of *why* and not simply *how* or *when*. This is especially important as we begin to appreciate the extensive degree to which nonverbal behavior is or can be managed. Determining the purpose of various behavioral patterns is not merely an exercise in after-the-fact understanding, but also a means by which predictions may be made about future interactions.

Although I think that a functional perspective can provide a practical and integrated framework for analyzing nonverbal behavior, I am less sanguine about the ultimate prospects for this functional model. In my own work (Patterson, 1973b, 1976, 1978a), it has been clear that each theoretical model or commentary has served to focus empirical research and critical analysis so that a new (and, one hopes, better) model might emerge. I think that a similar fate may be predicted for the specific dynamics of the functional model. This apparent modesty does not reflect a pessimism about or lack of confidence in my own work. Rather, I think it represents a reasonable expectation about the evolution of theory. I only hope that I have a hand in the next version.

Summary

This chapter provided an overview of a variety of general and specific issues relating to the functional perspective. The discussion included (a) an analysis of general advantages and disadvantages of the functional perspective, (b) a review of methodological issues involving research on the functional perspective, and (c) a consideration of specific substantive issues that merit attention. Characteristic of other critical discussion, more questions than answers were in evidence. My own biased evaluations stressed both the utility of a general functional perspective and the heuristic value of the sequential functional model. The utility of a functional perspective would seem to be evident even now, but an assessment of the value of the theory itself will necessarily develop more slowly. I hope that the functional model does stimulate new and important questions about nonverbal involvement. In fact, it may provide a useful general structure for analyzing all forms of social interaction.

Reference Notes

1. Heslin, R. *Steps toward a taxonomy of touching*. Paper presented at the annual meeting of the Midwestern Psychological Association, Chicago, May 1974.
2. Hayes, D. P., & Cobb, L. *Infradian periodicity in human social interaction*. Paper presented at the annual meeting of the American Psychological Association, New Orleans, September 1974.
3. Cook, D. L. *Public order in the U.S. Navy*. Unpublished manuscript, 1969. (Cited in E. Goffman, *Relations in public*. New York: Harper Colophon, 1972.)
4. Exline, R. V., & Eldridge, C. *Effects of two patterns of a speaker's visual behavior on the perception of the authenticity of his verbal message*. Paper presented at the annual meeting of the Eastern Psychological Association, Boston, 1967.
5. Wiemann, J. M. *An experimental study of visual attention in dyads: The effect of four gaze conditions on evaluation of applicants in employment interviews*. Paper presented at the meeting of the Speech Communication Association, Chicago, 1974.
6. Clore, G. *Attraction and interpersonal behavior*. Paper presented at the annual meeting of the Southwestern Psychological Association, Austin, 1969.
7. Patterson, M. L., & Holmes, D. S. *Social interaction correlates of the MPI extraversion-introversion scale*. Paper presented at the annual meeting of the American Psychological Association, New York, 1966.
8. Patterson, M. L., & Prevallet, R. I. *The effect of interpersonal expectancies on cognitions and behavior in a brief interaction*. Manuscript in preparation, 1983.
9. Reidhead, S., Ickes, W., & Patterson, M. L. *Personal pronoun use as an indicator of personality*. Manuscript in preparation, 1983.

References

Abelson, R. P. Psychological status of the script concept. *American Psychologist,* 1981, *36*, 715-729.

Aiello, J. R., & Aiello, T. D. The development of personal space: Proxemic behavior of children 6 through 16. *Human Ecology,* 1974, *2*, 177-189.

Aiello, J. R., & Cooper, R. E. Use of personal space as a function of social affect. *80th Annual Convention of the American Psychological Association,* 1972, *7*, 207-208.

Aiello, J. R., & Jones, S. E. Field study of the proxemic behavior of young school children in three sub-cultural groups. *Journal of Personality and Social Psychology,* 1971, *19*, 351-356.

Alagna, F. J., Whitcher, S. J., Fisher, J. D., & Wicas, E. A. Evaluative reaction to interpersonal touch in a counseling interview. *Journal of Counseling Psychology,* 1979, *26*, 465-472.

Albert, S., & Dabbs, J. M. Physical distance and persuasion. *Journal of Personality and Social Psychology,* 1970, *15*, 265-270.

Allen, D. E., & Guy, R. F. Ocular breaks and verbal output. *Sociometry,* 1977, *40*, 90-96.

Allgeier, A. R., & Byrne, D. Attraction toward the opposite sex as a determinant of physical proximity. *Journal of Social Psychology,* 1973, *90*, 213-219.

Altman, I. *The environment and social behavior.* Monterey, Cal.: Brooks/Cole, 1975.

Altman, I., & Taylor, D. A. *Social penetration: The development of interpersonal relationships.* New York: Holt, Reinhart & Winston, 1973.

Apple, W., Streeter, L. A., & Krauss, R. M. Effects of pitch and speech rate on personal attributions. *Journal of Personality and Social Psychology,* 1979, *37*, 715-727.

Argyle, M. *The psychology of interpersonal behavior.* Baltimore: Penguin Books, 1967.

Argyle, M. Non-verbal communication in human social interaction. In R. A. Hinde (Ed.), *Non-verbal communication.* Cambridge: Cambridge University Press, 1972.

Argyle, M., & Dean, J. Eye-contact, distance and affiliation. *Sociometry,* 1965, *28,* 289-304.

Argyle, M., & Kendon, A. The experimental analysis of social performance. In L. Berkowitz (Ed.), *Advances in experimental social psychology.* New York: Academic Press, 1967, 55-91.

Argyle, M., Lalljee, M., & Cook, M. The effects of visibility on interaction in a dyad. *Human Relations,* 1968, *21,* 3-17.

Aronson, E., & Carlsmith, J. M. Experimentation in social psychology. In G. Lindsey & E. Aronson (Eds.), *The handbook of social psychology* (Vol. 2). Reading, Mass.: Addison-Wesley, 1968.

Aronson, E., & Linder, D. E. Gain and loss of esteem as determinants of interpersonal attractiveness. *Journal of Experimental Social Psychology,* 1965, *1,* 156-171.

Ashton, N. L., Shaw, M. E., & Worsham, A. N. Affective reactions to interpersonal distances by friends and strangers. *Bulletin of the Psychonomic Society,* 1980, *15,* 306-308.

Bakan, D. *The duality of human existence.* Chicago: Rand McNally, 1966.

Bakeman, R., & Beck, S. The size of informal groups in public. *Environment and Behavior,* 1974, *6,* 378-390.

Baker, E., & Shaw, M. E. Reactions to interperson distance and topic intimacy: A comparison of strangers and friends. *Journal of Nonverbal Behavior,* 1980, *5,* 80-91.

Banks, D. L. A comparative study of the reinforcing potential of verbal and nonverbal cues in a verbal conditioning paradigm (Doctoral dissertation, University of Massachusetts, 1974). *Dissertation Abstracts International,* 1974, *35,* 2671A. (University Microfilms No. 74-25, 819)

Barker, R. G. *Ecological psychology: Concepts and methods for studying the environment of human behavior.* Stanford, Cal.: Stanford University Press, 1968.

Baron, R. A., & Bell, P. A. Physical distance and helping: Some unexpected benefits of "crowding in" on others. *Journal of Applied Social Psychology,* 1976, *6,* 95-104.

Barrios, B., & Giesen, M. Getting what you expect: Effects of expectation on intragroup attraction and interpersonal distance. *Personality and Social Psychology Bulletin,* 1977, *3,* 87-90.

Batchelor, J. P., & Goethals, G. R. Spatial arrangements in freely formed groups. *Sociometry,* 1972, *35,* 270-279.

Bauer, E. A. Personal space: A study of blacks and whites. *Sociometry,* 1973, *36,* 402-408.

Baum, A., & Greenberg, C. I. Waiting for a crowd: The behavioral and perceptual effects of anticipated crowding. *Journal of Personality and Social Psychology,* 1975, *32,* 671-679.

Baxter, J. C. Interpersonal spacing in natural settings. *Sociometry,* 1970, *33,* 444-456.

Baxter, J. C., & Rozelle, R. Nonverbal expression as a function of crowding during a simulated police-citizen encounter. *Journal of Personality and Social Psychology,* 1975, *32,* 40-54.

Beattie, G. W. Floor apportionment and gaze in conversational dyads. *British Journal of Social and Clinical Psychology*, 1978, *17*, 7-15.

Beier, E. G., & Sternberg, D. P. Marital communication: Subtle cues between newlyweds. *Journal of Communication*, 1977, *27*, 92-103.

Bem, D. J. Self-perception: An alternative interpretation of cognitive dissonance phenomena. *Psychological Review*, 1967, *74*, 183-200.

Bem, D. J. Self-perception theory. In L. Berkowitz (Ed.), *Advances in experimental social psychology* (Vol. 6). New York: Academic Press, 1972.

Berscheid, E., & Walster, E. *Interpersonal attraction* (2nd Ed.). Reading, Mass.: Addison-Wesley, 1978.

Birdwhistell, R. L. Contribution of linguistic-kinesic studies to the understanding of schizophrenia. In A. Auerback (Ed.), *Schizophrenia: An integrated approach*. New York: Ronald Press, 1959. (Cited in P. Watzlawick & J. Beavin. Some formal aspects of communication. *The American Behavioral Scientist*, 1967, *10*, 4-8.)

Bond, M. H. Effect of an impression set on subsequent behavior. *Journal of Personality and Social Psychology*, 1972, *24*, 301-305.

Boomer, D. S. Speech disturbance and body movements in interviews. *Journal of Nervous and Mental Disease*, 1963, *136*, 263-266.

Boomer, D. S. The phonemic clause: Speech unit in human communication. In A. W. Siegman & S. Feldstein (Eds.), *Nonverbal behavior and communication*. Hillsdale, N.J.: Erlbaum, 1978.

Boomer, D. S., & Dittman, A. T. Hesitation pauses and juncture pauses in speech. *Language and Speech*, 1962, *5*, 215-220.

Bourget, L. G. C. Delight and information specificity as elements of positive interpersonal feedback (Doctoral dissertation, Boston University Graduate School, 1977). *Dissertation Abstracts International*, 1977, *38*, 1946B-1947B. (University Microfilms No. 77-21, 580)

Bowlby, J. *Attachment and loss* (Vol. 1). New York: Basic Books, 1969.

Breed, G. The effect of intimacy: Reciprocity or retreat? *British Journal of Social and Clinical Psychology*, 1972, *11*, 135-142.

Brehm, J. W. *A theory of psychological reactance*. New York: Academic Press, 1966.

Buber, M. *Between man and man*. New York: Macmillan, 1965.

Buber, M. *I and thou*. New York: Scribner's, 1970.

Buck, R., Nonverbal communication of affect in children. *Journal of Personality and Social Psychology*, 1975, *31*, 646-653.

Buck, R. Nonverbal communication of affect in preschool children: Relationship with personality and skin conductance. *Journal of Personality and Social Psychology*, 1977, *35*, 225-236.

Buck, R. Nonverbal behavior and the theory of emotion: The facial feedback hypothesis. *Journal of Personality and Social Psychology*, 1980, *38*, 811-824.

Buck, R. W., Savin, V. J., Miller, R. E., & Caul, W. F. Communication of affect through facial expressions in humans. *Journal of Personality and Social Psychology*, 1972, *23*, 362-371.

Bugenthal, D. B., Henker, B., & Whalen, C. K. Attributional antecedents of verbal and vocal assertiveness. *Journal of Personality and Social Psychology*, 1976, *34*, 405-411.

Buss, A. R. Causes and reasons in attribution theory: A conceptual critique. *Journal of Personality and Social Psychology*, 1978, *36*, 1311-1321.

Buss, A. R. On the relationship between causes and reasons. *Journal of Personality and Social Psychology*, 1979, *37*, 1458-1461.

Byrne, D. *The attraction paradigm*. New York: Academic Press, 1971.

Byrne, D., Baskett, G. D., & Hodges, L. Behavioral indicators of interpersonal attraction. *Journal of Applied Social Psychology*, 1971, *1*, 137-149.

Byrne, D., Ervin, C. R., & Lamberth, J. Continuity between the experimental study of attraction and real-life computer dating. *Journal of Personality and Social Psychology*, 1970, *16*, 157-165.

Cacioppo, J. T., & Petty, R. E. Electromyograms as measures of extent and affectivity of information processing. *American Psychologist*, 1981, *36*, 441-446. (a)

Cacioppo, J. T., & Petty, R. E. Social psychological procedures for cognitive response assessment: The thought listing technique. In T. V. Merluzzi, C. R. Glass, & M. Genest (Eds.), *Cognitive assessment*. New York: Guilford Press, 1981. (b)

Campbell, A., & Rushton, P. Bodily communication and personality. *British Journal of Social and Clinical Psychology*, 1978, *17*, 31-36.

Cannon, W. B. The James-Lange theory of emotions: A critical examination and an alternative theory. *American Journal of Psychology*, 1927, *34*, 106-124.

Cappella, J. N. Mutual influence in expressive behavior: Adult-adult and infant-adult interaction. *Psychological Bulletin*, 1981, *89*, 101-132.

Cappella, J. N., & Greene, J. O. A discrepancy-arousal explanation of mutual influence in expressive behavior for adult and infant-adult interaction. *Communication Monographs*, 1982, *49*, 89-114.

Carver, C. S. A cybernetic model of self-attention processes. *Journal of Personality and Social Psychology*, 1979, *37*, 1251-1281.

Cary, M. S. Does civil inattention exist in pedestrian passing? *Journal of Personality and Social Psychology*, 1978, *36*, 1185-1193.

Chapman, A. J. Eye contact, physical proximity and laughter: A reexamination of the equilibrium model of social intimacy. *Social Behavior and Personality*, 1975, *3*, 143-155.

Chapple, E. D. *Culture and biological man: Explorations in behavioral anthropology*. New York: Holt, Rinehart & Winston, 1970.

Ciolek, T. M. Spatial arrangements in social encounters: An attempt at a taxonomy. *Man-Environment Systems*, 1978, *8*, 52-59.

Ciolek, T. M., & Kendon, A. Environment and the spatial arrangement of conversational encounters. *Sociological Inquiry*, 1980, *50*, 237-271.

Claiborn, C. D. Counselor verbal intervention, nonverbal behavior, and social power. *Journal of Counseling Psychology*, 1979, *26*, 378-383. (a)

Claiborn, C. D. Effects of counselor interpretation, restatement, and nonverbal behavior on perceptions of the counselor and the counselor's ability to influence (Doctoral dissertation, University of Missouri-Columbia, 1978). *Dissertation Abstracts International*, 1979, *39*, 5058B. (University Microfilms No. 7906855) (b)

Condon, W. S. An analysis of behavioral organization. *Sign Language Studies*, 1976, *13*, 285-318.

Condon, W. S., & Ogston, W. D. Sound film analysis of normal and pathological behavior patterns. *Journal of Nervous and Mental Diseases*, 1966, *143*, 338-347.

Condon, W. S., & Sander, L. W. Neonate movement is synchronized with adult speech: Interaction participation and language acquisition. *Science*, 1974, *183*, 99-101.

Cook, M. Anxiety, speech disturbance, and speech rate. *British Journal of Social and Clinical Psychology*, 1969, *8*, 13-21.

Cook, M. Experiments on orientation and proxemics. *Human Relations*, 1970, *23*, 61-76.

Cotton, J. L. Verbal reports on mental processes: Ignoring data for the sake of theory? *Personality and Social Psychology Bulletin*, 1980, *6*, 278-281.

Coutts, L. M., & Schneider, F. W. Visual behavior in an unfocused interaction as a function of sex differences. *Journal of Experimental Social Psychology*, 1975, *11*, 64-77.

Coutts, L. M., Schneider, F. W., & Montgomery, S. An investigation of the arousal model of interpersonal intimacy. *Journal of Experimental Social Psychology*, 1980, *16*, 545-561.

Dabbs, J. M., Jr., Evans, M. S., Hopper, C. H., & Purvis, J. A. Self-monitors in conversation: What do they monitor? *Journal of Personality and Social Psychology*, 1980, *39*, 278-284.

Daly, S. Behavioral correlates of social anxiety. *British Journal of Social and Clinical Psychology*, 1978, *17*, 117-120.

Daniell, R. J., & Lewis, P. Stability of eye contact and physical distance across a series of structural interviews. *Journal of Consulting and Clinical Psychology*, 1972, *39*, 172.

Derlega, V. J., Harris, M. S., & Chaikin, A. L. Self-disclosure, liking and the deviant. *Journal of Experimental Social Psychology*, 1973, *9*, 277-284.

Dittman, A. T. Developmental factors in conversational behavior. *Journal of Communication*, 1972, *22*, 404-423.

Dittman, A. T., & Llewellyn, L. G. The phonemic clause as a unit of speech decoding. *Journal of Personality and Social Psychology*, 1967, *6*, 341-349.

Dittman, A. T., & Llewellyn, L. G. Relationship between vocalizations and head nods as listener responses. *Journal of Personality and Social Psychology*, 1968, *9*, 79-84.

Dittman, A. T., & Llewellyn, L. G. Body movement and speech rhythm in social conversation. *Journal of Personality and Social Psychology*, 1969, *11*, 98-106.

Duke, M. P., & Nowicki, S., Jr. A new measure and social-learning model for interpersonal distance. *Journal of Experimental Research in Personality*, 1972, *6*, 119-132.

Duncan, S., Jr. Some signals and rules for taking speaking turns in conversations. *Journal of Personality and Social Psychology*, 1972, *23*, 283-292.

Duncan, S., Jr., & Niederehe, G. On signaling that it's your turn to speak. *Journal of Experimental Social Psychology*, 1974, *10*, 234-247.

Duval, S., & Wicklund, R. A. *A theory of objective self-awareness*. New York: Academic Press, 1972.

Edinger, J. A., & Patterson, M. L. Nonverbal involvement and social control. *Psychological Bulletin*, 1983, *93*, 30-56.

Efran, J. S. Looking for approval: Effects on visual behavior of approbation from persons differing in importance. *Journal of Personality and Social Psychology*, 1968, *10*, 21-25.

Efran, J. S., & Broughton, A. Effect of expectancies for social approval on visual behavior. *Journal of Personality and Social Psychology*, 1966, *4*, 103-107.

Eibl-Eibesfeldt, I. Similarities and differences between cultures in expressive movements. In R. A. Hinde (Ed.), *Non-verbal communication*. London: Cambridge University Press, 1972.

Ekman, P. Differential communication of affect by head and body cues. *Journal of Personality and Social Psychology*, 1965, *2*, 726-735.

Ekman, P. Universals and cultural differences in facial expressions of emotion. In J. Cole (Ed.), *Nebraska Symposium on Motivation, 1971* (Vol. 19). Lincoln: University of Nebraska Press, 1972.

Ekman, P. Facial expression. In A. W. Siegman & S. Feldstein (Eds.), *Nonverbal behavior and communication*. Hillsdale, N.J.: Erlbaum, 1978.

Ekman, P. About brows: Emotional and conversational signals. In M. Von Cranach, K. Foppa, W. Lepenies, & D. Ploog (Eds.), *Human ethology*. Cambridge: Cambridge University Press, 1979.

Ekman, P., & Friesen, W. V. Nonverbal leakage and clues to deception. *Psychiatry*, 1969, *32*, 88-106. (a)

Ekman, P., & Friesen, W. V. The repertoire of nonverbal behavior: Categories, origins, usage and codings. *Semiotica*, 1969, *1*, 49-97. (b)

Ekman, P., & Friesen, W. V. Hand movements. *The Journal of Communication*, 1972, *22*, 353-374.

Ekman, P., & Friesen, W. V. Detecting deception from the body or face. *Journal of Personality and Social Psychology*, 1974, *29*, 288-298.

Ekman, P., & Friesen, W. V. Measuring facial movement. *Environmental Psychology and Nonverbal Behavior*, 1976, *1*, 56-75.

Ekman, P., Friesen, W. V., & Scherer, K. R. Body movement and voice pitch in deceptive interaction. *Semiotica*, 1976, *16*, 23-27.

Ekman, P., Hager, J. C., & Friesen, W. V. The symmetry of emotional and deliberate facial actions. *Psychophysiology*, 1981, *18*, 101-106.

Ekman, P., & Oster, H. Facial expressions of emotion. *Annual Review of Psychology*, 1979, *30*, 527-554.

Ellsworth, P. C., & Carlsmith, J. M. Effects of eye contact and verbal content on affective response to a dyadic interaction. *Journal of Personality and Social Psychology*, 1968, *10*, 15-20.

Ellsworth, P. C., Carlsmith, J. M., & Henson, A. The stare as a stimulus to flight in human subjects: A series of field experiments. *Journal of Personality and Social Psychology*, 1972, *21*, 302-311.

Ellsworth, P. C., & Langer, E. J. Staring and approach: An interpretation of the stare as a nonspecific activator. *Journal of Personality and Social Psychology*, 1976, *33*, 117-122.

Ellsworth, P. C., & Ludwig, L. M. Visual behavior in social interaction. *Journal of Communication,* 1972, *22,* 375-403.

Ellsworth, P. C., & Ross, L. Intimacy in response to direct gaze. *Journal of Experimental Social Psychology,* 1975, *11,* 592-613.

Ericsson, K. A., & Simon, H. A. Verbal reports as data. *Psychological Review,* 1980, *87,* 215-251.

Exline, R. V. Explorations in the process of person perception: Visual interaction in relation to competition, sex, and need for affiliation. *Journal of Personality,* 1963, *31,* 1-20.

Exline, R. V. Visual interaction: The glances of power and preference. In J. K. Cole (Ed.), *Nebraska Symposium on Motivation* (Vol. 19). Lincoln: University of Nebraska Press, 1972.

Exline, R. V., Ellyson, S. L., & Long, B. Visual behavior as an aspect of power role relationships. In P. Pilner, L. Krames, & T. Alloway (Eds.), *Advances in the study of communication and affect* (Vol. 2). New York: Plenum, 1975.

Exline, R. V., Gray, D., & Schuette, D. Visual behavior in a dyad as affected by interview content and sex of respondent. *Journal of Personality and Social Psychology,* 1965, *1,* 201-209.

Exline, R. V., Thibaut, J., Hickey, C. B., & Gumpert, P. Visual interaction in relation to Machiavellianism and an unethical act. In R. Christie & F. Geis (Eds.), *Studies in Machiavellianism.* New York: Academic Press, 1970.

Exline, R. V., & Winters, L. C. Affective relations and mutual glances in dyads. In S. Tompkins & C. Izard (Eds.), *Affect, cognition, and personality.* New York: Springer, 1965.

Eysenck, H. J. *The biological basis of personality.* Springfield, Ill.: Charles C. Thomas, 1967.

Farrenkopf, T., & Roth, V. The university faculty office as an environment. *Environment and Behavior,* 1980, *12,* 467-477.

Feldstein, S., & Jaffe, J. A note about speech disturbances and vocabulary diversity. *Journal of Communication,* 1962, *12,* 166-170.

Feldstein, S., & Welkowitz, J. A chronography of conversation: In defense of an objective approach. In A. W. Siegman & S. Feldstein (Eds.), *Nonverbal behavior and communication.* Hillsdale, N.J.: Erlbaum, 1978.

Felipe, N. J., & Sommer, R. Invasion of personal space. *Social Problems,* 1966, *14,* 206-214.

Firestone, I. J. Reconciling verbal and nonverbal models of dyadic communication. *Environmental Psychology and Nonverbal Behavior,* 1977, *2,* 30-44.

Fisher, J. D., & Byrne, D. Too close for comfort: Sex differences in response to invasions of personal space. *Journal of Personality and Social Psychology,* 1975, *32,* 15-21.

Fisher, J. D., Rytting, M., & Heslin, R. Hands touching hands: Affective and evaluative effects of an interpersonal touch. *Sociometry,* 1976, *39,* 416-421.

Foot, H. C., Chapman, A. J., & Smith, J. R. Friendship and social responsiveness in boys and girls. *Journal of Personality and Social Psychology,* 1977, *35,* 401-411.

Foot, H. C., Smith, J. R., & Chapman, A. J. Individual differences in children's responsiveness in humour situations. In A. J. Chapman & H. C. Foot (Eds.), *It's a funny thing, humour*. London: Pergamon, 1977.

Forbes, R. J., & Jackson, P. R. Nonverbal behavior and the outcome of selection interviews. *Journal of Occupational Psychology*, 1980, *53*, 65-72.

Forston, R. F., & Larson, C. V. The dynamics of space: An experimental study in proxemic behavior among Latin Americans and North Americans. *Journal of Communication*, 1968, *18*, 109-116.

Freedman, N., Blass, T., Rifkin, A., & Quitkin, F. Body movements and the verbal encoding of aggressive affect. *Journal of Personality and Social Psychology*, 1973, *26*, 72-85.

Freud, S. Fragment of an analysis of a case of hysteria. In *Collected papers* (Vol. 3). New York: Basic Books, 1959. (Originally published, 1925.)

Friedman, H. S. Nonverbal communication between patients and medical practitioners. *Journal of Social Issues*, 1979, *35*, 82-99.

Fry, R., & Smith, G. F. The effects of feedback and eye contact on performance of a digit-coding task. *Journal of Social Psychology*, 1975, *96*, 145-146.

Fugita, B. N., Harper, R. G., & Wiens, A. N. Encoding-decoding of nonverbal emotional messages: Sex differences in spontaneous and enacted expression. *Journal of Nonverbal Behavior*, 1980, *4*, 131-145.

Fugita, S. S., Wexley, K. N., & Hillery, J. M. Black-white differences in nonverbal behavior in an interview setting. *Journal of Applied Social Psychology*, 1974, *4*, 343-350.

Gabrenya, W. K., Jr., & Arkin, R. M. Self-monitoring scale: Factor structure and correlates. *Personality and Social Psychology Bulletin*, 1980, *6*, 13-22.

Gale, A., Lucas, B., Nissim, R., & Harpham, B. Some EEG correlates of face-to-face contact. *British Journal of Social and Clinical Psychology*, 1972, *11*, 326-332.

Garfinkel, H. Studies of the routine grounds of everyday activities. *Social Problems*, 1964, *11*, 225-250.

Gatewood, J. B., & Rosenwein, R. Interactional synchrony: Genuine or spurious? A critique of recent research. *Journal of Nonverbal Behavior*, 1981, *6*, 12-29.

Geller, D. M., Goodstein, L., Silver, M., & Sternberg, W. C. On being ignored: The effects of the violation of implicit rules of social interaction. *Sociometry*, 1974, *37*, 541-556.

Giesen, M., & McClaren, H. A. Discussion, distance and sex: Changes in impressions and attraction during small group interaction. *Sociometry*, 1976, *39*, 60-70.

Giles, H. Social psychology and applied linguistics: Toward an integrative approach. *ITL: Review of Applied Linguistics*, 1977, *33*, 27-42.

Goffman, E. *The presentation of self in everyday life*. Garden City, N.Y.: Anchor, 1959.

Goffman, E. *Behavior in public places*. New York: The Free Press, 1963.

Goffman, E. *Interaction ritual*. Garden City, N.Y.: Anchor, 1967.

Goffman, E. *Relations in public*. New York: Harper Colophon, 1972.

Goffman, E. *Forms of talk*. Philadelphia: Univ. of Pennsylvania Press, 1981.

Goldstein, M., Kilroy, M., & Van de Voort, D. Gaze as a function of conversation and degree of love. *Journal of Psychology*, 1976, *92*, 227-234.

Greenbaum, P. E., & Rosenfeld, H. M. Varieties of touching in greetings: Sequential structure and sex-related differences. *Journal of Nonverbal Behavior,* 1980, *5,* 13-25.

Greenberg, C. I., Strube, M. J., & Myers, R. A. A multitrait-multimethod investigation of interpersonal distance. *Journal of Nonverbal Behavior,* 1980, *5,* 104-114.

Greene, L. R. Effects of field independence, physical proximity and evaluative feedback on affective reactions and compliance in dyadic interaction (Doctoral dissertation, Yale University, 1973). *Dissertation Abstracts International,* 1973, *34,* 2284B-2285B. (University Microfilms No. 73-26, 285)

Green, L. R. Effects of verbal evaluative feedback and interpersonal distance on behavioral compliance. *Journal of Counseling Psychology,* 1977, *24,* 10-14.

Hager, J. C., & Ekman, P. Methodological problems in Tourangeau and Ellsworth's study of facial expression and experience of emotion. *Journal of Personality and Social Psychology,* 1981, *40,* 358-362.

Hall, E. T. A system for the notation of proxemic behavior. *American Anthropologist,* 1963, *65,* 1003-1026.

Hall, E. T. *The hidden dimension.* New York: Doubleday, 1966.

Hall. E. T. Proxemics. *Current Anthropology,* 1968, *9,* 83-108.

Hall, J. A. Gender effects in decoding nonverbal cues. *Psychological Bulletin,* 1978, *85,* 845-857.

Hall, J. A. Voice tone and persuasion. *Journal of Personality and Social Psychology,* 1980, *38,* 924-934.

Hall, J. A., Roter, D. L., & Rand, C. S. Communication of affect between patient and physician. *Journal of Health and Social Behavior,* 1981, *22,* 18-30.

Harper, R. G., Wiens, A. N., & Matarazzo, J. D. *Nonverbal communication: The state of the art.* New York: Wiley, 1978.

Harrison, R. P. Nonverbal communication. In I. S. Pool, W. Schramm, N. Maccoby, F. Fry, E. Parker, & J. L. Fern (Eds.), *Handbook of communication.* Chicago: Rand McNally, 1973.

Harvey, J. H., & Tucker, J. A. On problems with the cause-reason distinction in attribution theory. *Journal of Personality and Social Psychology,* 1979, *37,* 1441-1446.

Hatfield, J. D., & Gatewood, R. D. Nonverbal cues in the selection interview. *Personnel Administrator,* 1978, *23,* 30-37.

Heider, F. *The psychology of interpersonal relations.* New York: Wiley, 1958.

Helson, H. *Adaptation-level theory.* New York: Harper & Row, 1964.

Henley, N. M. Status and sex: Some touching observations. *Bulletin of the Psychonomic Society,* 1973, *2,* 91-93.

Henley, N. M. *Body politics: Power, sex, and nonverbal communication.* Englewood Cliffs, N.J.: Prentice-Hall, 1977.

Heshka, S., & Nelson, Y. Interpersonal speaking distance as a function of age, sex, and relationship. *Sociometry,* 1972, *35,* 491-498.

Heslin, R., & Boss, D. Nonverbal intimacy in airport arrival and departure. *Personality and Social Psychology Bulletin,* 1980, *6,* 248-252.

Heslin, R., & Patterson, M. L. *Nonverbal behavior and social psychology.* New York: Plenum, 1982.

Hollandsworth, J. G., Jr., Kazelskis, R., Stevens, J., & Dressel, M. E. Relative contributions of verbal, articulative, and nonverbal communication to employment decisions in the job interview setting. *Personnel Psychology*, 1979, *32*, 359-367.

Hollender, M. H. The need or wish to be held. *Archives of General Psychiatry*, 1970, *22*, 445-453.

Holley, M. Field-dependence-independence, sophistication-of-body-concept, and social distance selection (Doctoral dissertation, New York University, 1972). *Dissertation Abstracts International*, 1972, *33*, 296B. (University Microfilms No. 72-20, 635)

Horowitz, M. J., Duff, D. F., & Stratton, L. O. Body-buffer zone. *Archives of General Psychiatry*, 1964, *11*, 651-656.

Hottenstein, M. P. An exploration of the relationship between age, social status, and facial gesturing (Doctoral dissertation, University of Pennsylvania, 1977). *Dissertation Abstracts International*, 1978, *38*, 5648B-5649B. (University Microfilms No. 78-06, 598)

Ickes, W. Sex role influences in dyadic interaction: A theoretical model. In C. Mayo & N. M. Henley (Eds.), *Gender and nonverbal behavior*. New York: Springer-Verlag, 1981.

Ickes, W. A basic paradigm for the study of personality, roles, and social behavior. In W. Ickes & E. S. Knowles (Eds.), *Personality, roles, and social behavior*. New York: Springer-Verlag, 1982.

Ickes, W., & Barnes, R. D. The role of sex and self-monitoring in unstructured dyadic settings. *Journal of Personality and Social Psychology*, 1977, *35*, 315-330.

Ickes, W., & Barnes, R. D. Boys and girls together and alienated: On enacting stereotyped sex roles in mixed-sex dyads. *Journal of Personality and Social Psychology*, 1978, *36*, 669-683.

Ickes, W., Patterson, M. L., Rajecki, D. W., & Tanford, S. Behavioral and cognitive consequences of reciprocal versus compensatory responses to pre-interaction expectancies. *Social Cognition*, 1982, *1*, 160-190.

Ickes, W., Schermer, B., & Steeno, J. Sex and sex-role influences in same-sex dyads. *Social Psychology Quarterly*, 1979, *42*, 373-385.

Imada, A. S., & Hakel, M. D. Influence of nonverbal communication and rater proximity on impressions and decisions in simulated employment interviews. *Journal of Applied Psychology*, 1977, *62*, 295-300.

Isenberg, S. J., & Bass, B. A. Effects of verbal and nonverbal reinforcement on the WAIS performance of normal adults. *Journal of Consulting and Clinical Psychology*, 1974, *42*, 467.

Izard, C. E. Differential emotions theory and the facial feedback hypothesis of emotion activation: Comments on Tourangeau and Ellsworth's "The role of facial response in the experience of emotion." *Journal of Personality and Social Psychology*, 1981, *40*, 350-354.

Jaffe, J., & Feldstein, S. *Rhythms of dialogue*. New York: Academic Press, 1970.

Jaffe, J., Sterm, D. N., & Peery, J. C. "Conversational" coupling of gaze behavior in prelinguistic human development. *Journal of Psycholinguistic Research*, 1973, *2*, 321-329.

James, W. *The principles of psychology*. New York: Dover, 1950. (Originally published, 1890.)

James, W. What is an emotion? In M. Arnold (Ed.), *The nature of emotion*. Baltimore: Pengrun, 1968. (Originally published, 1884.)

Jones, E. E., & Davis, K. From acts to dispositions: The attribution process in person perception. In L. Berkowitz (Ed.), *Advances in experimental social psychology* (Vol. 2). New York: Academic Press, 1965.

Jones, E. E., & Nisbett, R. E. *The actor and the observer: Divergent perceptions of the causes of behavior*. Morristown, N.J.: General Learning Press, 1971.

Jones, S. E. A comparative proxemics analysis of dyadic interaction in selected subcultures of New York City. *Journal of Social Psychology*, 1971, *84*, 35-44.

Jones, S. E., & Aiello, J. R. Proxemic behavior of black and white first-, third-, and fifth-grade children. *Journal of Personality and Social Psychology*, 1973, *25*, 21-27.

Jourard, S. M. An exploratory study of body-accessibility. *British Journal of Social and Clinical Psychology*, 1966, *5*, 221-231.

Jourard, S. M., & Friedman, R. Experimenter-subject "distance" and self-disclosure. *Journal of Personality and Social Psychology*, 1970, *15*, 278-282.

Justice, M. T. Field dependency, intimacy of topic and interperson distance (Doctoral dissertation, University of Florida, 1969). *Dissertation Abstracts International*, 1970, *31*, 395B-396B. (University Microfilms No. 70-12, 243)

Kahn, A., & McGaughey, T. A. Distance and liking: When moving close produces increased liking. *Sociometry*, 1977, *40*, 138-144.

Kasl, S. V., & Mahl, G. I. The relationship of disturbances and hesitations in spontaneous speech to anxiety. *Journal of Personality and Social Psychology*, 1965, *1*, 425-433.

Kazdin, A. E., & Klock, J. The effect of nonverbal teacher approval on student attentive behavior. *Journal of Applied Behavior Analysis*, 1973, *6*, 643-654.

Keating, C. F., Mazur, A., & Segall, M. H. Facial gestures which influence the perception of status. *Sociometry*, 1977, *40*, 374-378.

Keenan, A. Effects of nonverbal behavior of interviewers on candidates' performance. *Journal of Occupational Psychology*, 1976, *49*, 171-176.

Kelley, H. H. The warm-cold variable in first impressions of persons. *Journal of Personality*, 1950, *18*, 431-439.

Kendon, A. Some functions of gaze-direction in social interaction. *Acta Psychologica*, 1967, *26*, 22-63.

Kendon, A. Movement coordination in social interaction: Some examples described. *Acta Psychologica*, 1970, *32*, 100-125.

Kendon, A. The F-formation system: The spatial organization of social encounters. *Man-Environment Systems*, 1976, *6*, 291-296.

Kendon, A. Spatial organization in social encounters: The F-formation system. In A. Kendon (Ed.), *Studies in the behavior of social interaction*. Lisse, Holland: Peter deRidder Press, 1977.

Kendon, A. Looking in conversation and the regulation of turns at talk: A comment on the papers of G. Beattie and D. R. Rutter *et al. British Journal of Social and Clinical Psychology*, 1978, *17*, 23-24.

Kendon, A., & Cook, M. The consistency of gaze patterns in social interaction. *British Journal of Psychology*, 1969, *60*, 481-494.

King, M. J. Interpersonal relations in preschool children and average approach distance. *Journal of Genetic Psychology*, 1966, *109*, 109-116.

Kinzel, A. F. Body-buffer zone in violent prisoners. *American Journal of Psychiatry*, 1970, *127*, 59-64.

Kleck, R. E. Interaction distance and nonverbal agreeing responses. *British Journal of Social and Clinical Psychology*, 1970, *9*, 180-182.

Kleck, R. E., & Rubenstein, C. Physical attractiveness, perceived attitude similarity, and interpersonal attraction in an opposite-sex encounter. *Journal of Personality and Social Psychology*, 1975, *31*, 107-114.

Kleinfeld, J. S. Effects of nonverbally communicated personal warmth on the intelligence test performance of Indian and Eskimo adolescents. *Journal of Social Psychology*, 1973, *91*, 149-150.

Kleinfeld, J. S. Effects of nonverbal warmth on the learning of Eskimo and white students. *Journal of Social Psychology*, 1974, *92*, 3-9.

Kleinke, C. L. Compliance to requests made by gazing and touching experimenters in field settings. *Journal of Experimental Social Psychology*, 1977, *13*, 218-223.

Kleinke, C. L. Interaction between gaze and legitimacy of request on compliance in a field setting. *Journal of Nonverbal Behavior*, 1980, *5*, 3-12.

Kleinke, C. L., Meeker, F. B., & LaFong, C. Effects of gaze, touch, and use of name on evaluation of "engaged" couples. *Journal of Research in Personality*, 1974, *7*, 368-373.

Kleinke, C. L., & Pohlen, P. D. Affective and emotional responses as a function of other person's gaze and cooperativeness in a two-person game. *Journal of Personality and Social Psychology*, 1971, *17*, 308-313.

Kleinke, C. L., Staneski, R. A., & Berger, D. E. Evaluation of an interviewer as a function of interviewer gaze, reinforcement of subject gaze and interviewer attractiveness. *Journal of Personality and Social Psychology*, 1975, *31*, 115-122.

Kleinke, C. L., Staneski, R. A., & Pipp, S. L. Effects of gaze, distance, and attractiveness on male's first impression of females. *Representative Research in Social Psychology*, 1975, *6*, 7-12.

Kleinke, C. L., & Tully, T. B. Influence of talking level on perceptions of counselors. *Journal of Counseling Psychology*, 1979, *26*, 23-29.

Knapp, M. L., Hart, R. P., & Dennis, H. S. An exploration of deception as a communication construct. *Human Communication Research*, 1974, *1*, 15-29.

Knowles, E. S. Boundaries around group interaction: The effect of group size and member status on boundary permeability. *Journal of Personality and Social Psychology*, 1973, *26*, 327-331.

Knowles, E. S. Convergent validity of personal space measures: Consistent results with low intercorrelations. *Journal of Nonverbal Behavior*, 1980, *4*, 240-248.

Knowles, E. S., & Bassett, R. L. Groups and crowds as social entities: Effects of activity, size, and member similarity on nonmembers. *Journal of Personality and Social Psychology*, 1976, *34*, 837-845.

Knowles, E. S., & Johnsen, P. K. Intrapersonal consistency in interpersonal distance. *JSAS Catalog of Selected Documents in Psychology*, Fall 1974, *768*, 1-27.

Knowles, E. S., Kreuser, B., Haas, S., Hyde, M., & Schuchart, G. E. Group size and the extension of social space boundaries. *Journal of Personality and Social Psychology*, 1976, *33*, 647-654.

Konstadt, N., & Forman, E. Field dependence and external directedness. *Journal of Personality and Social Psychology*, 1965, *1*, 490-493.

Kruglanski, A. W. Casual attribution, teleological explanation: On radical particularism in attribution theory. *Journal of Personality and Social Psychology*, 1979, *37*, 1447-1457.

LaCrosse, M. B. Nonverbal behavior and perceived counselor attractiveness and persuasiveness. *Journal of Counseling Psychology*, 1975, *22*, 563-566.

LaFrance, M. Nonverbal synchrony and rapport: Analysis by the cross-lag panel technique. *Social Psychology Quarterly*, 1979, *42*, 66-70.

LaFrance, M., & Broadbent, M. Group rapport: Posture sharing as a nonverbal indicator. *Group and Organizational Studies*, 1976, *1*, 328-333.

LaFrance, M., & Ickes, W. Postural mirroring and interactional involvement: Sex and sex-typing effects. *Journal of Nonverbal Behavior*, 1981, *5*, 139-154.

LaFrance, M., & Mayo, C. Racial differences in gaze behavior during conversations: Two systematic observational studies. *Journal of Personality and Social Psychology*, 1976, *33*, 547-552.

LaFrance, M., & Mayo, C. *Moving bodies: Nonverbal communication in social relationships*. Monterey, Cal.: Brooks/Cole, 1978.

Laird, J. D. Self-attribution of emotion: The effects of expressive behavior on the quality of emotional experience. *Journal of Personality and Social Psychology*, 1974, *29*, 475-486.

Lamb, M. E. Proximity seeking attachment behaviors: A critical review of the literature. *Genetic Psychology Monographs*, 1976, *93*, 63-89.

Lamke, L. The influence of sex role orientation in initial interactions within same-sex dyads. Unpublished doctoral dissertation, Texas Tech University, 1979. (Cited in Ickes, W. Sex role influences in dyadic interaction: A theoretical model. In C. Mayo, & N. M. Henley (Eds.), *Gender and nonverbal behavior*. New York: Springer-Verlag, 1981.)

Lanzetta, J. T., Cartwright-Smith, J., & Kleck, R. E. Effects of nonverbal dissimulation on emotional experience and autonomic arousal. *Journal of Personality and Social Psychology*, 1976, *33*, 354-370.

Lazarus, R. S. A laboratory approach to the dynamics of psychological stress. *American Psychologist*, 1964, *19*, 400-411.

Lazarus, R. S. Emotions and adaptation: Conceptual and empirical relations. In W. J. Arnold (Ed.), *Nebraska Symposium on Motivation*. Lincoln: University of Nebraska Press, 1968.

Lee, D. Y., Hallberg, E. T., Hassard, J. H., & Haase, R. F. Client verbal and nonverbal reinforcement of counselor behavior: Its impact on interviewing behavior and postinterview evaluation. *Journal of Counseling Psychology*, 1979, *26*, 204-209.

Leibman, M. The effects of sex and race norms on personal space. *Environment and Behavior*, 1970, *2*, 208-246.

Leventhal, H. Emotions: A basic problem for social psychology. In C. Nemeth (Ed.), *Social psychology: Classic and contemporary integrations.* Chicago: Rand McNally, 1974.

Libby, W. L., Jr. Eye contact and direction of looking as stable individual differences. *Journal of Experimental Research in Personality,* 1970, *4,* 303-312.

Lippa, R. Expressive control and the leakage of dispositional introversion-extraversion during role-played teaching. *Journal of Personality,* 1976, *44,* 541-559.

Littlepage, G. E., & Pineault, M. A. Detection of deceptive factual statements from the body and the face. *Personality and Social Psychology Bulletin,* 1979, *5,* 325-328.

Littlepage, G. E., & Pineault, T. Verbal, facial, and paralinguistic cues to the detection of truth and lying. *Personality and Social Psychology Bulletin,* 1978, *4,* 461-464.

London, H. *Psychology of the persuader.* Morristown, N.J.: General Learning Press, 1973.

MacKay, D. M. Formal analysis of communicative processes. In R. A. Hinde (Ed.), *Nonverbal communication.* Cambridge, England: University Press, 1972.

Mahl, G. F. Disturbances and silences in the patient's speech in psychotherapy. *Journal of Abnormal and Social Psychology,* 1956, *53,* 1-15.

Mahl, G. F. Gestures and body movements in interviews. In J. M. Shlien (Ed.), *Research in psychotherapy 3.* Washington, D.C.: American Psychological Association, 1968.

Mahl, G. F. Body movement, ideation, and verbalization during psychoanalysis. In N. Freedman & S. Grand (Eds.), *Communicative structures and psychic structures.* New York: Plenum, 1977.

Maines, D. R. Tactile relationships in the subway as affected by racial, sexual, and crowded seating arrangements. *Environmental Psychology and Nonverbal Behavior,* 1977, *2,* 100-108.

Major, B., & Heslin, R. Perceptions of cross-sex and same sex nonreciprocal touch: It is better to give than to receive. *Journal of Nonverbal Behavior,* 1982, *6,* 148-162.

Mandler, G. *Mind and emotion.* New York: Wiley, 1975.

Mark, E. W., & Alper, T. G. Sex differences in intimacy motivation. *Psychology of Women Quarterly,* 1980, *5,* 164-169.

Maslow, A. *Motivation and personality.* New York: Harper & Row, 1954.

Maslow, A. *Toward a psychology of being.* New York: Van Nostrand, 1968.

McAdams, D. P. A thematic coding system for the intimacy motive. *Journal of Research in Personality,* 1980, *14,* 413-432.

McAdams, D. P., & Powers, J. Themes of intimacy in behavior and thought. *Journal of Personality and Social Psychology,* 1981, *40,* 573-587.

McBride, G., King, M. C., & James, J. W. Social proximity effects of galvanic skin responses in adult humans. *Journal of Psychology,* 1965, *61,* 153-157.

McCauley, C., Coleman, G., & DeFusco, P. Commuters eye contact with strangers in city and suburban train stations: Evidence of short-term adaptation to interpersonal overload in the city. *Environmental Psychology and Nonverbal Behavior,* 1978, *2,* 215-222.

McDowall, J. J. Interactional synchrony: A reappraisal. *Journal of Personality and Social Psychology*, 1978, *36*, 963-975. (a)

McDowall, J. J. Microanalysis of filmed movement: The reliability of boundary detection by observers. *Environmental Psychology and Nonverbal Behavior*, 1978, *3*, 77-88. (b)

McGovern, T. V. The making of a job interviewee: The effect of nonverbal behavior on an interviewer's evaluations during a selection interview (Doctoral dissertation, Southern Illinois University, 1976). *Dissertation Abstracts International*, 1977, *37*, 4740B-4741B. (University Microfilms No. 77-6239)

McGuire, W. J. The nature of attitudes and attitude change. In G. Lindzey & E. Aronson (Eds.), *The handbook of social psychology* (Vol. 3). Reading, Mass.: Addison-Wesley, 1969.

Mehrabian, A. Significance of posture and position in the communication of attitude and status relationships. *Psychological Bulletin*, 1969, *71*, 359-372. (a)

Mehrabian, A. Some referents and measures of nonverbal behavior. *Behavior Research Methods and Instrumentation*, 1969, *1*, 203-207. (b)

Mehrabian, A. Nonverbal betrayal of feeling. *Journal of Experimental Research in Personality*, 1971, *5*, 64-73.

Mehrabian, A., & Diamond, S. G. Effects of furniture arrangement, props, and personality on social interaction. *Journal of Personality and Social Psychology*, 1971, *20*, 18-30. (a)

Mehrabian, A., & Diamond, S. G. Seating arrangement and conversation. *Sociometry*, 1971, *34*, 281-289. (b)

Mehrabian, A., & Friar, J. T. Encoding of attitude by a seated communicator via posture and position cues. *Journal of Consulting and Clinical Psychology*, 1969, *33*, 330-339.

Mehrabian, A., & Williams, M. Nonverbal concomitants of perceived and intended persuasiveness. *Journal of Personality and Social Psychology*, 1969, *13*, 37-58.

Merton, R. K. The self-fulfilling prophecy. *Antioch Review*, 1948, *8*, 193-210.

Merton, R. K. *Social theory and social structure*. Glencoe, Ill.: Free Press, 1957.

Milgram, S. The experience of living in cities. *Science*, 1970, *167*, 1461-1468.

Mobbs, N. A. Eye-contact in relation to social introversion/extraversion. *British Journal of Social and Clinical Psychology*, 1968, *7*, 305-306.

Morris, D. *Intimate behavior*. London: Jonathan Cape, 1971.

Nevill, D. Experimental manipulation of dependency motivation and its effects on eye contact and measures of field dependency. *Journal of Personality and Social Psychology*, 1974, *29*, 72-79.

Newman, R. C., & Pollack, D. Proxemics in deviant adolescents. *Journal of Consulting and Clinical Psychology*, 1973, *40*, 6-8.

Nguyen, M. L., Heslin, R., & Nguyen, T. The meaning of touch: Sex and marital status differences. *Representative Research in Social Psychology*, 1976, *7*, 13-18.

Nguyen, T., Heslin, R., & Nguyen, M. L. The meanings of touch: Sex differences. *Journal of Communication*, 1975, *25*, 92-103.

Nichols, K. A., & Champness, B. G. Eye gaze and the GSR. *Journal of Experimental Social Psychology*, 1971, *7*, 623-626.

Nisbett, R. E., & Wilson, T. D. Telling more than we can know: Verbal reports on mental processes. *Psychological Review*, 1977, *84*, 231-259.

Noesjirwan, J. Contrasting cultural patterns of interpersonal closeness in doctors' waiting rooms in Sydney and Jakarta. *Journal of Cross-Cultural Psychology*, 1977, *8*, 357-368.

Noesjirwan, J. A laboratory study of proxemic patterns of Indonesians and Australians. *British Journal of Social and Clinical Psychology*, 1978, *17*, 333-334.

Notarius, C. I., & Levenson, R. W. Expressive tendencies and physiological response to stress. *Journal of Personality and Social Psychology*, 1979, *3*, 1204-1210.

O'Neal, E. C., Brunault, M. A., Carifio, M. S., Troutwine, R., & Epstein, J. Effect of insult upon personal space preferences. *Journal of Nonverbal Behavior*, 1980, *5*, 56-62.

Patterson, M. L. Compensation in nonverbal immediacy behaviors: A review. *Sociometry*, 1973, *36*, 237-252. (a)

Patterson, M. L. Stability of nonverbal immediacy behaviors. *Journal of Experimental Social Psychology*, 1973, *9*, 97-109. (b)

Patterson, M. L. An arousal model of interpersonal intimacy. *Psychological Review*, 1976, *83*, 235-245.

Patterson, M. L. Interpersonal distance, affect, and equilibrium theory. *Journal of Social Psychology*, 1977, *101*, 205-214. (a)

Patterson, M. L. Tape recorded cuing for time-sampled observations of nonverbal behavior. *Environmental Psychology and Nonverbal Behavior*, 1977, *2*, 26-29. (b)

Patterson, M. L. Arousal change and cognitive labeling: Pursuing the mediators of intimacy exchange. *Environmental Psychology and Nonverbal Behavior*, 1978, *3*, 17-22. (a)

Patterson, M. L. The role of space in social interaction. In A. Siegman & S. Feldstein (Eds.), *Nonverbal behavior and communication*. Hillsdale, N.J.: Erlbaum, 1978. (b)

Patterson, M. L. A sequential functional model of nonverbal exchange. *Psychological Review*, 1982, *89*, 231-249. (a)

Patterson, M. L. Personality and nonverbal involvement: A functional analysis. In W. Ickes & E. S. Knowles (Eds.), *Personality, roles, and social behavior*. New York: Springer-Verlag, 1982. (b)

Patterson, M. L., Jordan, A., Hogan, M. B., & Frerker, D. Effects of nonverbal intimacy on arousal and behavioral adjustment. *Journal of Nonverbal Behavior*, 1981, *5*, 184-198.

Patterson, M. L., Kelly, C. E., Kondracki, B. A., & Wulf, L. A. Effects of seating arrangement on small-group behavior. *Social Psychology Quarterly*, 1979, *42*, 180-185.

Patterson, M. L., Mullens, S., & Romano, J. Compensatory reactions to spatial intrusion. *Sociometry*, 1971, *34*, 114-121.

Patterson, M. L., Roth, C. P., & Schenk, C. Seating arrangement, activity, and sex differences in small group crowding. *Personality and Social Psychology Bulletin*, 1979, *5*, 100-103.

Patterson, M. L., & Schaeffer, R. E. Effects of size and sex composition on interaction distance, participation, and satisfaction in small groups. *Small Group Behavior*, 1977, *8*, 433-442.

Patterson, M. L., & Sechrest, L. B. Interpersonal distance and impression formation. *Journal of Personality*, 1970, *38*, 161-166.

Patterson, M. L., & Strauss, M. E. An examination of the discriminant validity of the social-avoidance and distress scale. *Journal of Consulting and Clinical Psychology*, 1972, *39*, 169.

Pattison, J. E. The effects of touch on self-exploration and the therapeutic relationship. *Journal of Consulting and Clinical Psychology*, 1973, *40*, 170-175.

Pedersen, D. M. Correlates of behavioral personal space. *Psychological Reports*, 1973, *32*, 828-830. (a)

Pedersen, D. M. Relations among sensation seeking and simulated and behavioral personal space. *Journal of Psychology*, 1973, *83*, 79-88. (b)

Pellegrini, R. J., & Empey, J. Interpersonal spatial orientation in dyads. *Journal of Psychology*, 1970, *76*, 67-70.

Pittenger, R. E., Hockett, C. F., & Danehy, J. J. *The first five minutes*. Ithaca, N.Y.: Martineau, 1960.

Rajecki, D. W., Ickes, W., & Tanford, S. Locus of control and reactions to strangers. *Personality and Social Psychology Bulletin*, 1981, *7*, 282-289.

Reece, M. M., & Whitman, R. N. Expression movements, warmth, and verbal reinforcement. *Journal of Abnormal and Social Psychology*, 1962, *64*, 234-236.

Roger, D. B., & Schalekamp, E. E. Body-buffer zone and violence: A cross-cultural study. *Journal of Social Psychology*, 1976, *98*, 153-158.

Rosenbloom, S. Openness-enclosure and seating arrangements as determinants in lounge design. In L. M. Ward, S. Coren, A. Gruft, & J. B. Collins (Eds.), *The behavioral basis of design, Book 1*. Stroudsburg, Penn.: Dowden, Hutchinson, & Ross, 1977.

Rosenfeld, H. M. Approval-seeking and approval-inducing functions of verbal and nonverbal responses in the dyad. *Journal of Personality and Social Psychology*, 1966, *4*, 597-605. (a)

Rosenfeld, H. M. Instrumental affiliative functions of facial and gestural expressions. *Journal of Personality and Social Psychology*, 1966, *4*, 65-72. (b)

Rosenfeld, H. M. The experimental analysis of interpersonal influence processes. *Journal of Communication*, 1972, *22*, 424-442.

Rosenfeld, H. M. Conversational control functions of nonverbal behavior. In A. W. Siegman & S. Feldstein (Eds.), *Nonverbal behavior and communication*. Hillsdale, N.J.: Erlbaum, 1978.

Rosenfeld, L. B., Kartus, S., & Ray, C. Body accessibility revisited. *Journal of Communication*, 1976, *26*, 27-30.

Rosenthal, R. *Experimenter effects in behavioral research*. New York: Appleton-Century-Crofts, 1966.

Rosenthal, R. On the social psychology of the self-fulfilling prophecy: Further evidence for pygmalion effects and their mediating mechanisms. New York: M.S.S. Information Corporation Modular Publication, 1974.

Rosenthal, R., & Jacobson, L. *Pygmalion in the classroom*. New York: Holt, Rinehart & Winston, 1968.

Rotter, J. B. Generalized expectancies for internal versus external control of reinforcement. *Psychological Monographs*, 1966, *80* (1, Whole No. 609).

Rubin, Z. Measurement of romantic love. *Journal of Personality and Social Psychology*, 1970, *16*, 265-273.

Rutter, D. R. Visual interaction and speech patterning in remitted and acute schizophrenic patients. *British Journal of Social and Clinical Psychology*, 1977, *16*, 357-361.

Rutter, D. R. Visual interaction in schizophrenic patients: The timing of looks. *British Journal of Social and Clinical Psychology*, 1978, *17*, 281-282.

Rutter, D. R., & Stephenson, G. M. Visual interaction in a group of schizophrenic and depressive patients. *British Journal of Social and Clinical Psychology*, 1972, *11*, 57-65.

Rutter, D. R., Stephenson, G. M. Ayling, K., & White, P. A. The timing of looks in dyadic conversation. *British Journal of Social and Clinical Psychology*, 1978, *17*, 17-21.

Schachter, S., & Singer, J. E. Cognitive, social and physiological determinants of emotional state. *Psychological Review*, 1962, *69*, 379-399.

Schaeffer, G., & Patterson, M. L. Studying preferences, behavior, and design influences in a university library. In P. Suedfeld, J. A. Russell, L. M. Ward, F. Szigeti, & G. Davis (Eds.), *The behavioral basis of design* (Book 2). Stroudsberg, Penn.: Dowden, Hutchinson, & Ross, 1977.

Schank, R. C., & Abelson, R. P. *Scripts, plans, goals and understanding.* Hillsdale, N.J.: Erlbaum, 1977.

Scheflen, A. E. Communication and regulation in psychotherapy. *Psychiatry*, 1963, *28*, 126-136.

Scheflen, A. E. The significance of posture in communication systems. *Psychiatry*, 1964, *27*, 316-331.

Scheflen, A. E. *How behavior means.* Garden City, N.J.: Anchor, 1974.

Scheflen, A. E., & Ashcraft, N. *Human territories: How we behave in space-time.* Englewood Cliffs, N.J.: Prentice-Hall, 1976.

Scherer, K., London, H., & Wolf, J. The voice of confidence: Paralinguistic cues and audience evaluation. *Journal of Research in Personality*, 1973, *7*, 31-44.

Scherer, S. E. Proxemic behavior of primary school children as a function of their socioeconomic class and subculture. *Journal of Personality and Social Psychology*, 1974, *29*, 800-805.

Scherer, S. E. The influence of linguistic style, interpersonal distance and gaze on attitude acquisition (Doctoral dissertation, University of Toronto, 1975). *Dissertation Abstracts International*, 1978, *38*, 4479B.

Scherwitz, L., & Helmreich, R. Interactive effects of eye contact and verbal content on interpersonal attraction in dyads. *Journal of Personality and Social Psychology*, 1973, *25*, 6-14.

Schlenker, B. R. *Impression management.* Monterey, Cal.: Brooks/Cole, 1980.

Schneider, D. J., Hastorf, A. H., & Ellsworth, P. C. *Person perception* (2nd Ed.). Reading, Mass.: Addison-Wesley, 1979.

Sheckart, G. R., & Bass, B. A. The effects of verbal and nonverbal contingent reinforcement upon the intelligence test performance of black adults. *Journal of Clinical Psychology*, 1976, *32*, 826-828.

Siegel, J. C. Effects of objective evidence of expertness, nonverbal behavior, and subject sex on client-perceived expertness. *Journal of Counseling Psychology*, 1980, *27*, 117-121.

Siegel, J. C., & Sell, J. M. Effects of objective evidence of expertness and nonverbal behavior on client-perceived expertness. *Journal of Counseling Psychology*, 1978, *27*, 188-192.

Siegman, A. W. The telltale voice: Nonverbal messages of verbal communication. In A. W. Siegman & S. Feldstein (Eds.), *Nonverbal behavior and communication*. Hillsdale, N.J.: Erlbaum, 1978.

Siegman, A. W., & Feldstein, S. (Eds.), *Nonverbal behavior and communication*. Hillsdale, N.J.: Erlbaum, 1978.

Siegman, A. W., & Pope, B. Effects of question specificity and anxiety producing messages on verbal fluency in the initial interview. *Journal of Personality and Social Psychology*, 1965, *4*, 188-192.

Silverthorne, C., Micklewright, J., O'Donnell, M., & Gibson, R. Attribution of personal characteristics as a function of the degree of touch on initial contact and sex. *Sex Roles*, 1976, *2*, 185-193.

Smith, D. E., Willis, F. N., & Gier, J. A. Success and interpersonal touch in a competitive setting. *Journal of Nonverbal Behavior*, 1980, *5*, 26-34.

Smith, E. R., & Miller, F. D. Limits on perception of cognitive processes: A reply to Nisbett and Wilson. *Psychological Review*, 1978, *85*, 355-362.

Smith-Hanen, S. S. Effect of nonverbal behaviors on judged levels of counselor warmth and empathy. *Journal of Counseling Psychology*, 1977, *24*, 87-91.

Snyder, M. Self-monitoring of expressive behavior. *Journal of Personality and Social Psychology*, 1974, *30*, 526-537.

Snyder, M. Impression management: The self in social interaction. In L. S. Wrightsman & K. Deaux (Eds.), *Social psychology in the 80's*. Monterey, Cal.: Brooks/Cole, 1981.

Snyder, M., & Swann, W. Behavioral conformation in social interaction: From social perception to social reality. *Journal of Experimental Social Psychology*, 1978, *14*, 148-162.

Snyder, M., Tanke, E. D., & Berscheid, E. Social perception and interpersonal behavior: On the self-fulfilling nature of social stereotypes. *Journal of Personality and Social Psychology*, 1977, *35*, 656-666.

Sobelman, S. A. The effects of verbal and nonverbal components on the judged level of counselor warmth (Doctoral dissertation, American University, 1973). *Dissertation Abstracts International*, 1974, *35*, 273A. (University Microfilms No. 74-14, 199)

Sommer, R. Studies in personal space. *Sociometry*, 1959, *22*, 247-260.

Sommer, R. The ecology of privacy. *Library Quarterly*, 1966, *36*, 234-248.

Sommer, R. Reading areas in college libraries. *Library Quarterly*, 1968, *38*, 249-260.

Sommer, R. *Personal space: The behavioral basis of design*. Englewood Cliffs, N.J.: Prentice-Hall, 1969.

Sommer, R. The ecology of study areas. *Environment and Behavior*, 1970, *2*, 271-280.

Sommer, R. *Tight spaces: Hard architecture and how to humanize it*. Englewood Cliffs, N.J.: Prentice-Hall, 1974.

Sommer, R., & Becker, F. D. Territorial defense and the good neighbor. *Journal of Personality and Social Psychology*, 1969, *11*, 85-92.

Stern, D. N. Mother and infant at play: The dyadic interaction involving facial, vocal, and gaze behavior. In M. Lewis & L. A. Rosenblum (Eds.), *The effect of the infant on its caregiver*. New York: Wiley, 1974.

Stewart, D. J., & Patterson, M. L. Eliciting effects of verbal and nonverbal cues on projective test responses. *Journal of Consulting and Clinical Psychology*, 1973, *41*, 74-77.

Stiles, W. B. Verbal response modes and dimensions of interpersonal roles: A method of discourse analysis. *Journal of Personality and Social Psychology*, 1978, *36*, 693-703.

Storms, M. D., & Thomas, G. C. Reactions to physical closeness. *Journal of Personality and Social Psychology*, 1977, *35*, 412-418.

Street, R., & Giles, H. Speech accommodation theory: A social cognitive approach to language and speech behavior. In M. Roloff & C. Berger (Eds.), *Social cognition and communication*. Beverly Hills, Cal.: Sage Publications, 1982.

Streeter, L. A., Krauss, R. M., Geller, V., Olson, C., & Apple, W. Pitch changes during attempted deception. *Journal of Personality and Social Psychology*, 1977, *35*, 345-350.

Strong, S. R., Taylor, R. G., Bratton, J. C., & Loper, R. G. Nonverbal behavior and perceived counselor characteristics. *Journal of Counseling Psychology*, 1971, *18*, 554-561.

Sullivan, H. S. *The interpersonal theory of psychiatry*. New York: Norton, 1953.

Summerhayes, D. L., & Suchner, R. W. Power implications of touch in male-female relationships. *Sex Roles*, 1978, *4*, 103-110.

Sundstrom, E., & Altman, I. Interpersonal relationships and personal space: Research review and theoretical model. *Human Ecology*, 1976, *4*, 47-67.

Sussman, N. M., & Rosenfeld, H. M. Influence of culture, language, and sex on conversational distance. *Journal of Personality and Social Psychology*, 1982, *42*, 66-74.

Swann, W., & Snyder, M. On translating beliefs into action: Theories of ability and their application in an instructional setting. *Journal of Personality and Social Psychology*, 1980, *38*, 879-888.

Tesch, F. E., Huston, T. L., & Indenbaum, E. A. Attitude similarity, attraction, and physical proximity. *Journal of Applied Social Psychology*, 1973, *3*, 63-72.

Tessler, R., & Sushelsky, L. Effects of eye contact and social status on the perception of a job applicant in an employment interviewing situation. *Journal of Vocational Behavior*, 1978, *13*, 338-347.

Thayer, S. The effect of interpersonal looking duration on dominance judgments. *Journal of Social Psychology*, 1969, *79*, 285-286.

Thayer, S., & Schiff, W. Gazing patterns and attribution of sexual involvement. *Journal of Social Psychology*, 1977, *101*, 235-246.

Thomas, A. P., & Bull, P. The role of pre-speech posture change in dyadic interaction. *British Journal of Social Psychology*, 1981, *20*, 105-111.

References

Timney, B., & London, H. Body language concomitants of persuasiveness and persuasibility in dyadic interaction. *International Journal of Group Tensions*, 1973, *3*, 48-67.

Tomkins, S. S. The role of facial response in the experience of emotion: A reply to Tourangeau and Ellsworth. *Journal of Personality and Social Psychology*, 1981, *40*, 355-357.

Tourangeau, R., & Ellsworth, P. C. The role of facial response in the experience of emotion. *Journal of Personality and Social Psychology*, 1979, *37*, 1519-1531.

Trout, D. L., & Rosenfeld, H. M. The effect of postural lean and body congruence on the judgment of psychotherapeutic rapport. *Journal of Nonverbal Behavior*, 1980, *4*, 176-190.

Washburn, P. V., & Hakel, M. D. Visual cues and verbal content as influences on impressions formed after simulated employment interviews. *Journal of Applied Psychology*, 1973, *58*, 137-141.

Watson, O. M., & Graves, T. D. Quantitative research in proxemic behavior. *American Anthropologist*, 1966, *68*, 971-985.

Watzlawick, P., & Beavin, J. Some formal aspects of communication. *American Behavioral Scientist*, 1967, *10*, 4-8.

Waxer, P. Nonverbal cues for depression. *Journal of Abnormal Psychology*, 1974, *56*, 319-322.

Wegner, D. M., & Giuliano, T. Arousal-induced attention to self. *Journal of Personality and Social Psychology*, 1980, *38*, 719-726.

Welkowitz, J., & Feldstein, S. Dyadic interaction and induced differences in perceived similarity. *Proceedings of the 77th Annual Convention of the American Psychological Association*, 1969, *4*, 343-344.

Whitcher, S. J., & Fisher, J. D. Multidimensional reaction to therapeutic touch in a hospital setting. *Journal of Personality and Social Psychology*, 1979, *37*, 87-96.

White, P. Limitations on verbal reports of internal events: A refutation of Nisbett and Wilson and of Bem. *Psychological Review*, 1980, *87*, 105-112.

Wicker, A. W. *An introduction to ecological psychology.* Monterey, Cal.: Brooks/Cole, 1979.

Wiener, M., Devoe, S., Rubinow, S., & Geller, J. Nonverbal behavior and nonverbal communication. *Psychological Review*, 1972, *79*, 185-214.

Wiener, M., & Mehrabian, A. *Language within language: Immediacy, a channel in verbal communication.* New York: Appleton-Century-Crofts, 1968.

Williams, E. Analysis of gaze in schizophrenics. *British Journal of Social and Clinical Psychology*, 1974, *13*, 1-8.

Willis, F. N. Initial speaking distance as a function of the speakers' relationship. *Psychonomic Science*, 1966, *5*, 221-222.

Willis, F. N., & Hoffmann, G. The development of tactile patterns in relation to age, sex and race. *Developmental Psychology*, 1975, *11*, 886.

Willis, F. N., & Reeves, D. L. Touch interactions in junior high students in relation to sex and race. *Developmental Psychology*, 1976, *12*, 91-92.

Willis, F. N., Reeves, D. L., & Buchanan, D. R. Interpersonal touch in high school relative to sex and race. *Perceptual and Motor Skills*, 1976, *43*, 843-847.

References

Witkin, H. A., & Goodenough, D. R. Field dependence and interpersonal behavior. *Psychological Bulletin*, 1977, *84*, 661-689.

Woodall, W. G., & Burgoon, J. K. The effects of nonverbal synchrony on message comprehension and persuasiveness. *Journal of Nonverbal Behavior*, 1981, *5*, 207-223.

Woolfolk, A. E., Abrams, L. M., Abrams, D. B., & Wilson, G. T. Effects of alcohol on the nonverbal communication of anxiety: The impact of beliefs on nonverbal behavior. *Environmental Psychology and Nonverbal Behavior*, 1979, *3*, 205-218.

Worchel, S., & Teddlie, C. The experience of crowding: A two-factor theory. *Journal of Personality and Social Psychology*, 1976, *34*, 30-40.

Word, C. O., Zanna, M. P., & Cooper, J. The nonverbal mediation of self-fulfilling prophecies in interracial interaction. *Journal of Experimental Social Psychology*, 1974, *10*, 109-120.

Yerkes, R. M., & Dodson, J. D. The relation of strength of stimulus to rapidity of habit-formation. *Journal of Comparative Neurology and Psychology*, 1908, *18*, 459-482.

Yngve, V. H. On getting a word in edgewise. In M. A. Campbell et al. (Eds.), *Papers from the sixth regional meeting, Chicago Linguistic Society*. Chicago: University of Chicago Department of Linguistics, 1970.

Young, D. M., & Beier, E. G. The role of applicant nonverbal communication in the employment interview. *Journal of Employment Counseling*, 1977, *14*, 154-165.

Zajonc, R. B. Social facilitation. *Science*, 1965, *149*, 269-274.

Zajonc, R. B. Feeling and thinking: Preferences need no inferences. *American Psychologist*, 1980, *35*, 151-175.

Zimmerman, L. E. S. First impressions as influenced by eye contact, sex, and demographic background (Doctoral dissertation, University of Nevada-Reno, 1976). *Dissertation Abstracts International*, 1977, *37*, 6414B-6415B. (University Microfilms No. 77-12, 978)

Zuckerman, M., DeFrank, R. S., Spiegel, N. H., & Larrance, D. T. Masculinity-femininity and encoding of nonverbal cues. *Journal of Personality and Social Psychology*, 1982, *42*, 548-556.

Author Index

Subject Index